Alabama and Mississippi Connections

Historical and Biographical Sketches of Families Who Settled on Both Sides of the Tombigbee River

By
Judy Jacobson

CLEARFIELD

Printed for
Clearfield Company, Inc. by
Genealogical Publishing Co., Inc.
Baltimore, Maryland
1999

Reprinted for
Clearfield Company, Inc. by
Genealogical Publishing Co., Inc.
Baltimore, Maryland
2000, 2001, 2003

International Standard Book Number: 0-8063-4857-7

Made in the United States of America

Table of Contents

Acknowledgments

I lived in Oktibbeha County, Mississippi, for twenty-one years. During that time, I worked for the public library and a university library and conducted genealogical research for out-of-towners. That led to becoming curator of the Oktibbeha Heritage Museum and writing a monthly column for the *Starkville Daily News* for the last five years I lived in the county. So many people-from the local genealogist to the university archivist-have helped.

While I was there, I got to know the history of the Alabama/ Mississippi border region pretty well. I also got to know the area libraries and courthouses pretty well. There are a lot of librarians and county clerks who also deserve my thanks, but there is no way I could ever name them all. However, I do want to specifically mention Louise Gilmore, Mattie Sink, and Lynn Mueller. This book would not have been possible if it had not been for their help.

In addition, I want to thank Jodi Jacobson, my archaeologist daughter, for keeping me on the "right road" concerning those earliest years and for showing me how to look at history from a different perspective. I also need to recognize the help I received from Dan ("Trey") Comfort Jordan III, Frances Lindigrin, Steven Carson, Dr. Donald Maxwell, Anna Beth Hewgley, and Flo Steven. My thanks also goes out to those anonymous helpers on the Internet whose dedication to genealogy and history has led to a plethora of information on the web. All of their contributions were very important.

Most of all, I would like to thank my best friend and husband, Harry Jacobson, for his support of my work and his acceptance of my research trips. He realizes that research and writing are the best kind of therapy for me.

Preface

Quite a bit has been written about America's two most famous western movements-first, across the Atlantic, and then, west of the Mississippi River to the Pacific Ocean, but little has been written about the in-between movement which took settlers from the Atlantic coast states west through either Georgia or Tennessee, through Alabama, into Mississippi before going beyond.

Although in 1800 there were only two states--Kentucky and Tennessee--west of the Appalachian Mountains, portions of the Alabama-Mississippi region were opened for settlement as early as 1798. Those who settled were a mixture of people. They were Tories and Rebels; Mormons and Evangelicals; Scotch-Irish, German, Dutch and French Hugenots. They were the people no one wanted,

Many moved west when they exhausted the supply of good available farm land in the Upper South, using primitive agricultural techniques which depleted nutrients from previously healthy land. Leaving their worn-out fields and, in some cases, bankruptcy behind them, they left to start again in the abundant and productive lands to the south and west.

Added to declining productivity of the land, the previously stable English markets for typically Southern products, such as tobacco, fell off drastically after the American Revolution when England levied stiff duties against her rebellious child. At about the same time, the 1793 invention of the cotton gin opened the Lower South to the production of this high price commodity.

In addition to the obvious economic and social reasons, the unsettled frontier proved to be seductive in those early years, making the first half of the nineteenth century unmatched as a time for expansion in the United States.

This is a book about those settlers who traveled the old Indian trails into Alabama. Later, during the Indian Wars, the trails were widened to military roads. When regular mail service was established, these were the free souls who began to feel civilization closing in on them and moved on again. One of them was Gideon Lincecum who discovered at one of his stops-

"There were at this place plenty of deer and turkey and the fishing was splendid ... but the immigrants were pouring in with their shot-guns and hounds and it was very plain to be seen that the game would soon be gone."

Soon afterwards, the Lincecum family moved on like the rest.

They were among the rootless ones, those following the opening of lands to the west, always looking for frontier lands and opportunities over the next hill. They went by horse, by wagon, by boat and by foot as the pioneers pushed westward.

It is almost as if mobility is a part of the American character, for it is still going on today.

In Explanation

Abbreviations

aft	after
b.	born
betw	between
bpt	baptized
br	brother
bur.	buried
c.	circa
circa	approximately
d.	died
dau	daughter
employ	employed as / at / by
eng	engaged
fthr	father
inv dtd	inventory of estate dated
m.	married
mthr	mother
nd	no date
np	no place
pos	possibly
prob	probably
R	range
repr	reprint
Sec	section
sis	sister
son	son
tw	twin
T	township
twp	township

vol	volume
wid	widow / widower
wll dtd	will dated
wll prb	will probated

Names

Before the 1850's, few Americans could read or write. Anyone who has worked with old records know that those who could write were not necessarily good spellers. So names in census and other early records frequently contained creative spellings.

Added to the educational problem was the "melting pot factor." Spelling a name quite foreign to you can be a challenge. And foreign names, especialy non-English ones, were frequently Anglicized.

For the sake of this book, one spelling for each name has been chosen to dominate. That does not mean it is the only correct spelling. It simply means that a particular spelling was chosen to lessen confusion.

Early Indian Land in Georgia
and the Mississippi Territory

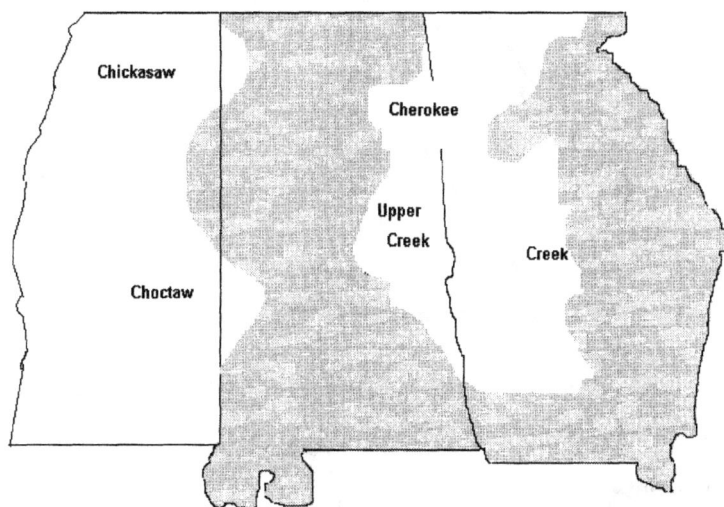

Chickasaw

Cherokee

Upper
Creek

Creek

Choctaw

Mississippi   **Alabama**   **Georgia**

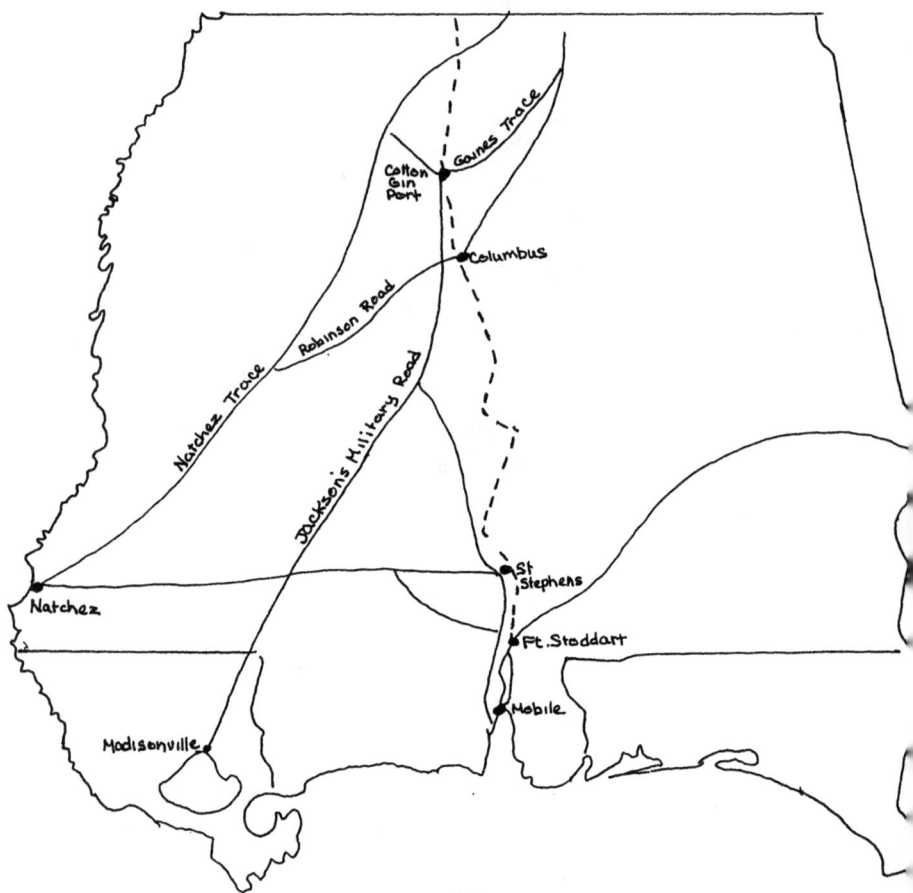

Cotton
Gin
Port

Gaines Trace

Columbus

Natchez Trace

Robinson Road

Jackson's Military Road

St
Stephens

Natchez

Ft.Stoddart

Mobile

Modisonville

Tombigbee River Division of the Mississippi Territory, with
the Roads and Towns of Early Alabama and Mississippi

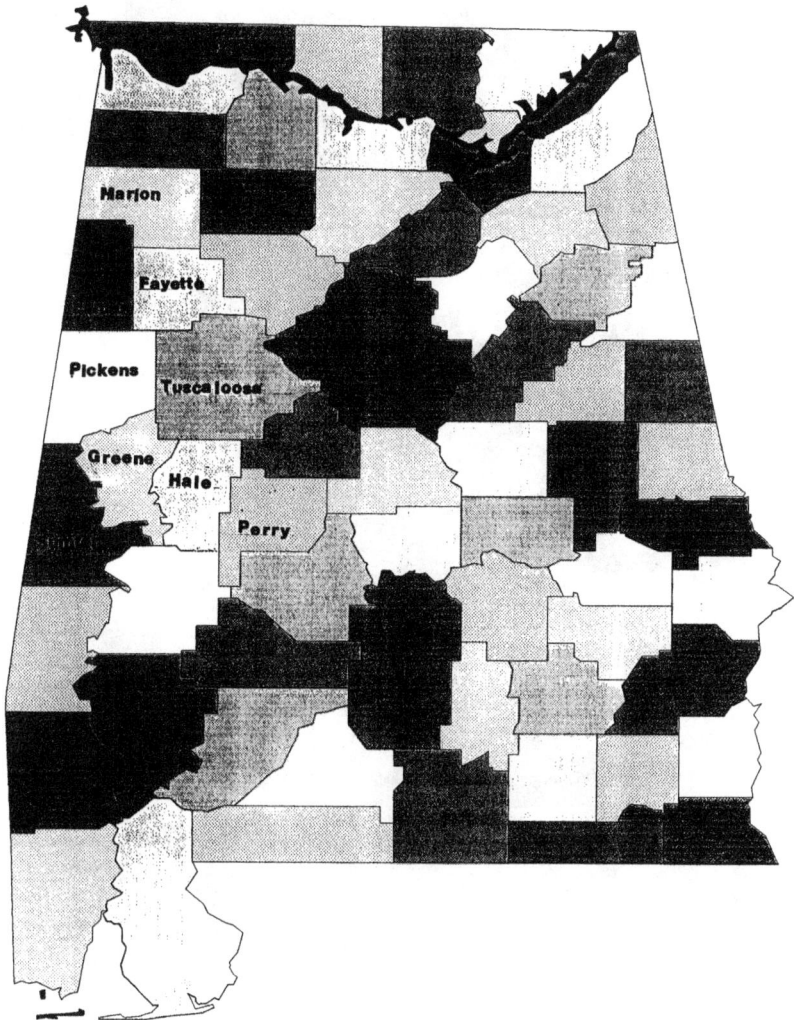

Present Day Alabama

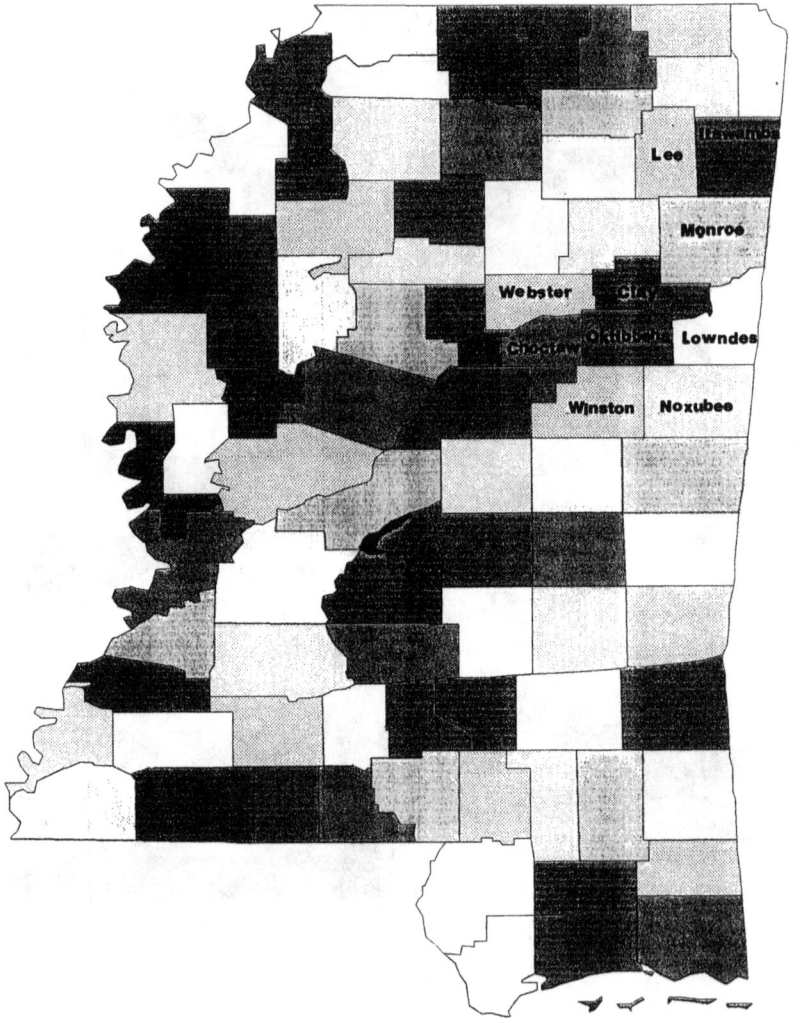

Present Day Mississippi

The Mississippi Territory

People have lived in the Mississippi Territory region for at least nine thousand years. Still, Hernando de Soto did not arrive in northeast Mississippi until the mid 1500's. De Soto was an aristocratic military veteran when King Charles V of Spain sent him to pacify and convert America's heathens and to return with riches. The King was to receive twenty per cent while de Soto was to keep eighty per cent of the "booty."

Although he was under orders to commit no atrocities, de Soto arrived in Mobile on October 18, 1540 after winning an expensive victory over the Choctaws. In 1541 he finally reached the Mississippi River. Although de Soto did not survive the expedition, other of his men did make it back with their accounts and de Soto's journal.

De Soto also has been blamed with importation of diseases which decimated the native population of the New World. And while in reality, European explorers did introduce diseases for which the natives had no biological defenses, it would be impossible to place the blame singularly on de Soto.

Ramenofsky reported in her 1992 *Archeology* article that de Soto had made only vague references to Indian illnesses in his journal. However, St. Cosme, a Jesuit who traveled down the Mississippi River 147 years later (in 1698) reported smallpox on the Arkansas side of the river. But there was no way to pinpoint when the disease was introduced or by whom.

What archaeologists have been able to determine was that between 1450 and 1550 there were a minimum of fifty large villages between Memphis, Tennessee and Natchez, Mississippi. Yet by 1600, there were only ten Indian villages left.

Other studies in the Mississippi Territory have uncovered similar devastation. Ramenofsky cited the introduction of European expedition diseases prior to 1600 as the only logical explanation.

The next to arrive were British traders who reached the upper Tombigbee River Valley by the 1680's and began to trade with the Chickasaws. Some of them ventured south into Choctaw territory. Then in 1682 LaSalle and de Tonti arrived. And D'Iberville was in the region in 1702.

The 1697 Peace of Ryswick first divided North America among the European powers, with France claiming the Mississippi Valley region - that area which extended from the Chattahoochee River on the east to the Mississippi River on the west. Consequently, the French were the first to establish permanent European settlements in that area, beginning in 1699 with a settlement at Biloxi. Then in the early 1700's, the French began courting the Chickasaws and Choctaws in an effort to counter British intrusion into the interior.

While the Gulf of Mexico, and the Mississippi and Tennessee River areas were explored and settled early by the French (1699-1763), British (1763-1781), and Spanish (1781-1798), the interior wilderness was pretty much left to the Indians. Settlement of those areas came about much slower. Nevertheless, the French did build a post on the Tombigbee near the mouth of Tibbee (Oktibbeha) Creek, the stream that formed the boundary between Choctaw and Chickasaw territory. "Ft. Tombecbe" remained a post into the early 1800's under the control of the French, the English, the Spanish, and, lastly, the Americans.

The British received much of the territory with the 1763 Treaty of Paris after their victory in the French and Indian War. France retained only New Orleans. After receiving Florida from Spain, the British divided that piece of land into East and West

Florida. The British ruled all their land between the Alleghenies and the Mississippi River in a highly paternalistic manner. King George III proclaimed

> We do hereby strictly forbid, on pain of our displeasure, all of our loving subjects from making any purchase or settlements whatever, or of taking possession of any of the lands above reserved without our special leave and license for that purpose first obtained.

They ordered any persons already in the territory to "remove themselves." Attempts were made to insure peace with the Indians. As might be expected, American settlers sitting in the Atlantic seaboard colonies were not happy with this British attempt to keep them out. But then settlement began to increase during the American Revolution when Loyalists from the colonies were allowed to flock into the British territory,

Also during the Revolution War, Spain took possession of Florida. So, by the 1783 Treaty of Paris, the Spanish had claimed much of the Gulf Coast region. Nevertheless, in the Treaty of 1795, Spain gave up everything north of the thirty-first parallel. Finally after much negotiation the Spaniards left East and West Florida completely in 1798.

After the British left the area, several of the original colonies claimed land, usually directly to their west. Eventually South Carolina ceded the fourteen mile strip along the northern Mississippi and Alabama boundaries it had claimed to the United States.

The state of Georgia claimed the land west of it and the area became known as the Yazoo Strip. In 1794 the Georgia legislature authorized the sale of more than twenty-one million acres of land in what would become Alabama and Mississippi for $500,000. It was purchased by four companies of speculators.

In 1798, the Mississippi Territory was formed. On April 24, 1802, the state of Georgia officially gave it to the U.S. government with the understanding that eventually the territory would become a state. Surveyors were sent out into the territory to record the land, climate, water and other important information. All persons holding land under British grants were required to file evidence of their claims.

The United States took possession of the entire area after the War of 1812, claiming in 1813 that the land controlled by the Spanish had been rightfully purchased from the French in the Louisiana Purchase. Most of that land was eventually sold for cash under the Land Act of 1820.

Since England, France and Spain, at one time or another, all had control over a portion of the territory and had granted land to their subjects; when the United States took control, it guaranteed the earlier land titles would be recognized. But difficulty in researching foreign claims, overlapping titles and frequent fraud made it nearly impossible for the United States to completely keep its pledge.

Alabama

The origin of the name Alabama always has been a matter of discussion among researchers. According to one view, the state was named for the Alabama Indians, a Creek (Muscogee) tribe that resided in the area of the upper Alabama River, shown on early French maps as Riviere des Alibamons.

De Soto referred to the tribe in 1540 when he first passed through the Muscogee Nation. Spellings varied. Depending upon whether the record was from the Spanish, French or British, it appeared as Albama, Alebamon, Alibama, Alibamou, Alibamon,

Alabamu or Allibamou. De la Vega called them the "Alibamo," the Knight of Elvas referred to them as the "Alibamu" and Ranjel alluded to them as the "Limamu."

Another theory was that the name of Alabama came from "Alba", the Choctaw word for "plants" or "vegetation", and "amo", the word for "to cut" or "to gather." The assumption was that the Choctaws called their neighboring tribe "vegetation gatherers."

In all likelihood, Alabama was not named for a translation from the Muscogee dialect of "Here we rest" as was commonly accepted in the 1850's. Still, in his writings, Alexander Beauford Meeks claimed the name came from "Hillibee" or "Hillaba" in the Muscogee dialect. However, experts have been unable to confirm such a connection.

During the American Revolutionary War, white inhabitants of Alabama remained loyal to the crown and a number of other loyalists moved into the area. Along with them came missionaries, traders and trappers. But few non-Tory settlers moved into the territory in those early days.

In 1802, the area of today's Alabama and Mississippi was given up by Georgia and South Carolina and became known as the Mississippi Territory. In fact, it was possible to be born in Georgia, to be married in Alabama and to die in Mississippi, without ever leaving the house.

During the War of 1812, the British used the Creeks, a branch of the Muscogee Indians, against the new American Republic and migration into the territory slowed even more. Frequent skirmishes occurred when the Creeks tried to resist white onslaught. The first major armed confrontation was at the Battle of Burnt Corn on July 27, 1813. The Creeks painted their war clubs and called it "The Red Sticks War." Andrew Jackson and the Tennessee militia defeated the hostile Indians at the

Battle of Horseshoe Bend, breaking the Creeks and opening land along the Tombigbee River to settlement.

After the war, the population in the Mississippi Territory land comprising the present state of Alabama exploded. An 1815 North Carolina legislature report approximated that 200,000 people had left that state during the previous twenty-five years, to settle in the Lower Mississippi Valley. But most came from other Southern states through Tennessee into Alabama, or down through the Carolinas and Georgia into Alabama.

Andrew Jackson was appointed to secure treaties from the Choctaws, Chickasaws and Cherokees. Beginning in 1816, white settlement was open to all Alabama land except Choctaw land west of the Tombigbee, Chickasaw land in the northwest corner and Cherokee and Creek/Muscogee land in the eastern third of the state.

The Cherokees came from mountain homes in northeast Alabama and were considered the most civilized of the tribes. The Chickasaws lived on the headwaters of the Tombigbee in the northwestern area of Alabama. Choctaws occupied the southwestern and western portion of the state. They were friendly with the French and other Europeans.

Originally the Muscogee Nation reached from the Atlantic to the Tombigbee River and included parts of Georgia, Alabama and Florida. They were the most formidable tribe and, in 1813 and 1814, they waged a bloody war against the whites. Finally the whites, Cherokees, Chickasaws, and Choctaws united to defeat them.

By 1817, three proposals had been developed by the federal government for handling the new territory:

1. Admit the Mississippi Territory as one state,

2. Divide the territory into two states along an east-west line,

3. Divide the territory into two states along a north-south line.

The division of the Northwest Territory into several states had set a precedent, so the third proposal was accepted. In 1817, the eastern portion of the Mississippi Territory was declared a separate territory to be called Alabama and the area of today's Mississippi was admitted to the Union as a state.

Unlike the migration to the New World, migration in the Mississippi region occurred during economically good times. During hard times, like the Panic of 1819, the influx dwindled. But during flush times, they just kept coming.

The land was fertile. Rev. Ashbel Simonton wrote in his journal that

> Between Montgomery and Marion (in the Perry County, Alabama area) is for the most part very rich and produces cotton in great perfection. The soil is a black loam and of such depths as to produce heavy crops year after year without discovering any signs of exhaustion.

Land offices were established in Alabama as a means for selling the land acquired in treaties. The land office for west-central Alabama remained open in Tuscaloosa from 1821 through 1866.

It was the first time in the United States that land was surveyed and laid out in sections, townships and ranges before being sold. After the survey, the land was put up for auction. Land not sold for at least $2.00 per acre was later sold separately.

Yet it was still a territory when poverty-stricken settlers, speculators and some fugitives began to pour into the area before the surveying had been completed. Consequently, many of the first white settlers were squatters. The Creeks threatened trouble because of these early invaders. In a political move, President Madison ordered the squatters be removed, but in the end, most were allowed to stay.

In fact, the growth was so quick that on December 14, 1819, Alabama was admitted to Union as the country's twenty-second state. The Chattahoochee River formed the new state's border.

In all, Alabama has had five capital cities. When the territory was first created in 1817, Saint Stephens in southwest Alabama was named temporary capital. The first constitutional convention and first session of the General Assembly met in Huntsville in 1819. But the legislature chose Cahaba (Cahawba) at the confluence of the Cahaba and Alabama Rivers for the second session and the new temporary capital in 1820. Since Cahaba proved to be easily flooded and often unhealthy, Tuscaloosa was named the capital city in 1826. But when population concentrations shifted, Montgomery, on the Alabama River, was named the next and final capital.

Fayette County

Fayette was created from portions of Pickens, Marion, and Tuscaloosa Counties on December 20, 1824. Nuzzled in the rolling hills of northwest-central Alabama, Fayette was named for Revolutionary War General de Lafayette. Settlers as early as 1819 and 1820 only encountered a few Indians, and they discovered river bottoms which furnished them with fine farm land.

The county seat of Fayette was originally known as Frog Level because of the surrounding swamp land. Then it was named Alfreda after the postmaster's wife. Next, the town was named Dicy after yet another postmaster's daughter. In 1821 the name was changed to Latona. And, finally, in 1898 the people voted to name it Fayette

Greene County

Greene County was established on December 13, 1819, out of 650 square miles of land given to the Federal government during the 1816 Choctaw Cession and originally part of Marengo and Tuscaloosa Counties. The rich alluvial land attracted settlers in hoards as early as 1817. It was named for Georgia's Revolutionary War General Nathaniel Greene who had been born in Rhode Island in 1740, but resided in Savannah, Georgia until his death in 1786.

Situated in west-central Alabama, Greene County bordered Tuscaloosa and Pickens Counties. The Tombigbee River formed the western and southern borders and the Tuscaloosa River the eastern border.

Although the first county seat was Erie, that town was eventually transferred to Houston County and, in 1838, Eutaw became county seat. It was named for the Revolutionary Battle of Eutaw Springs in South Carolina and was incorporated in 1841. A courthouse fire destroyed some of the early records in 1868.

A number of settlers probably arrived as early as 1812. Others who arrived had fought with Andrew Jackson at the Battle of New Orleans and had discovered the fertile soil of Greene County on their trip home. Among the earliest towns in Greene County were Boligee (organized 1816), Clinton (c. 1819), Forkland (1818), Mantua (1817), Mesopotamia (by 1818), Mt. Hebron (1818), Pleasant ridge (1819), Old Springfield (1818) and Tishabee (1817).

Lamar County

Originally a portion of Marion County, Alabama, became the western part of Fayette County. Then the area became a county itself on February 4, 1867 and was named Jones County after Fayette County resident E.P. Jones. It was abolished later that year and re-created in 1868 as Sanford County. In 1877 the name was changed to Lamar after Mississippi's Senator L.Q.C. Lamar. Lowndes and Monroe Counties in Mississippi and Marion, Fayette, and Pickens counties in Alabama bordered Lamar.

Swayne Courthouse, named for General Wager Swayne, military governor of the Chattahoochee District, became the first county seat in 1866. But in 1868 the name was changed to Vernon for Edmund Vernon from England.

Marion County

Marion County was created out of northwestern Alabama on February 13, 1818, and was named for General Frances Marion of South Carolina. It was a large county which included portions of what would become Fayette, Lamar, Walker and Winston Counties, Alabama. But before long it was discovered that much of the county's territory was inside Mississippi's borders and included portions of what would become Itawamba, Lowndes and Monroe Counties, Mississippi.

In 1830, the county's population was little more than four thousand people. But by 1860, the population had grown to 21,171, of which 11,182 were slaves. The county had thirty-five churches.

The first county seat for Marion County was Cotton Gin Port on the Tombigbee River, near present-day Amory. In as much as it was discovered that Cotton Gin Port was within the Mississippi borders, on December 6, 1819, Alabama temporarily moved the Marion County courts to Henry Grier/Greer's home and called for elections. But that area also was discovered to be in Mississippi. Eventually Hamilton was officially established as county seat in 1820.

Pickens County

Pickens County, Alabama became the western holding area for pioneers anxious for treaties to be signed and western Indian lands to be opened to settlers. When Gideon Lincecum went through in 1818, he found that

"The country between the Black Warrior and Tombecbee (sic) rivers - over which we were then traveling - had been disputed territory between the Mushkogees and Choctaws for a long time. Neither party dare be found hunting on that forbidden region, which accounts for the great number of wild beasts seen on our route. It was a delightful autumn - not a drop of rain fell during our entire passage through that dense wilderness, there the wheeled carriage had never before stamped its impress on the face of that virgin soil."

Pickens County was created out of Tuscaloosa County in December 1820. The northern and eastern portions were hilly, the south and west were level. Although its boundaries changed a number of times, they were permanently established in 1866.

The county was named for Revolutionary War General Andrew Pickens who was born in 1739 in Pennsylvania, but moved to South Carolina as a child. The first county seat was at Picken's Courthouse, eventually known as Pickensville; before being moved to Carrollton in 1830. Carrollton was named for the Honorable Charles Carroll.

The first settler in the area was Josiah Tilly from who arrived in 1817 at the site on the Tombigbee River, one-half mile from what would become Pickensville. Tilly had come from Tuscaloosa where he had lived for a year or two.

Instead of remaining with his family, Tilly spent much of his time with the Indians in Mississippi. In fact, when the Mississippi Choctaw Indians were sent west, Tilly joined them and was residing in the West with the Indians as late as 1855.

While Tilly was the first to follow the path, many others would follow. Those early settlers had to pack supplies on horses from Tuscaloosa and they became squatters since the land did not open for purchase until five years after Tilly's arrival.

As with Tilly, most of the earliest pioneers came from other southern states - mostly from South Carolina, but also from North Carolina, Virginia, Tennessee and Georgia. These settlers migrated South down the Tennessee River from Tennessee into northern Alabama and then down old Indian trails into Tuscaloosa, Greene and Pickens Counties. Still others came south through the Carolinas to Georgia and west into Alabama.

After only a few years, Pickens became almost crowded as these newcomers swarmed into western Alabama and dotted the landscape with their settlements. They brought with them their families and their slaves. By the early 1820's over five thousand people lived in the county.

Most were from well regarded families, some coming from plantations whose land had been drained of nutrients. Looking towards the fertile soil to the west, they settled on terraces along the creeks and rivers of Pickens County. Others were more enterprising, seeing the opening of Indian lands for its economic possibilities. Still others were looking for the freedom or adventure in the newly acquired western land. Most had the rugged self-reliance needed to survive and succeed.

But then the trails became roads and in 1837 stage coaches began to run three times a week between Pickensville and Tuscaloosa. The railroad didn't arrive in Pickens County until 1897.

Sumter County

Sumter County, Alabama, was formed in December 1832 out of ceded Choctaw Indian land and was named for General Thomas Sumter of South Carolina. In the west-central part of the state, Sumter is bordered by the state of Mississippi on the west and Tombigbee River on the east. Livingston became the county seat in 1833,

Tuscaloosa County

The grandfather of Alabama's western counties, Tuscaloosa, was created on February 6, 1818 in the Appalachian foothills and coastal plain originally inhabited by both Creek and Choctaw Indians. At the time, less than 300 people lived in the area. Two years later, Tuscaloosa County has over 5,000 whites and 2,200 slaves.

The original border went all the way to the Mississippi River. The name of the county originated with the Choctaw words "tuska" for "warrior" and "loosa" for "black". The Black Warrior River flowed through the county.

The county contained both Appalachian foothills and coastal plain. But most of Tuscaloosa County was broken, hilly land with just a thin layer of soil over clay - not the rich soil hoped for by the settlers.

The first white settlers had moved into the area by 1815. Among them were Joseph Tillery, John Clark, Pleasant Dearing, Patrick Scott, Jonathan and Thomas York, and William Wilson. But because of the convenience of the river and its access to Mobile, after 1816, settlers came pouring into the area.

In his later years, Gideon Lincecum would write about arriving in Tuscaloosa -

"Tuscaloosa was at that time (1818) a small log cabin village, but people from Tennessee were arriving daily, and in the course of that year it grew to be a considerable town.

There were in the town a set of young men who came out to explore the country, and Tuscaloosa being at that time the only place where provisions could be had, those men made that place the homepoint, from whence they went out and returned.

Tuscaloosa has wide bottoms, which at the time were densely clothed in the largest cane I ever saw in any country. The old Indian town of 'Tush-cah-loo-sa' lay a mile or more below where new Tuscaloosa is situated. The chief whom the place was named for dwelt there previous to the war with the Muskogees (Muscogees). He was a very dark colored Indian, and that fact named him ... 'Tuscah' is 'a warrior' and 'loosa' is 'black'. The white people spell it 'Tuscaloosa'."

Previously called "Falls of Black Warrior" or "Falls of Tuscaloosa", the city of Tuscaloosa was incorporated in 1819, with a population of 600. Even though no one owned land until the 1821 land sale, in January, 1820, white residents of the

"south fraction of Section 22 Township 21 Range 10 West"

assembled at the courthouse to elect seven town commissioners.

Tuscaloosa has always been the county seat except for a short period during the 1820's when it was moved to Newton. In fact, up until 1820, the town of Tuscaloosa was the center for the courts for all of Alabama territory west of it.

In 1819, Tuscaloosa lost to Cahaba for capital of the territory. Because Tuscaloosa continued to thrive, it finally became the capital in 1826.

But Alabama's population moved eastward as Creek Indian lands opened for settlement and Tuscaloosa shortly became inconveniently placed. An amendment to the constitution freed the legislature to pick another site further east. In 1846 Tuscaloosa lost out to Montgomery after sixteen ballots of the General Assembly.

Almost Alabama

Monroe County

Originally, Monroe sprang from three Indian land cessions. In August, 1814, the area east of the Tombigbee River was ceded by the Creeks after being defeated by General Andrew Jackson. Then the rest was ceded to the United States as part of Alabama in the treaty of September 20, 1816. The boundary set by Congress between the State of Mississippi and the Territory of Alabama was set to

> "run from the junction of Bear Creek with the Tennessee River, in a direct line to the Northwest corner of Washington Co., and thense (sic) South to the Gulf of Mexico, so as to intersect the confluence of the Pascagoula River."

But then in December 17, 1817, Congress suggested the eastern boundary of Mississippi be changed to extend

"To the bay of Mobile, and thence along the middle of the Tombigbee River, according to the meanders thereof, to the Cotton Gin Port, and thence due to north to the southern boundary line of the state of Tennessee."

Although that boundary was never adopted, many settlers moving into the territory just east of the Tombigbee believed they were in Alabama, not Mississippi.

So the Tombigbee River formed Alabama's western border. Originally, the river was known by the Chickasaw Indians as "Ming-co aye-u-pye, Ok'Hin-nah" or the "King's Bath River". And the Choctaws probably called it "Itta-om-bee-aye-ika-a-bee" meaning "coffin" or "box maker" and the French corrupted it to "Tombecbe".

In 1820 a survey uncovered the problem and on January 3, 1821, Gov. George Poindexter told the Mississippi Assembly that it appeared that

"a considerable population on the waters of the Tombigbee formally attached to Alabama"

fell within Mississippi borders. So in February, 1821, the state legislature officially accepted the area as part of Mississippi. That was the area which became known as Monroe County, while later, parts of it broke off to become other counties, such as Lowndes and Clay. But in the beginning it was all Monroe.

The county was actually organized at Henry Greer's home just outside of today's Columbus. In 1830, the county seat was Athens and, finally in 1849 it was moved to Aberdeen.

The town of Plymouth on the west side of the Tombigbee was at first called Peachland's, probably a faulty spelling of Pitchlynn, since John Pitchlynn was an early settler there. And

Because of Pitchlynn, it became a center of American influence. But after the cessions of 1816 and statehood in 1817, land on the east side of the river was open to settlement. But Plymouth, being on the west side of the Tombigbee, still belonged to the Choctaws and so attention turned across the river to Possum Town (Columbus) where Gideon Lincecum built his home in 1818.

The United State government built a cotton gin on the west bank of the Tombigbee near the present-day Amory in an effort to encourage the Chickasaw Indians in more agricultural pursuits. The town that grew up around it was named Cotton Gin Port and became a principal trading town for the Chickasaws.

There were only two towns in Monroe County in the 1820 Federal Census. And both Cotton Gin Port with its forty-nine inhabitants and Possum Town with its one hundred nine inhabitants were on the Tombigbee River.

Northerner Rev. Ashbel Green Simonton, the eventual founder of the Presbyterian Church in Brazil, visited Monroe County with his brother James several times in the 1850's and wrote in his journal that he found out that Aberdeen, the county seat, was a cultural center for the regions.

"We found quite a number of Aberdeen gentlemen congregated on the piazza, dressed up as only Aberdeeners can dress. They as much as any class I ever met seemed to think that dress makes the gentleman ... We could not beat it into our heads that we are out of Pennsylvania and out of The North. We could not conceive that in such a thinly settled country, and in a log house standing in the woods, any large school, much less a classical school could be got which would yield a fair salary. This is a mistake. Often Homer and Virgil are found in log huts, in copies whose well-worn covers show marks of diligent use."

Later, while sitting on a log in Monroe County, five miles from Aberdeen, Simonton wrote

"We are out on the prairie and buzzards are flocking around us as tame as turkeys. We are walking over a beautiful rolling prairie and often for miles nothing meets the eye, but fields of corn and cotton stretching away".

Lowndes County

Lowndes was organized on January 30, 1830 out of the southern 504 square miles of old Monroe County. Rivalry between Cotton Gin Port (near Amory) and Possum Town (Columbus) settlers resulted in the division of Monroe into two separate counties - Monroe and Lowndes. Lowndes was named for William Jones Lowndes, a member of Congress from South Carolina .

The county's first white settler was probably Simon Mhoon. In addition, there were missionaries at Mayhew Mission in the northwestern corner of the county. A 1958 article in the *Jackson Daily News* written by Anabel Power claimed that the first house erected in Columbus was a log cabin built in 1817 by Thomas Moore. But other sources claimed that Dr. Gideon Lincecum built the first house on the site of "Opossum" Town (Columbus). In his journal, Lincecum wrote that they went because

"No people have got in there (Columbus area) yet and that's worth something. I was pleased with (the) description of the wild uninhabited district of heavy forests, extensive canebrakes, cypress swamps and pretty river full of fish and beaver and otter. No marks of civilized destructiveness nor clattering bell nor yelping hound disturbed the maiden quietude of that dark forest ... The Choctaws were near the river on the opposite side, but no where on the east side was to be found any signs that the country had ever been occupied."

Gideon's family left Tuscaloosa on November 1, 1818. Upon arriving, the Lincecum family set up their last camp two miles southeast of what would become Columbus. The Choctaw had named the river the family had camped at the "Lookse-ok-pullila". "Lookse" was "a terrapin" and "ok-pullila" meant "floating on the water."

"It was full of blue-winged teal, swarming like wild pigeons ... Oh, that was a delightful camp: in a thick canebrake (sic), near that little river, where the harsh sounds of obtrusive civilization had never before alarmed the owls or savage beasts ... We heard the panthers scream; the racoons complained; the owls came near and hooted awfully; and the wolves howled all night."

Then on

"the afternoon of the twelfth day we reached the Tombigbee river, three miles above where Columbus now stands and there I made my camp. Father went two hundred yards below and pitched his tent ... After the road was made by the government from Nashville to Natchez, which crossed the river where Columbus now stands, I went down there to see what kind of place it was. I thought it was an eligible town site."

A post office was established in 1820 with service along Military Road to Muscle Shoals, Alabama, and, according to Anabel Power, Gideon Lincecum was the first postmaster.

Another route later that year connected Columbus with Tuscaloosa.

Columbus was incorporated as a town in 1822. William L. Moore serving as the first mayor. The first free public school in Mississippi was established there. Then the first county court convened in the new county seat of Columbus on April 12, 1830. By 1837, the town had a population of 3,500. Eventually it became quite prosperous. Nevertheless, in 1852, Rev. Simonton described the area around Columbus as

> "Mississippi life in earnest, seven or eight wagons
> drawn by oxen, horses and mules are wallowing about
> in the mud. One has upset. The roads are awful."

During the Civil War, Columbus became the state capital after Jackson was captured. And the country's first Decoration Day was observed there in 1866. Author Tennessee Williams was born in Columbus Episcopalian parsonage in 1911.

Many other early settlements - like, Moore's Bluff, Peachland, West Port, Cork and Nashville - are gone. But others with charming names - like, Kolola Springs, Waverly and Plum Nellie - have survived.

Mississippi

West of Tuscaloosa, Greene, Pickens and other Alabama counties was more Indian land sitting waiting to be taken. Probably the best of the land was the Black Prairie or Blacklands of eastern Mississippi. Its fertile black calcareous soil had rich agricultural potential.

Most of the interior Indian land was not open to whites for settlement when Mississippi became the twentieth state in the Union on December 10, 1817. The name Mississippi was taken from the river which received its name from the Algonquian word for "big river."

The earliest humans in Mississippi were probably Paleo-Indians, hunters from the Ice Age, who were there between 10,000 B.C. and 12,000 B.C. A variety of Indian cultures followed, including the Mississippian culture, which was there from 1000 A.D. to 1500 A.D. Mississippian was the culture to precede the Chocchumas and, then, the Choctaws in the territory.

The Chocchumas, a small tribe which spoke Choctaw, were mentioned by de Soto in his journal. In 1682 LaSalle and de Tonti went through the region. Then in 1702, D'Iberville wrote to the Chocchumas urging them to return to their village which was located

"three or four French leagues from Plymouth on the Tombigbee River."

Many believe the village that D'Iberville described was one uncovered in northern Starkville in Oktibbeha County, Mississippi.

In 1770, the Chocchumas were nearly exterminated by the Choctaws and Chickasaws and their land was divided between the other two tribes. After an 1816 treaty, the Tombigbee River became the eastern border of Indian land. So before 1830, central and northern portions of Mississippi, west of the Tombigbee River remained in Choctaw and Chickasaw hands.

Although still Indian territory, others than just Indians were living in the region. Traders and trappers were permitted to stay in the territory only if they converted to Choctaw citizenship. Some took Indian wives. And about the same time, there were also a number of African slaves in Choctaw territory.

As protection from their fiercer neighbors, the Choctaws of the early 1800's lived in compact villages. But as things calmed down their settlements became more scattered with farms and two-room log houses with dirt floors dotting hills and ridges. The Choctaws had an orderly democratic type of government consisting of a council with legislative and treaty-making powers. Officers, such as chiefs, were elected.

In 1775, James Adair estimated the total Choctaw population as 22,500. In 1836, the U.S. War Department estimated there were 18,500 Choctaws and 5,500 Chickasaws. The two tribes spoke the same language and lived in the western portion of the continent before migrating about 1400 A.D. to land which would become the state of Mississippi. Gatchet reported that the word "Choctaw" meant "Flathead". Other sources claimed it meant "charming voice".

According to Lincecum's journal, Mushulatubbe was the principal chief until the "Chahtas" (Choctaws) were moved west of the Mississippi River.

"He was a handsome man, about six feet in height and quite corpulent. He possessed a lively, cheerful disposition, and ... was good-natured and would get drunk. He was not much of an orator and to remedy that deficiency he had selected an orator to speak for him ...

"Mushulatubi was not very wealthy, having but a moderate stock of cows and horses and five or six Negroes. He was, however, certainly rich in his family relations. He had a house full of children and two handsome wives, who like himself, were healthy and somewhat corpulent ...

"It sometimes happened that the Ohio traveler would waylay and rob the Kentuckians and Tennesseeans within the limits of Mushulatubi's district. On hearing of the robbery he would raise his

warriors, rush out in pursuit and never fail to arrest
and bring the culprit to Columbus."

During the War of 1812, the Choctaws sided with the
United States. But in late 1813, Chief Mushulatubbe wrote to the
President of the United States informing him of the Choctaw war
effort and asking for help.

"Father, As our Agent has been absent from our
Nation for nine Moons past and from the difficulties
and troubles which my nation labors under being now
engaged in war in behalf of my father the President
against the Creeks I have thought proper to write to
you, and depute my friend and brother Mr. King whom
I know and who has lived in our country at the Agency
and whose talk I know is straight I wish you to listen to
it, as I make my talk in writing but short and refer you
to him for information.

"On the 4 instant I sent out a party against a
neighboring town of the Creeks and have returned
successful bringing home a quantity of their hair. And
on the 25 inst the Creeks came into this country and
killed one of my warriors. I have now ordered out a
large Army, which are to rendezvous at my council
house on the 11 of next month when I shall head
them in person and go into the Creek Nation
determined to storm their forts & conquer...

"My friend & Brother the bearer of this will tell
you our situation better than I can describe it to you
and whom I further beg leave to recommend to you as
my friend & has the confidence of this nation."

In addition to Mushulatubbe's signature, the letter was also
signed by John Pitchlynn, the U.S. Interpreter.

Then, in June, 1814, Chiefs Pushmataha and Mushulatubbe again wrote asking that a new agent be appointed. In the letter they wrote

"Father we long for a time to come when we shall be permitted to see you at the big white house to make known to you our grievances which we have long wished to tell you,

"Father, twelve winters ago you sent Mr. Dinsmoor amongst us to teach us to quit our wild habits and to follow the ways of our white brethren, which we have endeavored so far as we had examples set us, we are sorry to inform our father that the beloved man Mr. Dinsmoor has not done towards us as we know our father wished him to do, which has vexed our hears and made them cold towards him - he has lived but twelve moons in our country since our father sent him to live with us, and when with us it appears he cares but little about us.

"If agreeable to our father we would wish to have no more to do with Mr. Dinsmoor as we might as well want an Agent.

"Father our hearts are warm and our tongues are straight towards our father the President of the United States and his white Children, altho (sic) we have had many offers of presents promised to us to take up the hatchet against the U. States but we have adhered firmly to the treaty we made with our father sixteen winters ago at his beloved white house which we hope our conduct will prove as we are ready at any time to take up arms for our father the President against his enemies white or red."

In addition to John Pitchlynn who served as U.S. interpreter at the time, an 1813 list of persons permanently employed in the Choctaw Agency included their salaries and the times to which they had been paid.

"John Pitchlynn Interpreter @ 500 Drs a year paid to the 30 June 1812

Turner Brashears Interpreter @ 400 Drs a year paid to 31 March 1813

Mary Nail Weaver Instructor of Indians @ 30 Drs a month paid to 31 March 1813

Robert Ross Do paid to the same time

William Swain first smith 30 Drs a month and 50 cents a day subsistence Pd to 31 March 1813

James Standley Second smith 20 Drs. A month & subsistence 50 Cents a day pd to 31 March 1813

Edward Mitchell Wheelwright & loom maker on contract by the piece."

Long before man ever set foot in the area, animals had established trails to nourishment and water. When man arrived, those same trails also led him to the necessities of life. The trails followed water and the lines of smoothest passage. They led to the organization of great settlements along rich valleys, near bodies of water and along the ridges the trails followed.

When the white man arrived, he came on foot or horse. And soon those trails were widened to carry wagons bringing more settlers in the region.

After the War of 1812, it became apparent a road was needed to connect Nashville with New Orleans. It was commissioned by Congress in 1816 and construction began in May, 1817, using portions of those old Indian trails.

The Military Road was completed during the 1819-1820 winter under the direction of General Andrew Jackson, using a

Tombigbee River ferry crossing originally used by Indians. The Robinson Road, on the other side of the Tombigbee was completed circa 1824. It joined the Military Road in the Columbus area. Lincecum wrote that

> "Mushulatubi resided on the military road, which (previous to the advent of steamboats on the Mississippi River) was the great thoroughfare upon which returned the hosts of flatboat men from Ohio, Kentucky, Tennessee and Indiana. They were mostly footmen, who, after disposing of their cargo of produce at New Orleans, came up through the Chapta (Choctaw) country on their way to their (sic). I have often heard those weary footmen while passing my house - I also resided on the military road - speaking of the friendly demeanor and the kind hospitality they had received at the house of Mushulatubi."

David Folsom, a half Indian Choctaw Chief, also lived in a house along the Robinson Road in what would become Oktibbeha County, Mississippi. The road which also connected Columbus with Jackson, Mississippi was formally known as the Government Military Road, and informally as the Turnpike and, later as the "Old Pike."

During an 1811 Choctaw Council at the prairie home of Mushulatubbe, the eminent war Chief Tecumseh urged the Choctaws to join his coalition of Indians against the whites. Twenty-year-old Chief Folsom and Pushmataha were assigned to escort Tecumseh from Choctaw land "never to return on pain of death."

In addition, Folsom was instrumental in encouraging the whites to come into Indian lands. He encouraged missionaries from Massachusetts to establish a school for Indian children at Mayhew Mission in far northwest Lowndes County. Even though, like Folsom, some of the full blooded chiefs favored the school, they were hostile to the idea of religious instruction. But Folsom won.

Cyrus Kingsbury, a New England Presbyterian missionary, was sent by the American Board of Missions from Tennessee to begin a mission in Choctaw Indian country. Kingsbury went to Pigeon Roost in Choctaw County to consult with Chief David Folsom. They met with John Pitchlynn, the U.S. Government interpreter and together the three men selected the site for a mission, in the northwestern corner of Lowndes County.

A number of people were living in the area in 1820 when the Mayhew Mission School was actually established. Although most were Choctaws, a few were whites or black slaves. Columbus in Lowndes County, Mississippi, was just a trading post and Starkville in Oktibbeha County was non-existent.

In 1819, H.B. Cushman, the son of one of the missionaries at Mayhew wrote about the site that

"The beauty of the place is heightened by the extent of the prospect, the undulating form of the land, and the flocks ranging upon the prairie."

Eventually the mission grew to eight buildings, twelve missionaries and sixty-five to seventy students per year. The boarding school was supported by the church, the Federal government, and the Indians. The students tended the mission farm and did housework; cutting maintenance expenses. In addition to reading, writing, arithmetic and religion; boys learned skills such as black smithing, carpentry, furniture making, and agriculture work at the mission school. Girls learned housekeeping skills and sewing.

The Board of Missions had been surprised by the request by local Indians that missionaries be sent. One source reported that when Kingsbury wondered why the Indians would make such a request, they sent him to talk with the "Praying Negro". The slave, named Uncle Lester, explained that he had been converted to Christianity before his capture in Africa and had prayed for a mission so that the Indians could hear the same message. But Judge Carroll, in his *Historical Sketches of Oktibbeha County* reported that the Choctaws had learned about mission schools from the Cherokees and wanted to get one for themselves.

Nearly all of the missionaries at Mayhew were from New England. One of the earliest missionaries was Elizabeth Varnum, Kingsbury's first wife. After she died in 1822, Kingsbury was left to raise two sons. So he wrote the Board of Missions which sent him Electra May to be his next bride. Legend has it that Electra turned out to be so ugly, Kingsbury wept. But he did eventually marry her.

The missionaries erected a gristmill and blacksmith shop; and opened a mission farm. They also opened roads - two east to Columbus and Plymouth; two southwest to Osborne and Hebron, near present-day Starkville; and one south to the Folsom / Choctaw Agency area. Sub-missions were begun at Hebron and in the southeastern part of Oktibbeha County, near Agency.

Attempts to remove the Indians from their land began with the completion of the Louisiana Purchase. After the War of 1812, it became apparent the nation was fated to grow. And the Federal government began to aggressively work towards the relocation. General Andrew Jackson was even brought in to at first persuade and later to bribe and frighten the Indians into signing the Treaty of Doaks Stand on October 18, 1820.

Unfortunately, it was soon discovered that some of the land in northwestern Arkansas that had been promised to the Choctaws had already been settled by whites. After tribal leaders were given trips to Washington, clothes, jewelry and whiskey; they signed away their Arkansas lands for $6000 a year to be allocated for schools for the Indians.

After the September 27, 1830 Treaty of Dancing Rabbit (see APPENDIX 8), the Choctaws gave up claim to their land in Mississippi, opening the land south of the Tibbee Creek and west of the Tombigbee River for white settlement. In the October 20, 1832 Treaty of Pontotoc, the Chickasaw ceded land north of Tibbee Creek and west of the Tombigbee. The Indians were forced to leave their homes and move west along what would become known as the Trail of Tears. After the Indians' departure, the mission gradually disappeared. Kingsbury, known by the Indians as "Walking Wolf," followed his flock, arriving in Boggy Depot, Oklahoma in August of 1840.

The Treaty of Dancing Rabbit took its name from Dancing Rabbit Creek, the location selected for the signing of the treaty. Actually the Choctaw name for the creek was "Chunkfi-ahihlabok." "Chunkfi" meant "rabbit"; "a" was a location preposition, "Hihla" meant "to dance" and "bok" meant "creek". So the literal translation was "Rabbit-there-dances-creek."

In early September, 1830, the Choctaws owned twelve thousand square miles within the state of Mississippi. With the Treaty of Dancing Rabbit signed on September 27, 1830, all of that Choctaw land was ceded to the federal government in exchange for land in the west. Before that time, the interior of Mississippi had only been visited by a few white trappers, traders and missionaries.

After the treaty, settlers waiting along the Alabama border crossed into the new land. According to the treaty,

1. Indians would only leave if it was voluntary. They could go or stay as they pleased,

2. The whites would stay out of the ceded land and those already in it would be removed until the country was surveyed.

This treaty allowed for three types of land allotments to the Indians and their supporters (see Appendix 8). But the reality of it was something quite different. Many Choctaws indicated they wanted to stay on their land and were willing to conform to white man's laws. And in 1830, the Mississippi legislature gave Indians the same status as whites. All tribal laws, except for marriage contracts. were nullified. And whites using scare tactics began to warn the Indians they would probably become paupers and beggars. That did not seem impossible to the Indian. Yet the harassments and scare tactics continued proving the Indians to be more "civilized" than the white settlers.

So most of Indians did leave within the allotted three years. But even though the survey and the migration of settlers was not supposed to begin until all the Choctaws had left, in September 1833, President Jackson offered the land for sale with little notice. Speculators grabbed up land that already had Indians and other settlers living on it.

But it was not just the Indians who were defrauded. In 1835, the 23rd Congress 2nd Session looked into complaints off mismanagement of sales of Indian land by officers representing the government and speculators. According to Senate Document #151, of course

> "Speculators, who were summoned to give testimony... either declined or positively refused to appear before the commissioners and testify ... In some instances the commissioners were threatened with personal violence ... and all who testified were denounced and put in fear."

But settlers did testify and the document indicated that the "most extensive" fraud and mis-use of power occurred in Mississippi where Samuel Gwin served as land registrar for both the Mount Salus and the Chocchuma (Choctaw) Land Offices. In testimony after testimony it became obvious that Gwin had continuously and illegally

1. Told potential buyers that specific land had been sold when it hadn't and held it back for private, more lucrative sale,

2. Set aside good land for "friends or favorites,"

3. Sold land on credit, pocketing the interest charged,

4. Purchased land in their own name,

5. Used "partiality and favoritism between applicants" in selling the same piece of property,

6. Allowed a company of speculators to become a monopoly in holdings of good land.

Each Indian family had been allotted land in the treaty. But the confusion caused by the President's premature land sale, the poor morals of land agents, the avarice of speculators and the lack of sophistication on the part of the Indians all added to depriving the few Indians left in Mississippi the land to which they were entitled.

In Oktibbeha County, Mississippi, sixty Choctaw families made claims, but only fourteen with Indian names sold land between 1834 and 1842. No further account of Indians appeared in Oktibbeha County records. Except for those who intermarried with whites, most of the Choctaws followed the same trails west that many of the whites would follow a short time later.

Actual surveying began in 1832 and lasted until 1840. But the first sales were made in January, 1831 when the Pontotoc Land Office sold 266,000 acres at an average of $1.88 per acre.

In 1834 and 1835, the Columbus Land Office sold eighty acre tracts of land for $1.25 per acre. While many of those who settled earlier were squatters forced to move on when public domain land was sold, a fair number did acquire title to the land they claimed. But even they could not escape the lure of "greener pastures".

Drawn westward, these visionary Americans followed the trails forged by so many before them - down from the Carolinas to Georgia, over to west-central Alabama, into Mississippi and, finally on to Arkansas, Louisiana and Texas.

Choctaw County

Choctaw was an irregularly shaped county established on December 23, 1833 and named for the Indian tribe. Originally a square and twice as large, Webster and Montgomery Counties would later take over much of the area, leaving only 372 square miles in Choctaw County.

According to J.P. Coleman's history, the center of the county was

"twenty miles east and twenty miles north of the geographical center of the state of Mississippi".

So it could be said Choctaw was in the north of the state, but barely, and in the east, but again barely.

In 1806, Congress allocated six thousand dollars for the building of a five hundred mile road from a foot-and-bridle path which cut through both Webster and Choctaw Counties on its way from Nashville, Tennessee to Natchez, Mississippi. It was named the Natchez Trace.

In 1812, French Canadian Louis LeFleur established a "stand" or tavern at French Camp along the Natchez Trace. However, with the invention of the steamboat and the construction of the Military / Robinson Road, before long the Trace had fallen into disuse. While the road existed, whites traveled up and down the Trace, but only the Indians occupied the interior of Choctaw County territory.

After the Treaty of Dancing Rabbit, the Indians were to be removed between 1831 and 1833. Then the land was to be surveyed and deeds for tracts of land were to be conveyed. But as with other counties, settlers in what would become Choctaw County ignored the order to wait for the survey and entered the land.

It's first county seat was Greensboro, which later became part of Webster County. Judge Colemen claimed that Greensboro received its name from some early settlers who had come from Greensboro, North Carolina. Greensboro sat on a ridge, one mile east of Culla Beeta Creek.

When Montgomery County was formed from Choctaw County in 1871 the Choctaw County seat was moved to the more central site of Ackerman. G.W. Gunter donated forty acres on which the town was built.

Clay County

De Soto and his men may have been the first Europeans to visit Clay County. Journals from his expedition report de Soto crossing the Tombigbee River in December 1540. First a snowstorm struck. Then on March 4, 1541, the Chickasaws launched a bloody attack on the Spanish explorers, killing many of them. It has been suggested these events all took place in what would become Clay County, Mississippi.

French and English traders arrived in the 1690's. The French built "Ft. Tomjbecbe" on Tibbe Creek. It remained a post of the French, English, Spanish and, finally, the Americans into the 1800's.

Irregularly shaped, Clay became a county on May 12, 1871, but the bill was vetoed by Gov. Alcorn. Legislation creating the county in 1872 was upheld by the Supreme Court. The county was formed out of 399 square miles of Lowndes, Oktibbeha and Chickasaw Counties and originally named Colfax County after Vice President Schuyler Colfax (1823-1885). Considered a bit of a radical Republican, Colfax served in the House of Representatives before becoming Speaker of the House in 1863. The name of the county was changed to Clay in honor of the less controversial Henry Clay in 1876. The city of West Point, which received its charter in 1858 after the arrival of the Mobile and Ohio Railroad, has always been the county seat.

The land which went in to the county marked the southern border of the old Chickasaw Indian territory. Tibbee Creek formed Clay's southern border with Lowndes and Oktibbeha. It was a grasslands area with Northeastern prairie soil. John Pitchlynn was one of the earliest settlers. On January 23, 1837, another settler wrote

"Never had I seen so grand a sight. The ground was covered with snow. The deer went running and skipping in every direction over the treeless expanse."

Itawamba County

The French arrived in the rolling countryside of Itawamba County with Bienville in 1736. Although he came with six hundred soldiers, Bienville discovered the British had arrived before him, possibly as traders.

Early British settler James Logan Colbert married a Chickasaw woman and had a son named Levi who became

Chief Itawamba circa 1750. When the Chickasaws moved west, most of the Colbert family went with them.

With the Tombigbee River running the length of it, the land was situated perfectly for trading with the Indians. Then in 1802, the Natchez Trace, a road running between Tennessee and Natchez on the Mississippi River, was cleared through Itawamba, adding to its attractiveness as a trading center.

Other whites also arrived long before the Chickasaw land was opened for settlement. By 1810, one Indian agent estimated that 4-5,000 white settlers had scattered throughout Chickasaw land.

The Indians finally agreed to move west in the October 20, 1832 Treaty of Pontotoc. In the treaty, Chickasaws referred to themselves as "oppressed" and chose to go "rather than submit to this great evil."

Itawamba was organized as a county in 1836. But it was still little more than a wilderness. In his 1839 diary, Josiah Hinds described his life in Itawamba,

> "We are among strangers in a strange land, and in a
> wilderness, where but a short time since, was heard
> the yell of the savage ... One cabin only to shelter us
> and our little ones ... no churches to worship God."

Lee County

Lee County was originally part of Chickasaw Indian territory. The land was some of the rich Black Prairie belt in northeastern Mississippi. But the area also became the bloodied site of two Civil War battles - the battles at Brice's Crossing and at Harrisburg.

In October 26, 1866, Lee was established from 449 square miles originally within the boundaries of Itawamba and Pontotoc County. It was named for General Robert E. Lee.

Tupelo was chosen as the county seat on April 15, 1867, because of its location in the center of the county. It also became the junction point of the Mobile & Ohio and the St. Louis & San Francisco Railroads.

Noxubee County

Noxubee was one of the sixteen counties formed by the Choctaw Cession. Established on December 23, 1833, Noxubee County's name came from an Indian word meaning "stinking water". Its 659 square miles rested in the fertile Black Prairie region of Mississippi, with the Noxubee River running jaggedly through it.

The famous treaty was signed on September 27, 1830 in Noxubee, at a spot between two prongs of the Dancing Rabbit Creek. Maj. John H. Eaton and Col. John Coffee represented the United States government. Six thousand Indians were also present at the talks.

Noxubee became a county in 1833 along with the other counties drawn from the Choctaw Cession. The first court in the county was held in the log home of Joseph H. Frith of Macon.

Oktibbeha County

Established on December 23, 1833, Oktibbeha County was formed from Choctaw territory. Supposedly the name of the county came from an Indian word for "bloody water" or "ice in water there" depending upon the source. Hebron became the first county seat. But then Starkville received a post office and it became county seat.

At first Starkville was named Boardtown. Some say the name came from the clapboard buildings in the town. Others claim the name was given because of the board sidewalks. And according to yet another explanation, the name was given because of lumber mills in the area.

When Starkville was named as county seat, a hewn log courthouse and jail were built. The courthouse also served as a school. And to keep down the number of jail breaks, the jail was constructed with no windows or doors. Prisoners were lowered down into the jail through a hole in the roof.

The first home in the county was built in the early 1820's by David Folsom on or near the Old Robinson Road. It was a large home of hewn logs which Folsom maintained as an inn. Folsom was known for his efforts in establishing schools and missions in the area. Before that time, few outsiders or non-Indians lived in Oktibbeha County.

The community of Folsom sprang up near the chief's home before the Choctaws were forced out of the area and Chief Folsom sold his property and moved west with the Indians. Travelers along the Robinson Road on their way to Jackson or New Orleans stopped for the night at the Folsom Inn. The town of Folsom was thriving even before the county was ever chartered. In fact, in 1834, of the sixty-nine votes cast in the county, thirty were from Folsom, thirty from Starkville and nine from Mayhew.

Judge Carroll described the town of Folsom as "a lowly place, with much drinking and fighting." In the 1840's Ned Martin stabbed a man but the injured man recovered. And when another citizen attempted to assassinate a neighbor late one night, he fired at an object on his neighbor's porch and fled to

Alabama. It was three months before he learned he had assassinated a water bucket.

But where Folsom was destined to die, Starkville was destined to grow. A May 30, 1835 advertisement in *Southern Argus Newspaper* offered lots to be sold on July 4th in Starkville

"25 miles west of Columbus, short distance from Oktibbeha River, which river has already been navigated by barges of 200 barrels burthen."

Yet in the eyes of Rev. Simonton, Starkville was not much better then Folsom. He wrote in his journal that

"Loaferism abounds here among old and young. Planters come in day after day and sit in back rooms or in front of the stores and talk hour after hour in foolish if not improper conversation."

Folsom and Starkville were both stops for the slave traders. They would camp in tents and send out notices announcing their arrival to the planters in the area.

As the town of Folsom was dying out in the 1840's, just a mile away on the Robinson Road, the town named Choctaw Agency was growing. It began as a government trading post established to maintain contact with the Indians whose council house was just two and one-half miles southeast of Agency. It was situated on a high ridge overlooking the Noxubee River.

The post included a two story house whose lower story was a prison, complete with stocks for pinioning prisoner's legs. There was also a government store and stables at the post. It remained as a government post until 1832.

In the mid-1850's, the town named Agency, also sometimes called Raw Hide, flourished. Frequent stage coaches brought a steady stream of passengers. On July 12, 1854, Rev. Simonton described a stage ride he took.

"Hurrying out I found in (the stage) quite a number of passengers but still a little more room left. In we climbed, three on each seat and one or two on top. The weather was oppressively hot, the thermometer standing about one hundred in the shade, and to make our case complete, the roads were so dusty as almost to produce suffocation. Being companions in misery and jammed up so closely together, in self defense and to while away the slow hours, we soon struck up an intimate acquaintance with each other."

As a trading center, Agency exceeded Starkville in its volume of trade. One of the many stores, Baskerville and Co., was a seventy foot long, two story building. In fact, the town was important enough to attract Jefferson Davis to speak at the Agency community center in the mid-1850's.

In fact, Agency prospered until the Mobile and Ohio Railroad was built seven miles east in Lowndes County. The unfortunate placement of the railroad did not immediately kill off the town though. Considerable business was still conducted there into the 1860's and 70's. In fact in 1870, Agency had a population of 4160 compared to Starkville's 3160 population.

But Agency did eventually suffer from not having the train and slowly declined. The last store closed in 1887 when the owner died. A doctor practiced there before moving to Starkville in 1894.

Webster County

Webster was named for statesman Daniel Webster in 1882. But the county was originally established in 1874 under the name Sumner. It was carved out of the portions of Choctaw County north of the Black River and parts of Montgomery

County. The early boundary between Choctaw and Chickasaw lands cut across the northeast corner of the Webster County.

Greensboro, which had been county seat of Choctaw County, suddenly found itself in Sumner County. Then after Greensboro was burned during the Civil War, it fell into disrepair, finally becoming somewhat of a haven for criminals. However, court continued to be held in Greensboro until 1876.

Because of its geographic position in the county, Walthall was named county seat instead of Greensboro. Walthall was named for General E.C. Walthall.

Winston County

Winston County was originally a center of Choctaw life. In fact, a Choctaw council house stood at Pinney Shook on Section 33 Township 13 Range 11.

The known first white settler in the area was Irishman James Bell who traveled from Williamsburg County, South Carolina. During the Revolutionary War, Bell had fought with the British before moving westward in disgust and bitterness over the rebel victory.

So when Bell settled in what would become Winston County, it was with the hope that he would never see another white man. Unfortunately, that was not to be, but James and his Indian wife managed to keep their family away from too much white influence.

In 1820, another Irishman, James Wilson, was living eight miles southwest of today's Louisville, where he eventually ran an inn and tavern. The only road in the county was the Robinson Road, but Wilson's inn was no where near it.

Surveying of Winston County was completed on schedule in 1833. But, as with other counties, crowds of speculators swarmed into it ahead of time. The first election of county officers occurred in August 1834.

Adair Family

Some Adairs claim a family tree traced back to include the sister of Julius Caesar and other dignitaries such as William the Conqueror, the Kings of Scotland and John Fitzgerald Kennedy. Those who connect themselves with John F. Kennedy have supposedly traced their ancestry back to the Fitzgeralds.

According to that genealogy, in 14th century Ireland, Robert Fitz-Gerald (son of Gerald) was born in Athdara in County Limerick. Athdara was an important town, with churches and castles. "Ath" meant "ford" and "dara" meant "oak tree." So Dr. James Barnett Adair suggested that Robert Fitzgerald's home community of Athdara had probably been organized near an oak tree at the ford of a river.

If there was any truth to family lore, Robert moved from Athdara because of a family feud in which he may have killed a kinsman. And, according to tradition, Robert Fitzgerald replaced his surname with Athdara, in honor of his hometown, and moved to Galloway, Scotland where he shortened it to Robert Adair/Adare.

But that is only one explanation of the origin of the name. Adair may have also come from the Gaelic "Edzeur" meaning "Edgar" or "rich appearance." And in Ireland the name might have been given to the grandson of someone with the name "Daire."

Whatever the source of his name, once in Scotland Robert Adair killed a robber named Currie and was given Currie's property as a reward. He built a castle there and called it Kinhilt. The motto for the Adairs of Kinhilt and Lord Waveny was "Loyal a la Mort" (Faithful Unto Death).

Yet another Adair genealogy claimed some Adairs came from Ulster (Northern) Ireland - a stronghold for the Scotch-Irish. And at least some of the Adair/Adare/Adaire/Odere families in these genealogies did settle near Scotch-Irish settlements in America.

The Thomas Jefferson Adair Family

Thomas Jefferson Adair, Sr.

  m1 Rebecca Brown

  m2? Anne Catherine Laustdatter Mattisen?

  d. Mississippi; c. 1856

  Children

    Samuel Jefferson (see below)

    Margaret Ann - b. Laurens, South Carolina; c. 1804

      m. William Richey (b. Laurens, South Carolina d. Parowan, Iron County, Utah; 1870), son of Robert and Rebecca Belton Richey; Pickens County, Alabama; February 10, 1820

      d. February 10, 1850

      Children

James	Emily Melissa
Joseph	John Belton
Rebecca Smith	Martha Ann
Eliza Jane	William Belton
Robert	Benjamin W.

    Eliza Jane - b. West Carthage, Rutherford County, Tennessee; November 11, 1811

      m1 Samuel Carson (b. St. Clair or Lowndes County, Alabama; November 22, 1805 d. Alabama; 1836-37), son of Franklin and Jane Carson; Alabama; c. 1829

      m2 Moses Pearson; c. 1838

      m3 John Price (b.Lynchburg, Lincoln County, Tennessee; November 20, 1815 d. Washington,

Washington County, Utah; January 11, 1839) c.
1844

d. Washington County, Utah; August 16, 1892

Children by Samuel Carson

> John   Elizabeth
>
> Valentine   William

Children by Moses Pearson

> Margaret Jane - b. Pickens County,
>> Alabama; July 13, 1839
>>
>> m. David Lewis; January, 1855

Children by John Price

> Rebecca Ann George Thomas
>
> John Wesley Hyrum Wiley

Thomas Jefferson, Jr. - b. Indiana; 1814

> m. Mary Vancil
>
> r. Arizonia

Mary Ann - b. Pickens County, Alabama; July 5, 1822

> m. John Mangum III (b. Springfield, St. Clair
> County, Illinois; June 10, 1817 d. Alpine, Apache
> County, Arizonia; May 23, 1885), son of John
> and Rebecca Canida Mangum; Noxubee
> County, Mississippi; c. 1840
>
> d. Georgetown, Kane County, Utah; May 9, 1892
>
> Children
>> William Perry Laney Ann
>>
>> Rebecca Frances Martha Elizabeth

Sarah - m. William Adair and/or William Mangum

Samuel Jefferson Adair

> b. Laurens County, South Carolina; March 28, 1806

m. Jemima Catherine Mangum (b. Ohio; October 14, 1809
d. Mt. Pisgah, Union County, Iowa; September 31, 1848),
dau of John and Rebecca Canida; Pickens County,
Alabama; December 3, 1829
d. Nutriuso, Apache County, Arizonia; July 6, 1889
Children

>William Jefferson - Pickens County, Alabama; August
>>27, 1830
>>d. Mt. Pisgah, Union County, Iowa; October 31,
>>1846
>John Milton - b. Pickens County, Albama: January 8,
>>1833
>>m. Eliza Jane Richey; 1855
>>d. Lincoln County, Nevada; June 1899
>Thomas - b. Alabama; c. 1835
>>r. Ozark, Itawamba County, Mississippi
>>m. Malinda (b. Alabama; 1836)
>>Children
>>>Perren - b. Alabama; c. 1855
>>>Rachel - b. Mississippi; c. 1858
>Rebecca Frances - b. Pickens County, Alabama; July
>>8, 1835
>Permelia Jane (tw) - Pickens County, Alabama; June
>>27, 1837
>>m. Charles Decatur Searle; Payson, Utah;
>>December 25, 1855
>>d. Dry Fork, Uintah County, Utah; December 16,
>>1883
>George Washington (tw) - b. Pickens County,
>>Alabama; June 27, 1837

m. Ann Catherine Chestnut; 1861

d. Bloomfield, San Juan County, New Mexico;
September 9, 1909

Samuel Newton - b. Itawamba County, Mississippi;
December 11, 1839

m. Helen Genette Brown; Washington County,
Utah; December 15, 1863

d. Luna, Catron County, New Mexico; May 16,
1924

David Secrist - b. 1840

d. March 22, 1867

Joseph Jasper - b. Itawamba County, Mississippi;
1842

d. Mt. Pisgah, Union County, Iowa; September 8,
1846

Rufus Columbus Burlison - b. Itawamba County,
Mississippi; February 9, 1844

d. Utah; August 2, 1858

Jamima Katherine - b. Desmoines, Polk County, Iowa;
April 6, 1846

m. Fredrick Dickinson Rugg; Washington
County, Utah; January 11, 1866

d. Murray, Salt Lake County, Utah; April 15,
1926

Ezra Taft - b. d. Mt. Pisgah, Union County, Iowa; April
1848

Thomas Jefferson Adair of this genealogy was possibly a
descendant of James Adair I of the following genealogy. Like
James, Thomas was from Laurens County in the western

piedmont region of South Carolina. Much of that backcounty area was settled by Scotch-Irish. The first white settler in Laurens County was John Duncan who had spent a few years in Pennsylvania before settling in Laurens in 1753.

When Thomas' daughter Margaret Ann Adair was born there in 1804, Laurens County was booming with tailors, mills, building contractors, doctors and eighty-one registered whiskey distilleries.

After his son Samuel's 1806 birth, Thomas Adair and his family followed the northern route into Alabama - through Tennessee, stopping at Maury/Rutherford County. He was listed along with William Adair as a juror in Pickens County, Alabama, circa 1824. A Rebecca Adair and "Fereby" Clark were granted land in Sec 22 T20 R15W in Pickens County, Alabama, on November 28, 1834. On November 10, 1835, Thomas Jefferson Adair received land in nearby Sec 20 T20 R15W. His son Samuel was granted eighty acres of land in Sec 9 and Sec 15 T20 R15W in 1836. James and William Adair received land in other townships and ranges. A Joseph also received land in T20 R15W like the Adairs of this genealogy. It would seem logical that Joseph was a member of Thomas and Samuel's family.

From Alabama, the family moved west into Itawamba County, Mississippi by 1839. According to Itawamba marriage records, Samuel Adair was registered as a "Christian Minister" on April 5, 1841. At about the same time, much of the family must have joined the Mormon Church, because Samuel was listed as performing the marriages of members of several other Mormon families. The Adairs were supposedly converted and baptized into the Church of Jesus Christ of Latter Day Saints by

James Richey. Eliza Jane Adair was baptized in the church in November 1844.

Although others in the family joined the church, Thomas Adair, Sr. did not. And when the others moved on, Thomas remained behind in Mississippi. A "Jamima" (b.c. 1861), wife of Rev. J. B. Adair was buried in November, 1883 in New Chapel Cemetery in Itawamba County. So not all the other Itawamba Adairs had joined the Mormon Church and moved west. Thomas Jefferson Adair, Sr. died in Mississippi circa 1856.

The ones who left Mississippi moved west with Brigham Young's groups. The route followed by these Mormons was a exhausting one. Because of this, Brigham Young set up settlerments as stopping points along the route between the starting point of Nauvoo in Illinois, and the destination point on the Great Salt Lake in Utah. Church members were left at each of these settlements to plant fields for food and to give other aid to those Mormons who followed.

The first settlement established was at what would become Council bluff, Iowa. The second was at Mt. Pisgath, Union County, Iowa.

It was there that Thomas' son Samuel Jefferson Adair and his family stopped for at least two years. Mt. Pisgah was not an attractive place to stop. On June 15, 1846, Louisa Barnes Pratt wrote of it in her journal that

"The tents are scattered everywhere. Poor people here..."

The Adairs may have been delayed manning the settlement, helping subsequent groups traveling the Mormon Trail.

Whatever the reason for their stay, the family's time in Mt. Pisgah was costly. On September 8, 1846, Samuel's son Joseph

Jasper Adair died at age four. On October 31, 1846, Samuel's son William Jefferson Adair died. He was sixteen years old. Then, on September 31, 1848, Samuel's wife, Jemima Catherine Mangum Adair died in Mt. Pisgah at the age of thirty-nine.

By 1855 the Samuel Jefferson Adair family had joined the other Mormons in Utah. It was then that Samuel's daughter Permelia Jane Adair married Charles Searle on December 25, 1855 in Paipon, Utah.

The Thomas Jackson Adair Family

Bozeman Adair, Sr.
> b. Virginia; c. 1771
>
> d. Paulding County, Georgia; 1857
>
> Children
>> Bozeman (see below)
>>
>> Whitmill
>>
>> Mitchell
>>
>> William Andrew
>>
>> John Bluett
>>
>> James Lee

Bozeman H. Adair
> b. Madison County, Georgia; August 27, 1826
>
> m. Elizabeth Adeline DeLoach (b. South Carolina; January
> 6, 1830 d. Lamar County, Alabama; March 1, 1892)
>
> d. Lamar County, Alabama; April 22, 1880
>
> Children
>> Thomas Jackson (see below)

Thomas Jackson Adair
> b. Paulding County, Georgia; October 20, 1865
>
> m. Beulah Eudora Smith (b. Lamar County, Alabama;
> February 27, 1876 d. Monroe County, Mississippi), dau of
> Lemuel Rand and Arrah Belle Neeley Smith
>
> d. Monroe County, Mississippi; January 29, 1960
>
> bur. Pleasant Grove Cemetery; Bartahatchie, Mississippi
>
> Children
>> Trice Paul   Exa Fay   Carey Adine

Lamar Lomax   Jewell Lucille   John Neely
Garnett Knox   Arrah Louise

Bozeman/Boseman Adair, Sr. of this genealogy was born in Virginia circa 1771, possibly the son of William and Sarah Ann Adair. A William Adair had moved from Virginia to Wilkes County, Georgia, circa 1775. Bozeman moved to Madison County, Georgia before the 1826 birth of his son Bozeman, but died in Paulding County, Georgia, west of Atlanta, in 1857.

The Thomas Jackson Adair family made their move from Alabama to Mississippi later then other families in this book. Thomas' first two children, Trice and Carley were born in Alabama in 1898 and 1899 respectively. But his third child Jewell was born in Monroe County, Mississippi in 1901 and was a lifelong resident of the Bartahatchie community.

The James Adair Family

James Adair I

    b. Antrim County, Ireland; 1680

    emig. 1730

    Children

        James II - b. 1709

        Joseph - b. 1711

            m. Sarah Laferty

            r. South Carolina, Georgia and Alabama

            Children

Joseph, Jr.	Leah Ramage
James	Sarah
Mary Owens	Benjamin

        William - b. 1719

            r. Kentucky

The James Adair family genealogy is perplexing. What is known is that James Adair I had three sons. The Old Ninety Six and Abbeville District had a record for a John Adair who died before May, 1784, leaving a wife Sarah and children James, Joseph and Benjamin Adair. The inventory of the estate was completed by June 9, 1784. This could have been the Joseph Adair (b. 1711), the son of James I shown above. The wife's and children's names and the expected birthdate match.

Other sources have given Susannah Long as Joseph's second wife and have listed Joseph, Jr.'s birthdate as 1773. But Joseph, Sr. would have had to have been sixty-two years old when his son and namesake was born.

The Adairs of this genealogy may have been Scotch-Irish. In 1768, James and Joseph Adair received patents for land on Duncan Creek in Laurens County, South Carolina, just west of the Scotch-Irish Waxau Colony. And a Joseph Adair helped build a Presbyterian church in South Carolina in 1763, according to *History of the Presbyterians in South Carolina*. The Duncan Creek Presbyterian Church was officially organized in 1766.

The Scotch-Irish were an interesting people. They were often stereotyped as irreverent people who loved their leisure and their whiskey. Although they were Presbyterians, they were Dissenters and Non-Conformists who were open to newer religions. They did anything they liked, anytime and anywhere. They could out drink, out chew, out race, out hunt and out dance anyone. These were the people who produced son-of-a-guns like Andrew Jackson, Patrick Henry and Sam Houston.

At age seventy, a Joseph Adair, Sr. served as commissary for Col. Casey's Regiment in the Revolutionary War. As mentioned earlier, more than likely, there was an intervening generation named Joseph between Joseph Adair (b. 1711) and Joseph Adair (b. 1773). And perhaps it was this Joseph II who was commissary in the war.

To make things more perplexing, a William Adair, who also died before May, 1784, mentioned a James, Joseph, Sarah and Benjamin Adair in his Abbeville District will. However, the relationship was not given. Could William of this will have been the brother of one of the Josephs above?

What is known is that James Adair I was probably born in 1680 to Thomas Adair of County Antrim, Ireland. James I and his three sons migrated to the colonies in 1730. Temporarily leaving his father and brothers in Pennsylvania, James II went to

Charleston, South Carolina where circa 1735, he went into partnership with an Indian trader named Golphin.

That was the beginning of a career which would continue for forty years. James Adair became a trusted friend of the Muscogees, Cherokees and Choctaws. His relationship with the Chickasaws lasted for twenty-four years. Consequently, he often served as a diplomat and peacemaker between the whites and Indians in the Alabama-Mississippi region.

The trading between his English associates and the Indians proved to be profitable. Goods were brought in through Charleston and carried by pack through the wilderness to the Indians. Despite his business dealings with them, James Adair deplored the British neglect of the Indians and wrote about the easy ways with which the Indians lived with the traders. In the 1760's he wrote the Chickasaws industry extended to

> "no further than to support a plain simple life, and secure themselves from the power of the enemy, and from hungar and cold..."

However,

> "instead of reforming the Indians, the monks and friars corrupted their morals; for in the place of inculcating love, peace, and good-will to their red pupils, as become messengers of the divine author of peace, they only impressed their flexible minds with an implacable hatred against every British subject, without any distinction ... Many evils are produced by sending out ignorant and wicked persons as clergymen."

As an educated man who studied the Indian languages and made vocabularies of the various dialects, James Adair even attempted to compare and find similarities between these languages and ancient Hebrew, which he had studied as a younger man.

He wrote a five hundred page *History of the American Indian* which was published in London in 1775 and edited by Samuel Cole Williams. In his book, Adair attempted to prove that the American Indians were a part of the lost tribes of Israel.

James Adair died in 1783.

An Elizabeth Adair (b.c. 1780-90) who was of mixed White and Cherokee parentage, married Emmanuel York (c. 1760 - 1834) in Jefferson County, Alabama. Elizabeth may have been a descendant of James or his brother Joseph. Elizabeth Adair and Emmanuel York had a daughter Mary "Polly" who married Wiley Bagwell in 1823 in Jefferson County, Alabama.

Bagwell Family

John? Bagwell
>   Children
>   >   Daniel (see below)
>   >   John - r. Lunenburg County, Virginia; 1764
>   >   William
>   >   James - r. Spartanburg, South Carolina; 1780
>   >   Littleton/Littlejohn - r. Spantenburg, South Carolina;
>   >   >   1787 and 1793
>   >   Jackson ?
>   >   Richard - r. Brunswick County, Virginia; 1782
>   >   >   Children
>   >   >   >   Drury

Daniel Bagwell
>   b. 1720
>   m. Elizabeth
>   r. Brunswick County, Virginia; 1757
>   r. Wake County, North Carolina; 1800
>   d. prob Wake County, North Carolina; c. 1801
>   Children
>   >   William - b. Halifax, North Carolina; c. 1757
>   >   >   m. Elizabeth (1760-1830)
>   >   >   r. Greenville, Pendleton District, South Carolina;
>   >   >   1816 & 1820
>   >   >   d. 1848
>   >   >   Children
>   >   >   >   John - b. near Raleigh, North Carolina

> d. Princeton, Laurens County, South Carolina

Jesse

Frederick I - b. Virginia or Halifax, North Carolina; circa 1759 - 1762

> m. Mary "Polly" Hill (1752-aft 1850); North Carolina; March 27, 1781
>
> r. Fayette County, Alabama; 1834 and June 1, 1840
>
> d. Fayette or Shelby County, Alabama; February 13, 1851
>
> bur. prob Pleasant Hill Cemetery, Berry, Fayette County, Alabama
>
> Children (7)
>> Frederick
>>
>> Crawford?
>>
>> Daughters

John/John Daniel - b. Halifax, North Carolina; c. 1761

> m. Rachel Shambley / Chamblee
>
> d. 1855
>
> bur. Sweetwater Cemetery, Duluth, Georgia
>
> Children

Blake	Robert Johnson
Mary "Polly"	John Daniel Jr.
Larkin	Mathew Warren
Henson	James William
Redmond	Daniel
Clara Kitty	Patsy
Berry	

> Children

John Daniel	William E.
Martha Jane	James Madison
Delany	George Franklin
Mary Amelia	Dr. Alfred Assury
Ida Caldonia	Albert Phillips

Nathan - b. Halifax, North Carolina; c. 1765
r. Pendleton District, South Carolina
d. 1838/9

Early Bagwells came from England and Ireland. The name was probably originally Backwell and may have been the surname given to people who lived in "back of the well" or at the "back well". Another possible origin would be a combining of "Baega" (meaning "Badger") and "Welle" (meaning "spring" or "stream"). Since then, spellings have included variations of Bakewell, Bacwel, Begwell, Bagswell, Bagwsl and Bagwell.

The first Bagwells in America were Thomas and Henry, residents of Jamestown, Virginia in 1608. The first Daniel of this genealogy was probably a descendant of one of these Bagwells.

Daniel's father may have been named John. In 1787 a John Bagwell, Jr. proved in court that injuries to his back were caused by the spurs of James Lee during a fight in Spartenburg County, South Carolina. Since Daniel's brother Littleton/Littlejohn was in Spartenburg at the time, it would be possible that John Jr. was also there and that he was Daniel and Littleton's brother. Or perhaps John Jr. and Littlejohn were the same person.

Littleton/Littlejohn appeared to have been the first to have moved westward. In 1824, the home of a Littleton Bagwell was designated as a voting precinct in Fayette County, Alabama. His nephew Frederick Bagwell would eventually also move there.

On June 21, 1757, the Daniel of this genealogy was in Brunswick County, Virginia, where "Danl Bagwell" was

> "summoned to the next court to make his excuse if any he has why he should not be deemed a soldier in the militia".

By 1760, Daniel Bagwell had followed Indian trails and trading paths south from Virginia and could be found in Halifax County, North Carolina, where sons William, Frederick, John Daniel and Nathan were born. A lot of Irish, Scottish, Welsh and English settled in the foothills of the Carolinas in the mid-1700's.

According to *Bagwell: The Family History Book*, during the American Revolution, William and Frederick fought for the United States, joining regiments in Bute and Wake Counties, North Carolina, respectively. After the war Daniel's brother Richard and nephew Drury were acknowledged as having given supplies to the American side.

John also served in the Revolutionary War, fighting with his brother William under General Ash in the Battle of Brier Creek. In September 1832, John filed a Revolutionary War application in which he swore he fought as a substitute first for his father, then for Jesse Richards, then for Thomas Bunch and finally for Arthur Pope. Moreover, he reported that he was in the Battle of Stono and at Gate's defeat at Camden.

After the war, most of Daniel's family moved to the Greenville and Spartenburg, South Carolina area. His son William arrived in the Pendleton District in 1816.

Daniel's son Frederick Bagwell I had more wanderlust than his brothers. At the beginning of the American Revolution he was in Wake County, North Carolina. At one point, he also may have lived in Johnston County, North Carolina. But in 1803, he was in Pendleton District, South Carolina and, in 1820 in Gwinnett County, Georgia.

In 1827, he drew land in the lottery but, for some reason, he did not collect it. Instead, he moved his family to Alabama, where, in 1834, he applied for his Revolutionary War pension and, in 1838, he lived in Fayetteville, Fayette County, Alabama. In 1840 he was receiving an annual pension of $50.00 at age eighty. After his 1851 death, his widow Mary continued to receive the $50.00 a year.

In Pamela Bagwell's history of the family, she lists Frederick I (b.c. 1759) and Mary (b.1752) Bagwell as the parents of Frederick Jr. (b. 1818) who follows in "Possibly Related Bagwell Family #1". That would have made Frederick Jr's parents 59 and 66 years old at his birth.

Because of this dilemma, its improbable that Frederick and Mary were the parents of Frederick Jr. While Frederick Jr. may have been a descendant of Frederick I, it is far more likely that there was another generation between them. Furthermore, the father may have been someone named Frederick.

Frederick Bagwell I died in Shelby County, Alabama on February 13, 1850.

Possibly Related Bagwell Family #1

Frederick Jr. - b. April, 1818
>m. Nancy Caroline Gaines (1823-1891), dau of Silas (1796-1838) and Elizabeth Arnold (1798-1879) Gaines; c. 1838/9
>d. 1899
>Children

Berry Judson	Mary E.
Harriet "Hannah"	James
William H.	Nancy Caroline
Louisa Jane	Martha Ann
Silas Gaines	Robert Arnold
John Lewis	

Possibly Related Bagwell Family #2

Fredric T. Bagwell
>b. September 5, 1853
>m. Rachel Weeks (1856-1954), dau of Hiram S. and Jane Johnson Weeks; Winston County, Mississippi; December 23, 1875
>d. May 24, 1921
>bur. Popular Flats Cemetery, Winston County, Mississippi
>Children
>>Lula Jane - b. 1876
>>>m1 Corley
>>>m2 Coleman
>>>d. 1968
>>Ella Elizabeth - b. 1880
>>>m. Coleman

d. 1915

Anna Elnora - b. 1882

 m. Williams

 d. 1956

Virgie Rachel - b. January 28, 1890

 m. John Benjamin Taylor (1891-1957), son of Egbert and Alice Gaston Taylor; November 8, 1914

 d. 1979

 bur. Popular Flats Cemetery, Winston County, Mississippi

 Children

Burton	Bonnie
Alliemae	J.B.
Gladys	Ester
Freeman	Morris
Bessie Alene	Mattie Dorris

Ida Pearl - b. 1892

 m. Arnett

Belle - b. 1894

 m. Roberts

 d. 1975

Possibly Related Bagwell Family #3

_____ Bagwell

 b. England

 Children

  Frederick (see below)

Frederick Bagwell

    b. South Carolina; 1799

    m. Margaret Ann Crawford (b. Alabama; c. 1802 d. 1874)

    r. Alabama; 1817

    r. Choctaw County, Mississippi; 1836

    d. Choctaw County, Mississippi; 1864

    Children

        John (see below)

        H.H. - b. Alabama; c. 1821

            m. Louisa (b. Mississippi; c. 1823)

            Children

                William   James   Jane

                Sarah

        Henry - b. Alabama; c. 1823

            m. Angeline (b. Georgia c. 1828)

            Children

                William   Emma   Margaret

        James - b. Alabama; c. 1828

        Peter - b. Alabama; c. 1835

        Elizabeth - b. Alabama; c. 1837

        William - b. Mississippi; c. 1838

        Martin - b. Mississippi; c. 1841

John Bagwell

    b. Alabama; January 3, 1833

    m. Sarah Frances Turner (b. 1842), dau of Frank Turner of
Oktibbeha County, Mississippi; 1858

    r. Winston County, Mississippi; 1870

    Children

        Sarah - b.c. 1861

William Frank - b.c. 1864

    m. E.V. Cork; Choctaw County, Mississippi; December, 1888

Martin Fred - b. 1864

    m. Miss I.F. Adams; Choctaw County, Mississippi; October 29, 1885

Henry H - b.c. 1866

    m. M.J. Evans; Choctaw County, Mississippi; January, 1888

John P. - b.c. 1868

    m. J.D. Jackson; Choctaw County, Mississippi: January, 1891

Abe - b. 1870

Anna L. - m. N. D.H. Cork; Choctaw County, Mississippi; December 1891

Lena - m. B.G. Dotson; Choctaw County, Mississippi; February, 1894

Robert - m. Bettie Lanthrif; Choctaw County, Mississippi; February, 1902

Effie May - m. L.D. Oswalt; Choctaw County, Mississippi; December, 1898

Lora

May

Marcus

Joe Lee

Jane - m. pos James Shaw

Blaikie / Blackie / Blaickie / Blakie Family

John Blaikie
> b. Scotland
>
> m. Janet Dickson
>
> Children
>> Alexander (see below)

Alexander Blaikie I
> b. County Berwick, Scotland; c. 1791
>
> m. Mary Somers (b. September 29, 1801); Colmslie, Melrose Parish, Scotland; June 13, 1823
>
> d. Lauder, Scotland; August 4, 1863
>
> Children
>> Alexander II (see below)
>>
>> Margaret - b.c. 1825
>>
>> Mary - b.c. 1826
>>
>> Janet - b.c. 1823
>>
>> Isabella - b. 1831
>>
>> John - b. 1836; Melrose, Scotland
>>> m. Ann White (Dunse, Scotland; b.c. 1837) , dau of David and Elizabeth White
>>>
>>> Child
>>>> Alexander
>>
>> George - b. Lauder, Scotland; 1840/41

Alexander Blaikie II
> b. Haddington, Haddingtonshire (East Lothian), Scotland; August 27 or September 29, 1837
>
> bapt. November 5, 1837

m1 Christena White (b. Dunse, Scotland; c. 1840 d. St. Louis, Missouri; 1874), dau of David and Isabella White; November 5, 1858; Yester Manse, County Haddington, Scotland

m2 St. Louis, Missouri

d. Missouri; November 11, 1920

Children

> Alexander III (see below)
>
> Isabella - b. Lauder Parish, Scotland; July 26, 1863
>
>> m. Elias Benjamin Merrill; Alabama; April 24, 1861
>>
>> d. March 11, 1890
>>
>> Children
>>
>>> Bessie
>>>
>>> Roy
>
> Mary - b. Lauder Parish; Scotland; September 19, 1866
>
>> d. St. Louis, Missouri; 1871
>
> Christina - b. 1869
>
>> d. St. Louis, Missouri; 1872

Alexander Blaikie III

> b. Long-Newton, Yester Parish, Haddingtonshire, Scotland; May 15, 1859
>
> m. Martha Holland (Hodges) Merrill (b. December 4, 1863 d. November 17, 1953), dau of Greenberry and Elizabeth Halley Merrill; Alabama; 1882
>
> d. Blount County, Alabama; 1882
>
> bur. Providence Cemetery, Hayden, Blount County, Alabama

Children

Alexander Greenberry	Edward
Hobart Donahue	Conabell Udora
Ola Collins	Grace Olympic
Frances Ethel	Essie Leora (tw)
Dessie Leona (tw)	

While the usual migration pattern was from the Atlantic seaboard states into Alabama and then on to Mississippi and the west, the Blaikie/Blackie/Blaickie/Blakie family of this genealogy did it somewhat backwards.

The family originated in Scotland, where the Blaikies were members of the Lamont Clan who settled in Lanarkshire. In the early 1500's, a William Blakye was at Newbattle Abbey. And a David Blakie was in Lanark, Scotland in the late 1500's.

Alexander II of this genealogy was born in Haddington, Scotland to Alexander I and Mary Somers Blaikie. Haddingtonshire (later East Lothian) was a county in south-eastern Scotland, bounded on the last by the Firth of Forth and the North Sea. Haddington parish was the equivalent of its county seat. Alexander Blaikie I was listed as a dyker in the 1841 and 1851 censuses. The marriage of Alexander II was registered in Yester Parish.

> "On 27 December 1858 at Yester Manse, county of Haddington, marriage (after Banns) was solemnized between us according to the forms of the church of Scotland; Alexander Blaickie aged 21, Longnewton, Yester, bachelor, mason, The son of Alexander Blakie and Mary Somers."

AND

"Christina White, Salton, parish of Yester, aged 18, spinster, domestic servant, the daughter of David White, farm steward and Isabella White."

Their son Alexander Blaikie III was born just four and one-half months later. In Long-Newton, Yester.

Long-Newton was one of the hamlets in Yester, Haddingtonshire, just north of Berwickshire where the Blaike's originated. Yester, whose post office was Gifford, was a 14 square mile parish.

In 1867 the family was living on Lauder Row. Alexander I had died, but Mary, his widow, was there. Down the street her sons Alexander II and John were living with their families in houses across the row from each other.

Later Alexander Blaikie II moved his family to Craighouse, on the road to Stowe, while he worked in Manchester, England during the summer. He built dry stone dykes (mortarless rock fences) which were used around fields. More important fences of the time were built with mortar.

Alexander Blaikie was able to save a good amount of money and was able to build a large home for his family. But, according to his son, Alexander was "defrauded" and lost both the house and his savings. While working on the castle at Waterloo, he hired lawyers and had a judgement made in his favor concerning the fraud. Yet he was never able to collect a cent

In 1866, the family moved in with Christina's parents in Edinburgh and then to Hillhouse Field in Leith, Scotland. All the while Alexander II was working at the Leith Docks.

But 1867 brought a major change in the lives of the Alexander Blaikie's family. It was that year that Blaikie was contacted by Col. William Bell Montgomery of Oktibbeha County, Mississippi.

The Blaikie family left Liverpool just before Christmas 1867 on board the new ship *Denmark*. As steerage passengers, the Blaikie family had to supply their own bedding and water buckets. After seventeen days at sea which included a major snow storm, the ship docked in New York. The family immediately boarded a train which took them to Cairo, Illinois. Another train took them to Mayhew Mission, Lowndes County, Mississippi where the family was forced to spend the night.

On February 13, 1868, the Blaikie family set out for "Squire" Montgomery's plantation near Starkville in Oktibbeha County. The Blaikies lived with the Montgomerys while Alexander worked building chimneys and house pillars, and walling up cisterns, and generally bringing new life into buildings that had become decayed during the Civil War.

The next year Alexander built a house for his family near the Montgomerys. Blaikie rented farm land for which he hired hands to work while he continued with his brick work.

While financially the family prospered, Alexander's wife Christina was growing weaker. So the family moved to St. Louis, Missouri, in Spring, 1870. At first the only job Alexander could find was that of a night watchman. Eventually, though, he got a job as foreman at Christy Clay Works.

Even though he had finally found employment more in keeping with his skills, personal adversity just continued. Alexander's daughter Mary died in St. Louis in 1871, daughter Christina in 1872, and wife Christina in 1874. After a few months, Alexander took what was left of his family back to Mississippi and to his friends, the Montgomerys.

Trying to boost the income of the old agrarian South following the Civil War, Col. Montgomery had become an advocate of moving dairy cattle onto the depleted cotton land of Mississippi. As a firm believer in diversification, Montgomery urged other plantation owners to stop battling the grass in their cotton fields and use it to feed cows. There is a story that Montgomery, like a Johnny Appleseed, would fill his pockets and saddlebags with grass and clover seeds and spread them in uncultivated areas as he traveled through Oktibbeha County.

In the long run, Montgomery's efforts had a dramatic effect on the economy of the area. But further, Starkville's industrial picture changed with the addition of creameries and a Borden plant.

Montgomery was just getting started. It was thought that the heat of Mississippi summers would not be conducive to dairy farming, but Montgomery was determined to prove that was not true.

So upon Alexander Blaikie's return to Mississippi in 1875, Montgomery put his latest idea to work by hiring Blaikie to build an underground dairy at Mhoon Farm in Oktibbeha County. It was like a gigantic root cellar, where butter could be churned and dairy products could be kept cool, even in the middle of a Mississippi summer.

After the completion of the underground dairy, Alexander allowed the Perrys, a childless neighbor couple, to take in his surviving daughter Isabelle, while he and his son Alexander III returned to St. Louis. After Mr. Perry's death, Isabelle joined her brother and father.

The family worked off and on in Starkville during the last third of the 1870's. But in 1880 they removed to Blount Springs,

Alabama, where Blaikie built Montgomery a small dairy and made other improvements to the land there.

In 1883 Alexander Blaikie II returned to St. Louis where he married for the second time. He lived there until his death in 1920.

Alexander III and his sister Isabelle remained behind in Blount County, Alabama. They married, raised families of their own, and eventually died there.

Blaylock/Blailock/Blalock Family

John William Blalock

  b. Accomac County, Virginia; 1671

  m1 Mary Terrell (d. 1697); 1691

  m2 Elizabeth Millington (1671-1745); Hanover County, Virginia; 1698

  d. Louisa County, Virginia; 1745

  Children

    Richard I (see below)

Richard Blalock/Blaylock I

  Children

    Richard II (see below)

    John William   Ann

    Millington   William

    Elizabeth   David

Richard Blalock II

  b. Hanover County, Virginia; 1722

  m. Rachel Hardin (b. South Carolina; c. 1784   d. Cumberland County, North Carolina; by 1801); North Carolina; 1745

  d. Cumberland County, North Carolina; 1805

  Children

    Richard II (see below)

    Hardy/Hardin - b. Greensburg or Barnwell County, South Carolina; 1768/72

m. Mason Long (b. Barnwell County, South Carolina, 1772; d. Barnwell County, South Carolina; November 1808); 1791

d. Harnett County, South Carolina; 1853

Children

    Elizabeth - b. 1794

        m. William W. Collins

        d. 1840

    Levi - b. South Carolina; 1797

        m. Sarah Tyler

        d. Mississippi; 1881

    Sarah (Sally) - b. 1795

        m. William Joiner

        d. 1865

    Hardin II - b. South Carolina; 1799

        m1 Caroline Long; bur. Lee County, Alabama; 1839

        m2 Nancy Blaylock, dau of John Blaylock; Russell County, Alabama; May 16, 1840

        d. Russell County, Alabama; 1854

        Children

Female	John H.
Levi	Harriet
Patrick P.	James
Elizabeth	William
Burrell	Missouri

    Amelia - b.c. 1800

    Samuel - b.c. 1800

    James - b.c. 1800

Ebenezer - b.c. 1800

> Charles
> William
> Anne

Richard Blaylock III

> b. Barnwell, South Carolina; c. 1747
> m. Sarah Mason (b. Barnwell, South Carolina; c. 1750 d. 1818/1820)
> d. Barnwell, South Carolina; c. 1818
> Children
>> Richard III (see below)
>> John
>> Hardin

Richard Blaylock IV

> b. Orangeburg, South Carolina; 1770
> m. Martha Long (b. Barnwell, South Carolina; 1774 d. Dallas County, Alabama; betw 1840-1848)
> d. Dallas County, Alabama; December 13, 1838
> Children
>> Nathaniel (see below)

John	James V.	Osmund
Julia Ann	Barney	Martha
Washington	Wade	Richard V
Sarah	Hardin	Levi

Nathaniel Blaylock

> b. Orangeburg, South Carolina; February 2, 1806
> m. Sarah Dalton (b. South Carolina; by 1817)

r. Oktibbeha County, Mississippi; 1850

d. aft 1854

Children

    Jasper (see below)

    Catherine - b. South Carolina; c. 1841

    William - b. betw 1831/1845

        m. Elizabeth (b. Alabama; c. 1832)

        d. Mississippi by 1870

        Children

            William M. "Bill" - b. Mississippi; c. 1852

                m. Nancy (b. Alabama c. 1853)

                Children

Hester/Marshall	Daisy G.
Leslie E.	Roseta/Pearl
Ivy Irene	Carrie/Myrele

            Benjamin - b. Mississippi; c. 1854

                m. Cora Reed; Webster County, Mississippi; December 19, 1891

            Mary C. - b. Mississippi; 1856

            Elmira and/or Sarah J. - b. Mississippi; c. 1858

            Julia A. - b. Mississippi; 1860

                m. John Franklin Land; Webster County, Mississippi; December 31, 1891

    James - b.c. 1844

    Beverly M. - b.c. 1846

        r. Choctaw County, Mississippi; 1863

    Frederick - b.c. 1847

    John - b.c. 1849

Jasper Blaylock

    b. Alabama; c. 1838

    m. Nancy Jane (b. June 30, 1842; d. August 1, 1940; bur. Mt. Vernon Cemetery, Tomnolen, Mississippi)

    d. betw 1891-1900

    Children

        William N. - b. Mississippi; c. 1868

        Sarah/Sallie - b. Mississippi; c. 1870

        Charles E. - b. Mississippi; c. 1872

        Henry David - b. Mississippi; February 1, 1880

            d. January 24, 1961

            bur. Edwards Springs Cemetery, Webster County, Mississippi

        James W. - b. Mississippi; c. 1874

            m. Ella Johnson; Webster County, Mississippi; January 16, 1895

        Jenneta/Jannett/Jenette E. - b. April 3, 1876

            m. P.R. Johnson (February 10, 1874-April 20, 1939) February 16, 1896; Webster County, Mississippi

            d. March 22, 1971

            bur. Mr. Vernon Cemetery, Tomnolen, Webster County, Mississippi

        Simeon Basco - betw 1877-1880

            m. Mary Jane Forbes (d. 1904; bur. Mt. Vernon Cemetery, Tomnolen, Mississippi)

Some early Blalock/Blalack/Blailock/Blaylock/Blacklock/ Blackloke/Baylock/Balock/Blaylark/Blellock/Blelack/Blaloc/ Blailoch probably received that surname because of his dark or lead colored hair or locks, with "blay" meaning "ash colored" and "lock" meaning "hair". Or the name might have come from the Old English "blaec locc" as used to refer to the occupation blacksmith. "Bleloch" meant "blue lake" to the Scots.

One of the Blaylock arms was "Vert a saltere between four pheons on a chief or lion passant gules." At least one Blaylock crest originated in France and several others in Northern England or Scotland.

Scotland seemed to have had its share of Blaylocks. William "Blakloche" was at the monastery at Dumfernlin, Scotland. In 1637, Joet "Blakloc" was Burgess of Dumfries, Scotland.

Whatever the origin, for the purpose of this genealogy, the Blaylock spelling was used. According to Colleen Blaylock Green, an editor of the Blaylock family newsletter, several Blaylocks appeared in early American records. A Patrick "Blalock" was in Jamestown in 1635, Richard Blaylock arrived in Massachusetts in 1620 and four Blaylock brothers were in the Cape Fear region of North Carolina in the early 1700's. Green believed this last group were descendants of Scot Highlanders.

Many of the early American Blaylocks descended from Thomas Blalock who emigrated from England to Accromac County, Virginia in 1622. He probably came from the Cumberland area of England on the Scottish border. Other Blaylocks were found in Scotland. Thomas arrived in Virginia with a group of seventy-five settlers headed by Captain William Epps.

A number of those early Blaylocks intermarried with the Cherokees. Their names could be found on Indian rolls and their dead in Cherokee graveyards.

Although John William Blaylock of this genealogy was born in Accomac County, Virginia, by his 1698 marriage to Elizabeth Millington he was in Hanover County, Virginia. John and Elizabeth were members of the Church of England in St. Paul's Parrish of Hanover County.

But it was in Hanover County were the Blaylock genealogy became confusing. John and Elizabeth supposedly had Richard, John William, William, Ann, Elizabeth, Millington and David - all born after 1710. However, had John William been the father of the Richard born in 1722, the father would have been 51 years old when his son was born. Moreover, there was a Richard Blaylock born circa 1690 to John and Mary Blaylock. That Richard was listed as having four sons - Richard II, David, John and Millington.

The most plausible solution to the problem would be that John William (b. 1671) and his wife Mary Terrill or Elizabeth Millington had a son named Richard I (b.c. 1690) who then became the father of John William (b. 1710), William, Millington, David, Ann, Elizabeth, and Richard II (b. 1722).

To add to the confusion, in 1704 there was a planter named John Blaylock living in St. Peter's Parish of New Kent County, Virginia, with William Millington, Sr. and William Millington, Jr. While he might have appeared to be the John William Blaylock of this genealogy, in reality the children of John of New Kent were named John Jr. (B. 1685), Kade (b. 1687), Sarah (b. 1689), Richard (b. 1690) and Jeremiah (b. 1692).

There also were a number of Hardin and Millington Blaylocks in the area. In fact, according to one genealogist, there may have even been a Millington Blaylock who emigrated from

Cumberland, England to Virginia in the late 1600's, and he apparently had a son named John.

The men of the Blaylock family of this genealogy married later in life than was usual at the time. The Nathaniel Blaylock family began their route west in South Carolina where Nathaniel probably married Sarah who was nine years his junior. His first child, Jasper, was born in Alabama when Nathaniel was approximately thirty years old. A William C. "Blalock" was born in Pickens County, Alabama in 1845, may also have been Nathaniel and Sarah's son.

A Jasper N. "Blalack", who was probably the Jasper of this genealogy, was a corporal in Company E of Mississippi's 31st Infantry. And probably because of the Civil War, Jasper married late and his first child was born when Jasper was approximately thirty-one years old. By the 1870 census, Jasper had married Nancy and his children William and Sarah had been born. They were living in what would become Webster County. Although he was thirty-three years old; Jasper owned no real estate and had only $400 worth of personal property.

At some point Jasper's family settled in Tomnolen, a town six miles southwest of Eupora and a mile north of the Big Black River. The town was established in 1866 on Nolen family property and was named after Jim Tom Nolen, a member of that family. The Georgia Pacific was constructed through town in 1888/89, attracting people living near the old county seat of Greensboro closer to the railroad and to the new courthouse in Walthall. By the time Jasper died, the area boasted a post office, several large stores, a livery, two churches, a lumber mill and a school.

In 1870 a Vachel Blaylock (approximately four years younger than Jasper) lived in the Cumberland area of Choctaw County. Although Cumberland would become part of Webster County and was quite near where the Blaylocks were living, no connection was found.

This was an area that was switched from county to county quite frequently. Oktibbeha became a county in 1833. In 1871 the northern portion of it was added to pieces of three other county's and made into Colfax County. Then in 1876, that county was renamed Clay County. Likewise, portions of Choctaw County went into the making of Sumter County, which eventually became Webster County.

In 1878, Jasper's school aged children (Willie, Sally and Charlie) appeared in the superintendent of education's list of educable children in the Ross School District. But in 1890, Sallie, James, Jannett, Simeon and David were in the Arcadia District. The younger ones appeared again in the 1900 list in "T2 R8."

Jasper and his wife were buried in the Mount Vernon Cemetery near Mary Jane, the wife of Jasper's brother Simeon Blaylock, and Simeon and Mary Jane's infant daughter. However, according to Curtis' Webster County history, in 1891, "J.N. (Jasper), N.J. (Nancy Jane), S.A. and Ella Blalack" were charter members of the Edwards Springs Church. Jasper's son Henry Blaylock eventually was buried there.

And like Jasper, three of his brothers; Beverly, William and James; also were in the 31st Mississippi Infantry, but they were all in Company I. While William and James enlisted at Saltillo, Beverly enlisted at Bankston in Choctaw County on November 1, 1863. But his confederate military career was short. On April 5, 1864 he was listed as suffering from "dibilitas" at the "First

Mississippi CSA Hospital" in Jackson, Mississippi. Then, the July 12 entry reported that Beverly had been "sick for 2 months" because of "diaherrea following measles."

By the 1860 census, brother William Blaylock had settled his family in the Lodi community in Montgomery County, just west of the eventual Webster County line. When William Sr. died, his widow and children continued to live in the Lodi area. Elizabeth Blaylock had two employees - Mariah and James Collins - in the 1870 census. Mariah was listed as disabled, but still could do housework. James did farm labor.

According to the Webster County history book, William and Elizabeth's daughter Julia and her husband John Franklin Land were

> "sad because many members of the Land and
> Blaylock families as well as other Mormon neighbors
> of the Lodi community migrated to Utah when the
> Federal government started enforcing laws against
> polygamy."

But which members of the Blaylock family practiced polygamy and traveled west was not noted.

Not all Blaylocks went west. On January 16, 1908, a newspaper reported that "Daisy and Ivy Blalock", daughters of Julia's brother William Jr. were living in Winona, Mississippi, but visiting their cousins "Mr. and Mrs. Jessie Patridge in Eupora".

The Blaylocks were close to the Patridge family. When their Uncle Benjamin married Cora Reed in 1891, W.T. "Pateridge" was a bondsman. Benjamin was thirty-seven years old at the time.

Bolton Family

James Bolton Jr.

    b. North Carolina; c. 1812

    m. Susan (b. North Carolina; betw 1814 - 1816)

    r. Pickens County, Alabama; 1850

    Children

        Elijah (see below)

        Helena - b. Alabama; c. 1836

        Rebecca - b. Alabama; c. 1835

        Wiley - b. Alabama; c. 1838

        Eli - b. Alabama; c. 1844

        Elizabeth - b. Alabama; c. 1847

        Catherine - b. Alabama; c. 1847

Elijah Bolton

    b. Pickens County, Alabama; c. 1850

    m. Margaret A. Lavender Story (b. Alabama; c. 1841), dau of John Smith and Julia Ann Frances Lavender, wid of David W. Story; Greene County, Alabama; September 19, 1867

    r. Courtland, Panola County, Mississippi; 1893

    Children

        Luther - b. aft 1872

            r. Courtland, Panola County, Mississippi

            d.c. 1956

        Josephine - r. Courtland, Panola County, Mississippi; 1893

        John - b. aft 1872

            r. Courtland, Panola County, Mississippi; 1893

Robert - r. Courtland, Panola County, Mississippi;
1893

Harriet E. - m. Abner W. Brewer

r. Courtland, Panola County, Mississippi; 1893

The James Bolton/Boulton, Jr. of this genealogy may have been descended from James (b.c. 1738) and Sarah Bolton of Wake County, North Carolina or one of their nine children. Their son James (b.c. 1775) had thirteen children, including a son named James. The James Boulton (b. 1738) may have been born in Virginia. That James removed to Bertie County, North Carolina in 1744. In 1754, he was in Granville, North Carolina and in 1761 a landowner in Bute County (later Wake). He died there in 1813.

Although the James Bolton of this family history was born in North Carolina, his family was in Alabama by 1828 when James received land on Section 29 Township 22 Range 13W in Pickens County from the "Tuskaloosa" land office. James Bolton also received Pickens County land in Sec 32 T22 R13W. That land was assigned to James and a Benjamin Bolton on November 28, 1834.

In the same general area of Pickens County (Sec7 T22 R14W) lived the Robert Story family. Later Robert Story's son David and James Bolton's son Elijah would separately marry Margaret Lavender.

At the same time, a number of Bolton's were living in tha area who could have been related to the Bolton's of this genealogy. There was an Elder James S. Bolton in neighboring Fayette County who served as pastor for Emmaus Primitive Baptist Church and Union Primitive Baptist Church. A wagon maker named Joseph Bolton (b.c. 1795; South Carolina) and his wife Milly (b.c. 1798) were living on land in Tuscaloosa County that Joseph had purchased from William and Patsy Cole on July 12, 1825. Joseph and Milly had a son named James (b.c. 1820).

Other Boltons in the same age bracket in Alabama at that time included a Benjamin Bolton who had served as a private in the North Carolina line in the Revolutionary War, died February 12, 1843 in Dallas County, Alabama. During the Creek War of 1836 and 1837, a John and an Eli Bolton served as privates in Gunn's Company, Webb's Battalion of the Alabama Mounted Volunteers. A Michael Bolton served in the First Battalion of the Alabama Military Infantry and Sevier Bolton was a private in the Second Alabama Mounted Volunteers.

James Bolton's family was in the southern division of Pickens County, Alabama in the 1850 Federal Census. His son Elijah had been born circa 1850. In the 1855 state census, a James "Boulton" was living in Pickens County, Alabama with two males age 21 and under, one male age over 21, one female age 21 and under, and one female age over 21. Other adult "Boultons" listed in Pickens County in that 1855 state census were Allison (0101), Anderson (3121), M.B. (0121), Madison (3151) and William (2212).

James' son Elijah Bolton married the young widow, Margaret A. Lavender Story in 1867 in her father's Greene County, Alabama home. If all the dates were correct, Elijah was approximately seventeen years old and Margaret was twenty-six. Margaret's first husband David Story had died during the Civil War.

The family moved to Mississippi, where Margaret died. Some of Elijah's family eventually moved on to Texas. But others continued to live in Mississippi. Elijah's son Luthur settled and ran a store in Edwards, Mississippi, east of Vicksburg.

Carson Family

Franklin Carson
> m. Jane
> Children
>> Samuel (see below)

Samuel Carson
> b. St. Clair or Lowndes County, Alabama
> m. Eliza Jane Adair (b, West Carthage, Rutherford County, Tennessee; November 11, 1811 d. Washington County, Utah; August 16, 1892), dau of Thomas Jefferson and Rebecca Brown Adair; Alabama; 1829
> r. Pickens County, Alabama; 1830
> d. Alabama; c. 1836
> Children
>> John - b. Alabama; March 22, 1830
>>> d. 1830
>> Valentine - b. Pickens County, Alabama; November 8, 1831
>>> d. Parowan, Iron County, Utah; September 25, 1898
>> Elizabeth - b. "Carroltown", Pickens County, Alabama; August 10, 1833
>>> m. David Lewis; Salt Lake City, Utah; August 4, 1852
>>> m. pos three more times
>>> d. Parowan, Iron County, Utah; June 23, 1901
>> William - b. Pickens County, Alabama; October 4, 1835

d. September 15, 1847

As unflattering as it may sound, Carr / Kerr was a Scottish name stemming from a wasteland or low swampy ground. So the first person with the Carson surname could have been the son of someone who lived in such a place.

One early Carson was John, son of James and Rebecca Carson, who emigrated to North Carolina from Fermanagh County, Ireland in the mid 1750's. He settled in Marion County and, then Burke County, North Carolina. His son Samuel Price Carson was the first Secretary of State for the Republic of Texas.

But the Carson of this genealogy began with Franklin and Jane Carson who lived in Alabama, probably in the early 1800's. A "Francis" Carson was in the southern district of Pickens County, Alabama for the 1830 census, along with John and William Carson. Could Francis have been Franklin, father of Samuel, of this genealogy? Since the Samuel of this genealogy had a son born in Pickens in 1835, there was a good chance he was the Samuel who appeared in the 1830 census for Pickens as number seven on page one hundred twelve.

But by 1840 the only Carsons in Pickens County were two named Nancy. In the 1850 census the two Nancys, ages forty-six and forty-seven, and a William, age thirty, were in Pickens County with their families.

But Samuel's family was not listed, even though Samuel and Eliza's children were born in Alabama, probably all in Pickens County between 1830 and 1835. Their son John died there as an infant. And Samuel Carson died shortly after the birth of his fourth child, William Carson, in 1835. His widow Eliza married Moses Peason circa 1838.

In 1841 and 1843 the family was with still another new stepfather, John Price, in Itawamba County, Mississippi. Other Carsons also lived in Itawamba (see APPENDIX 1).

Eliza Jane Adair Carson Pearson Price was baptized in the Church of Christ of the Latter Day Saints on November 11, 1844, about the time of her third marriage. The family moved west to Utah with other members of the Mormon Church.

But these were southerners, used to southern winters and many from the Mississippi group died along the trail during the winter of 1846-47. Those who survived still suffered a great deal at the Mormon posts at Winter Quarters, Iowa and Fort Pueblo.

The Mississippians also had problems adjusting to their fellow Mormons. Mormon journals recorded that while on the trail during June, 1847, the Mississippi Mormons had to be reproved for reading, playing the fiddle, hunting and playing cards while a sermon was being delivered in camp.

Samuel and Eliza's son William Carson died along the trail on September 15, 1847. He wasn't quite twelve years old. Valentine and Elizabeth Carson made it to Utah, as did their mother.

But those early years in Utah were not easy ones for the settlers. The years of 1855 and 1856 brought the fear of starvation following a drought and the infamous grasshopper infestation. In 1857, the Mormons were accused of sedition against the United States and 2500 Federal troops were sent along the Mormon Trail to Utah. The Mormons were calling it the "Utah War", but before any blood was shed, a peace was brokered.

The Carson children settled in Parowan, Iron County, Utah. Valentine died there in 1898, Elizabeth in 1901.

Duke Family

Unknown
>   Children
>>   Elijah (see below)
>>   Sarah - b. Alabama; November 4, 1834
>>>   m. George W. Bolles (b. Germany; May 4, 1832
>>>   d. Choctaw County, Mississippi; January 1, 1916)
>>>   d. July 12, 1918
>>>   bur. Fellowship Church Cemetery, Choctaw County, Mississippi
>>>   Children
>>>>   Sarah - b.c. 1859
>>   Nancy

Dr. Elijah Duke
>   b. Pickens County, Alabama; July 8, 1834
>   m1 ?
>   m2 Georg(e)anna Berry (b. Alabama; c. 1843), dau of Thomas D. and "Cindarillar" L. (b. Georgia; c. 1812) ; Oktibbeha County, Mississippi; November 6 or 7, 1865
>   d. Webster County, Mississippi; October 18, 1885
>   bur. Old Cumberland Cemetery, Cumberland, Webster County, Mississippi
>   Children
>>   Steven Thomas - b. November, 1859
>>>   m. Mary E. Burchfield (b.c. 1862), dau of Thomas and Frances Burchfield of South

Carolina; Webster County, Mississippi; October
3, 1881

r. Choctaw County, Mississippi; 1850

d. Purdon, Texas; January 30, 1910

Mary - b. Mississippi; c. 1868

John - b. Mississippi; c. 1870

Elijah - b. Mississippi; c. 1872

Martha - b. Mississippi; c. 1874

William - b. Mississippi; c. 1875

Charles (?tw) - b. Mississippi; February, 1880

Elisha (?tw) - b. Mississippi; February, 1880

Although the Duke surname may have originated with the name Marmaduke, meaning "sea leader", the surname more likely came from a person of noble birth. In English the title was "Duke", in French it was "le duc".

One early Duke was Peter Duke who was master on Sir Francis Drake's 1585/86 voyage. On that trip Drake stopped at St. Augustine, Florida, and Roanoke Island. So Peter was presumably the first Duke to set foot in the New World.

In the 1880 census, Elijah (b. 1834) of this genealogy reported that his parents were both born in Georgia. Coincidentally, in 1850 there was an Elijah Duke family in Thomas Georgia. But in the Elijah in that census was fifty-five years old with no son named Elijah living in the home. The Elijah of this genealogy would have been sixteen in 1850.

Moreover, Elijah was supposedly born in Pickens County, Alabama in 1834. So his parents had made the move to Alabama by that time. In 1830 a Reason Duke (age 30-40), Pleasant Duke (age 30-40) and Mrs. M. Duke (age 40-50) all headed households in Tuscaloosa County, Alabama. The 1840 Pickens County census had a Reason and an Alford Duke who might have been related to Elijah. An adult male named Robert Duke was living alone in the 1855 Alabama State census for Pickens County. A James Duke, with four males under 21, three males over 21, four females under 21 and one female over 21 also lived in Pickens County at the time.

And although either Robert or James Duke could have been related to Elijah, by that time the Choctaw land in Mississippi had opened to settlement and Elijah's family could have moved west already. In 1850, Elijah (age 16) was living separated from his family in Mississippi. Perhaps his parents had died. Perhaps he was working as a laborer. For whatever reason, a teenage Elijah Duke was living in Chickasaw County with H.B. Bonds (age 40) and his family.

Then in 1860, Dr. Elijah Duke (age 27) was living in Oktibbeha County, in the home of German immigrant George W. Bolles (age 26) and his family. George's wife was Sarah Duke Bolles, probably Elijah's sister.

Curious enough, in the 1860 Oktibbeha County census, as in Pickens County, Alabama, a Pleasant Duke and his family were living in Starkville. Pleasant (age 62, born in Tennessee) and his wife Martha (age 62, born in Georgia), Rufus (age 26, born in Alabama), and Mary (age 23, born in Alabama) were living on lot number 535. At the same time, Sarah Duke Bolles (age 24, born in Alabama) and her brother Elijah Duke (age 27, born in Alabama) were living on lot number 599 (see APPENDIX 2). Can it be merely a coincidence that Pleasant and Elijah were near each other in Picken's County, Alabama in the 1830's and in Oktibbeha County, Mississippi in 1860?

Another possibile sister of Elijah's was Nancy Berry. Between June 1, 1849 and June 1, 1850, Isham Berry (age 22), son of Thomas and "Cindariller" Berry, married an eighteen year old named Nancy. A Nancy Duke - same age and birthplace as Isham's wife - had lived near the Bonds family in Chickasaw County when Elijah Duke lived with them in 1850.

Fifteen years later, Isham Berry's little sister Georganna would become Elijah Duke's second wife. So it would not be improbable to discover that Nancy Berry was Elijah's sister. In 1850, Nancy Duke's mother or grandmother was listed as "Hicksey" Duke (age 60), born in North Carolina.

Listed as a physician in censuses, Elijah probably attended medical school. When he registered as a doctor in the Webster County Circuit Clerk's office in 1882 he reported as having attended "Eclestic Medical Institution".

Elijah Duke enlisted in the confederate army at Montpelier, Mississippi. Although Montpelier was in Chickasaw County at the time, it eventually became part of Clay in 1871. Clay was organized from land from several surrounding counties and was first named Colfax County.

Cumberland where Elijah's family settled was in Webster County, but bordered the land which became part of Clay. At one point, Chickasaw, Oktibbeha and Choctaw met Webster County only one-half mile north of Cumberland. Borders moved. Births in one county, marriages in a second and deaths in a third could all have taken place in the same house.

The Duke cemetery was located in that area, just northeast of Pheba. Could the tombstone there for W.C. Duke (December 2, 1818 to October 12, 1872 or 1877) have belonged to Elijah's father?

Immediately following the Civil War, Cumberland , originally named Choctaw Ridge, became a trading, educational, and industrial center. Cumberland Male and Female College was established in Old Cumberland circa 1875 with Dr. Duke as president of the board of trustees.

In 1880, Georganna Duke and eight children were living in Webster County, Mississippi. Georganna's mother, sixty-eight year old "Cinda" Berry and a servant were also living with them.

Then in 1883, Elijah purchased forty acres in Sec26 T20 R11E, north of Mathiston in Webster County. He paid $40. But two years later Elijah was dead. He was buried in the Old Cumberland Churchyard and his tombstone read -

Sacred
To the Memory of
Eld. Eligah Duke M.D.
Born
In Pickens Co. Ala.
July 8, 1834
Died
In Winston Co., Miss
October 1885

Gamble/Gammill Family

Samuel Gamble/Gammill
> b.c. Ireland; 1740-50
>
> m. Jane
>
> d. Abbeville District, South Carolina; June, 1804
>
> wll dtd. Abbeville District, South Carolina; October 19, 1800
>
> Children
>> Robert (see below)
>>
>> John
>>
>> Samuel
>>
>> 6 daughters

Robert Gammill
> b. South Carolina; 1788
>
> m. Margaret Holland (b. South Carolina; November 25, 1790 d. Clarkson, Webster County, Mississippi; June 27, 1860); South Carolina; c. 1808
>
> r. Choctaw County, Mississippi; 1844
>
> d. Clarkson, Webster County; Mississippi; March 23, 1865
>
> Children
>> Charles Matterson (see below)
>>
>> Thomas Jefferson - b. South Carolina; c. 1808
>>
>> James Alexander b. South Carolina; c. 1814
>>> r. Choctaw County, Mississippi; 1840
>>
>> Ivy Wesley - b. Tuscaloosa or Pickens County, Alabama; March 16, 1818
>>> m1 Eliza Harris (b. Tennessee; c. 1822 d. aft 1850); Choctaw County, Mississippi; c. 1842

m2 Nancy Cox; Choctaw County, Mississippi; c. 1870

m3 Unknown

d. Webster County, Mississippi; October 28, 1881

Children

William James Margaret

Eli - b. Pickens County, Alabama; 1821

m. Charlotty (b.c. South Carolina; c. 1819); Choctaw County, Mississippi; c. 1843

Children

Sarah Emily John

James

Sarah - b. Pickens County, Alabama; b. 1822

m. Elijah Holland (b. Jackson County Mississippi; March 16, 1820 d. aft 1870); son of Jacob and Drusilla Dearman Holland; Choctaw County, Mississippi; c. 1840

d. aft 1870

Permelia A. - b. Pickens County; 1825

m. James McBride; Choctaw County, Mississippi; c. 1845

d. Webster County, Mississippi; 1906

Jane - b. Pickens County, Alabama

m. William Ezell; Choctaw County, Mississippi; betw 1851-1859

Joseph - b. Pickens County, Alabama; 1830

r. with H.W. Nolen family; Choctaw County, Mississippi; 1850

d. Arkansas; aft 1865

Margaret - b. Pickens County, Alabama; 1831

    m. Samuel Kirkpatrick; Choctaw County, Mississippi; betw 1851-1859

Robert - b. Pickens County, Alabama; c. 1832

    r. Carroll County, Mississippi

Winney - b. Pickens County, Alabama; 1837

    m. Alse High; c. 1855

Charles Matterson Gammill

    b. South Carolina; January 24, 1810

    m1 Sarah Daniel (b. South Carolina; April 28, 1818 d. November 3, 1862); Pickens County, Alabama; January 27, 1835

    m2 Mary Ann Ivy

    d. Mississippi; aft 1850

    Children by Sarah

        Jacob Wilson (see below)

        Robert M. - Alabama; September 20, 1837

            d. February 19, 1862

        Charles - b. Alabama

            d. 1840

        Martha Jane - b. Mississippi; January 11, 1843

            d. October 15, 1862

        Adaline/Emiline - b. c. 1847

        Henry - b. 1847?

        Thomas Jefferson - b. June 21, 1849

        Wesley - b. 1860

    Children by Mary Ann

        Sarah Jane - b. May 4, 1865

        Joseph Marion - b. August 11, 1869

r. Aberdeen, Mississippi

Jacob Wilson Gammill
    b. Pickens County, Alabama; October 22, 1835
    m. Caroline Elizabeth Rains (b. July 24, 1834 d. March 24, 1906, dau of John Shaglin and Elizabeth Rains; Choctaw County, Mississippi; November 10, 1853
    d. March 16, 1891
    bur. Antioch Methodist Cemetery, Choctaw County, Mississippi
    Children
        Sarah Elizabeth - b. September 25, 1854
            m. Robert Joseph Stephens
            d. March 3, 1908
        Cyrus W. - b. June 25, 1856
            d. August 7, 1857
        Emily C. - b. October 1, 1857
            m. Frank Dudley
            d. May 19, 1899
        Robert Wilson - b. March 15, 1859
            m. A.M. Dickerson; Choctaw County, Mississippi; October 13, 1882
            d. October 22, 1904
        Joseph M. - b. March 25, 1866
            d. February 7, 1872
        Martha C. - b, June 13, 1867
            d. October, 1867
        Benjamin Franklin - b. May 21, 1869
            m. Florina Cochron/Cochran (1869-1930); December 9, 1889

d. April 19, 1910

Children

Charlie Wilson	Rufus Lynch
Joseph Franklin	Verona Evelyn
Alma Florence	Curtis Claude
Cullen Dean	infant dau
infant son	

The name of this family has been recorded as Gammill/ Gamel/Gamil/Gamble. A "Gamble" was considered a respectable man. The name may have originated from the old Norse "Gamall" meaning "old." The "Gammill" spelling will be used for the purpose of this genealogy.

Samuel Gammill was born in Ireland in the mid-1700's. A book by Janie Reville asserted that Samuel actually arrived in the United States between 1763 and 1773. Evidently, he had arrived in South Carolina by 1780 when he joined the South Carolina Militia. He served in the militia for the the Old Ninety-Six District until 1783. The Old Ninety-Six was eventually divided into five counties and, in 1785, the portion in which Samuel lived became Abbeville County, South Carolina. It was an area of rolling foothills bordered on the west by Georgia. The name Abbeville came from Hugenot settler John de la Howe's home in France.

In 1843, Robert Gammill and many of his children - Charles M., Robert, Ivy W. Gammill, and possibly Benjamin F. - were on the Choctaw County, Mississippi taxpayer list. Then in 1844, Robert, Sr. and his sons Charles and Ivy were taxpayers in Choctaw County, Mississippi. The "B.F. Gammill" living there at the same time may have been an earlier Benjamin Franklin

Gammill then the one born in 1869. Then in 1849, "Westly," Eli and Robert were on the Choctaw County taxpayer list.

Samuel's son Robert Gammill, was a slave owner who moved his family from South Carolina to Pickens County, Alabama circa 1818 and to Clarkson, Mississippi sometime after 1837. Robert's son moved between the 1840 Alabama birth of his son Charles and the 1843 Mississippi birth of his daughter Martha Jane.

Three of Robert Gammill's sons served in the Confederate Army. Charles Matterson was with Choctaw County's Drane's Company of the Mississippi Calvary (Choctaw Reserves), Ivy with Company K of the 35th Regiment of the Mississippi Infantry, and Robert with Company C of the 20th Regiment of the Mississippi Infantry.

In May, 1864, an R.M. Gammill purchased the west half of the southwest quarter of Sec21 T18 R11E of Choctaw County, Mississippi. He purchased the property from D.S. Easley for $50.

Although Charles Matterson Gammill's son Robert M. supposedly died in 1862, Charles' father Robert did not die until 1865. And Charles had a brother named Robert (date of death unknown).

Goachy Family

Because of lack of a lineage, it was decided to present this family differently from the others in this book. The family was chosen to be included because it demonstrated the dangers all the families in this book faced.

Correct spelling and origin of the surname was not known. First names were not known. Ancestry was not known. The small amount of information known about the family came directly from the diary of Peter Pitchlynn.

"September 23, 1837 - We left Rush Creek camp yesterday morning at about 7:00 and proceeded on our route westward - and encamped in the point of timber that made into this prairie which we have named Buffalo Prairie. It is the first large prairie after leaving Washita Prairie. The road runs along on the dividing ridge between the Red and Wahita rivers and is a crooked route, but the only one that can be traveled well - for on either side it is a rough and brushy country. We had some very fine views of the country on both sides of the road from the high knobs on the ridge. On arriving here, we found a camp of whites, and to us an interesting one. They had been prisoners among the Pawnees - a young woman about twenty-one years of age and her infant and two little brothers - one about nine years old and the other about seven. Fortunately they had been bought by Mr. Spaulding and were on their way home under his protection. We asked the young lady many questions respecting her captivity and her narrative was as follows:

'We moved to Texas from north part of Alabama, and settled high up on the Colorado. My father's name was Goachy. The Pawnees came to our house one morning. Three of my little brothers were at the spring with my child (a girl), there they killed one of my little brothers, and then came to the house. I was in the house and my mother was out - I heard her scream. When I ran out I saw several Indians had hold of her - they struck her down and shot eight arrows into her breast and they shot her with a gun and scalped her.

'My father and my oldest brother were out, with a wagon hauling wood. I saw them killed. They shot at me but missed me. Seeing they had my infant and two little brothers prisoners, I ran to one of them and gave myself up. I done this hoping they might not kill me and that if I should live I might see what became of my babe and little brothers. They stripped me of my clothes and gave me an old worn out blanket to cover my nakedness and to screen by babe from the weather, and made me walked bare footed through the prairies. We were three weeks on the road, and every night my hands were tied behind together. When I came in they made me and my little brothers hold the scalps of my mother and father and two brothers, while they danced around us and mocked at us. We were then divided out - my babe taken from me and I did not see her for two months.'

While she was thus telling about her infant she hugged and kissed the little child with mournful look, often calling it by many lovely epithets. She then renewed her narrative:

'I was put to hard work. They were clearing ground and I had to grub and burn brush. I was abused and whipped everyday. Oh, I tell you they are hard masters. But there was nothing that went so hard with me as that of being separated from my child. I knew not where it was, but I know it was not well treated. I can't tell you the half of my sufferings.'

I then spoke to her little brother, the eldest one, and asked him how he was treated. His answer was,

'Bad enough, and the worst of it, I was two months longer among them than the rest.'

'What did you eat?'

'Beans and corn, it was all they had, but we did not have enough of that, for sometimes we ate but once in three days, and then did not get enough.'

I asked him how he would like to lived among such Indians as we were. He quickly replied,

'Very well.'

He is a smart lively boy. In fact the whole family have the appearance of being well raised, and how fortunate they have been after being cast away as it were by fate to thus be redeemed and have the prospect of now being in the society of their own people again. Relations they have none. The young woman had a languid and melancholy cast, the little boys looked like poor orphans indeed. I did not learn as much about their fate as I wished to. But certainly I never felt more sympathy for any family than this family of prisoners."

Holland Family

____ Holland
Children
    Charles (see below)
    Jacob - b. Maryland; betw 1761 and 1763
        m. Sarah Miller (d. May 31, 1851)
        d. Greene County, Alabama; October 1, 1852
        bur. Hebron Churchyard, Greene County, Alabama
        Children

Charles	Polly
Hannah	Sarah
Jane	Elizabeth
Peggy	

    Thomas - Maryland; December, 17, 1763
        d. Blount or Limestone County, Alabama; aft 1840
        Children
            Thomas Jr. - r. Blount County, Alabam

Charles M. Holland, Sr.
    b. Netherlands; April 2, 1758
    m. _____ Smith
    r. Abbeville District, South Carolina
    d. Choctaw County, Mississippi; 1846
    bur. New Hope Cemetery; Clarkson, Webster County, Mississippi; December 25, 1838
    Children
        Charles Miller (see below)

Margaret - b. South Carolina; November 25, 1790

> m. Robert Gammill (b. South Carolina; March 23, 1865 d. Clarkson, Webster County, Mississippi), son of Samuel and Jane (Gamble) Gammill; South Carolina; c. 1808
>
> d. Clarkson, Webster County, Mississippi; June 27, 1860
>
> Children

Thomas Jefferson	Eli
Perelia A.	James Alexander
Charles Matterson	Jane
Ivy Wesley	Joseph
Sarah A.	Margaret
Robert	Winnie

Absalom - b. South Carolina; c. 1791

> m. Elizabeth Douglas (b. South Carolina; 1793 d. Choctaw County, Mississippi; aft 1850); Madison County, Alabama; July 12, 1814/5
>
> r. Pickens County, Alabama; 1821
>
> r. Choctaw County, Mississippi; 1838
>
> d. Choctaw County, Mississippi; aft 1870
>
> Children

Thomas	Elizabeth
Jacob	Louise
Absalom	Maude
Catherine	

Elizabeth - b. South Carolina; August 25, 1792

> m. James Paxton (b. Virginia; October 29, 1780 d. Webster County, Mississippi; March 12, 1865)

d. Webster County, Mississippi; September 4, 1882

bur. Clarkson Cemetery, Webster County, Mississippi

Children

Susan	Charles
Samuel A.	James
Joseph S.	Margaret
Mary Ann	Sarah Jane
Ruth Matilda	Benjamin
Frances	

Jacob (Rev.) - South Carolina; b. July 14, 1794

m. Druscilla Dearman (b. South Carolina; 1793 d. Lauderdale County, Mississippi; 1885); Alabama; November, 19, 1818

d. Choctaw County, Mississippi; February 15, 1872

Children

Elijah	William
Elizabeth	Effie
Andrew Jackson	Jacob
Eleanor	Charles Harris
Sarah Ann	Thomas J.
James D.	Elias Herron
Martha Melvina	Henry D.

Sarah - b. 1804

m. Ignatius Dudley (1799-1864); c. 1820

d. Choctaw County, Mississippi; 1867

Children

Elizabeth	Charles M.

John Taylor	Harriet
Caroline	Sarah A.
Mary	James Jacob
Thomas Benton	George Washington

Reuben A. - b. betw 1800-1810

    m. Mary Dearman; Tuscaloosa County, Alabama; August 20, 1831

    r. Choctaw County, Mississippi; 1840

    d. aft 1840

Charles Miller Holland, Jr.

    b. Ninety-Six District, South Carolina; April 7, 1793

    m. Dicy/Dicey Childress (b. South Carolina; December 12, 1799 d. Webster County, Mississippi; November 3, 1877), Madison County, Alabama, (Mississippi Territory); May 16, 1816

    d. Webster County, Mississsippi; April 15, 1879

    Children

        William Miller - b. Pickens County, Alabama; 1817

            m. Eleanor ____; Choctaw County, Mississippi; c. 1842

            r. Choctaw County, Mississippi; 1850

        George "Humphers"/Humphries - b. Pickens County, Alabama; June 26, 1819

            m1 ____ Daniel; Oktibbeha County, Mississippi; c. 1842

            m2 Mary Starnes (b. Alabama; March 16, 1825); dau of Jacob and Jane Russell Starnes; c. 1847

            m3 Charity Ann Stephens Vaughn (wid); August 26, 1860

d. Jackson, Mississippi; February 16, 1875

bur. New Hope Cemetery, Webster County, Mississippi

Children

Emily	Franklin
David	

David Childress - b. Pickens County, Alabama; 1821

m1 Sarah Hopkins

m2 Sarah Shaffer

m3 Adaline Miles

d. Choctaw County, Mississippi; aft 1870

Children

George P.	Sarah Eliza
David W.	Mary Agnes
Charles H.	Dorothy
Dicey	Virginia
Lissie	Cora
Nellie	Beulah

Sarah Agnes - b. Pickens County, Alabama; February 13, 1822

m. Joseph W. Starnes; Choctaw County, Mississippi; by 1850

d. Choctaw County, Mississippi; February 6, 1905

Jacob W. - b. Pickens County, Alabama; 1825

m. Choctaw County, Mississippi; c. 1855

r. Choctaw County, Mississippi; 1850

d. Webster County, Mississippi; aft 1873

Dr. Charles K. - b. Pickens County, Alabama; 1829

> m. Margaret ____; Choctaw County, Mississippi;
> 1857
>
> Calhoun County, Mississippi; August 16, 1909

Waymon R. - b. Pickens County, Alabama; 1834

> m. Caroline ____; Choctaw County, Mississippi;
> c. 1860
>
> d. Texas; aft 1870

Mary Jane - b. Choctaw County, Mississippi; 1838

> m. Samuel L. DeLoach; Choctaw County,
> Mississippi; September 29, 1858
>
> d. Webster County, Mississippi; October 25,
> 1911
>
> bur. New Hope Cemetery, Webster County,
> Mississippi

Henry Harrison - b. Choctaw County, Mississippi;
June 26, 1840

> m. Mary Ruth Williams; Oktibbeha County,
> Mississippi; November 18, 1867
>
> d. Walthall, Webster County, Mississippi;
> October 25, 1911
>
> bur. New Hope Cemetery, Webster County,
> Mississippi

Levi?

Alpha?

Nebachne?

Charles Holland was the eldest of three sons of Dutch parents who arrived in Maryland in 1761. A Jacob "Hollan" who took the oath of allegiance in 1778 in Cecil County, Maryland, may have been Charles' father.

Supposedly, the original family name was not Holland. Some sources claimed it was changed to that to honor the family's homeland when they first arrived in their new county. Nevertheless, the surname Holland was frequently found in The Netherlands. In order to have traced a family named Holland there, the name of the town had to also have been known, since archives were kept in the individual cities, not nationally.

Charles' family had moved to Ninety-Six District of South Carolina by 1770. The Old Ninety-Six District was so named because its British fort was exactly ninety-six miles south of the Cherokee Indian capital of Keowee. The Old Ninety-Six District was eventually divided into several districts, including Abbeville, Edgefield and Laurens.

When the Hollands arrived, the Old Ninety-Six was a bustling frontier area bordered on the west by the Savannah River. And while they were there, Old Ninety-Six became the site of an early Revolutionary War land battle when on November 18, 1775, eighteen hundred loyalists attacked about six hundred patriots under Major Andrew Williams. The fighting lasted for several days before both sides called a truce. However, patriot fervor was high and the truce was broken when they mounted an offensive that swept over the royalists' resistance.

Later, General Greene lay siege on the British at the Old Ninety-Six fort. Although the British loyalist managed to hold on, shortly after the siege the British abandoned the heavily damaged fort.

All three Holland brothers served in the Revolutionary War with the South Carolina Militia. Brother Thomas was only fourteen years old when he joined the militia under Capt. Thomas Weems and Col. Andrew Pickens. Another brother was not much older when he enlisted.

Charles Holland volunteered as a private in September 1776 to fight in the militia under Capt. James McCall and Maj. Andrew Williams. McCall was eventually taken prisoner by the Indians.

But Charles and his brothers continued to fight the Tories and Indians in the battle at Vanna Creek, Georgia in 1778. Charles was wounded in the knee in that battle. In 1780 he fought in the battles of Ramsour's Mill and Hanging Rock. He was shot in the groin at the August, 1780 battle at Hanging Rock, South Carolina, but was healed enough to fight in the battle of King's Mountain on October 7, 1780.

However, during the Battle of Cowpens in South Carolina in 1781, Charles received a sword wound which would affect him for the rest of his life. Before that battle the American military in the South was in terrible shape. When Maj. General Nathaniel Greene was named commander of the Southern Army, which consisted of 2500 men, only 1000 were fit for duty. According to Wood, only 800 of those "were properly clothed and equipped.". But they had no discipline and were entertaining themselves by pillaging and terrorizing civilians.

But the Battle of Cowpens turned everything around. Cowpens was an area of some rolling and some flat ground with stands of trees, but no underbrush. It was there that Generals Tarleton for the British and Morgan for the patriots pitted their troops against each other. The outcome was a substantial victory for the Americans, giving a boost which continued until the end of the war.

Despite his injuries, Charles Holland went on to fight at battles at William's Fort, Hammon's Old Store and Bullock's Plantation. At Bullock's Plantation he lost all his possessions, but in 1783 the State of South Carolina compensated him for his losses.

Charles Holland inventoried the estate of Joseph Brown (Box 12 Packet 240) on October 30, 1802 in the Abbeville District of South Carolina. On August 13, 1808, Charles, along with Samuel Linton, purchased a portion of the estate of "Stuteley" Cauley (Box 21, Pack 463) in Abbeville. A little later, his brother Jacob Holland witnessed the will of Titus Murray (Box 65, Packet 1556) on March 19, 1813.

In his history of Pickens County, Clanahan reported that a Charles Holland was one of the earliest settlers in Pickens County and served as a commissioner in 1824. Clanahan reported that Charles

> "Was a highly respected gentleman, a plain planter of some means, and was for many years the executor of the will of his father, the late Jacob Holland of this (Pickens) county. He made frequent visits to this county and the court of which he was one judge. His father resided at Sipsey and died in 1852, aged nearly ninety years."

This Clanahan also reported that "the house of Charles M. Holland" became an "election precinct in the county of Pickens, - (on Sipsey)". He was probably given that job because in 1830 he had been appointed to a judgeship. While this Charles Holland could have been Charles Sr. or Jr. of this genealogy, he more likely was the son of Jacob Holland who died in 1852. If so, he would have been the nephew of the Charles M. Holland Sr. (d.

1846). And Clanahan seemed to confirm this when he reported that the Charles Holland he was reporting about moved to Panola County, Mississippi in 1836.

Sometime after the war, Charles M. Holland, Sr. of this genealogy, went to Tuscaloosa, Alabama and was living there on October 13, 1832, when he applied for a pension. He enrolled for his pension on July 2, 1833 and received $80 a year. He was in Pickens County, Alabama in 1835, but by 1838 he had moved to an area of Choctaw County which would eventually become Webster County, Mississippi. In 1840 his pension was $85 per year. And on May 17, 1843 his Revolutionary War Pension was transferred from Tuscaloosa, Alabama to Mississippi.

Charles' brother Thomas Holland, who also served in the South Carolina Militia during the American Revolution, enrolled for his pension on June 13, 1833, and was granted $76.66 per year. According to pension records, he was living in Limestone County, Alabama, on June 1, 1840.

The third brother Jacob had also fought for South Carolina. And like Charles, Jacob Holland settled in Greene County, Alabama.

Several members of the Charles Holland family married into the Starnes family. J.W., Mary and Roxie Starnes all married Hollands. And, like the Starnes, the Hollands moved that westward trail through Alabama into Mississippi.

But before going to Mississippi, his son Charles Miller Holland, Jr. served as a corporal under Captain William Johnson in Mississippi Territory's 7th Battalion during the War of 1812. He fought in the attack on Mobile and the storming of Pensacola and the Battle of New Orleans.

After going to Mississippi, Charles Miller Holland, Jr. settled his family on the Big Black River where he owned and ran grist, cotton gin and lumber mills with the help of his slaves. Around 1837, Holland built a large plantation house on bounty land he had received for his service during the War of 1812.

The 1844 Choctaw County, Mississippi Tax Rolls included a number of Hollands, including Absalom, Charles M., David C., Elijah, George, Jacob, Thomas and William. But both Charles M. Holland Jr. and Sr. should have both been living in Choctaw County. Charles M. Holland, Sr. died there in 1846.

According to the 1850 Choctaw County census, Charles Jr.'s sons David (age 29) and Jacob (age 25) were millers living with their parents and younger siblings in the Eastern Division. David Childress was the Assistant Marshall of the district. Their father Charles M. Holland, Jr. had seven slaves.

In 1868, with Mississippi under military rule, George H. Holland, son of Charles Miller, Jr., was a delegate to a constitutional convention in Jackson. It was known as the "Black and Tan Convention" because of the large numbers of blacks and carpetbaggers in attendance.

Lampkin Family

William Lampkin

    b. North Carolina; September 16, 1773

    m. Rosanna Woods (b. Washington County, Tennessee; January 1, 1780 d. Madison County, Alabama; May 27, 1831), dau of Michael Wood

    d. Madison County, Alabama; August 30, 1822

    Children

        Robert Allison (see below)

        Mary "Polly" - b. May 20, 1800

            m. Elijah Hogan

            d. July 14, 1882

            bur. Odd Fellows Cemetery, Starkville, Oktibbeha County, Mississippi

        Louisa - m. Robert Baker and/or James Walton (b. Chester District; August 12, 1799)

        William - d. young

        Alexander Woods - m. Margaret Barnett

        Esther - d. young

        Washington Campbell - m. Martha Norsworthy

        Minerva - m. Robert Baker

Robert Allison Lampkin I

    b. Washington County, Tennessee; November 30, 1809

    m1 Cemantha/Simantha Rand (b. Franklin County, Alabama; March 1, 1812 d. December 29, 1874), dau of John and Martha Curtis Rand; Franklin County, Alabama; July 30, 1835 m2 Mary E. Heath (d. December 27, 1903 bur. Odd Fellows Cemetery, Starkville, Oktibbeha County, Mississippi); Starkville, Oktibbeha County, Mississippi; June 8, 1875

r. Oktibbeha County, Mississippi; 1850

d. Starkville, Mississippi; April/May 17, 1885

bur. Odd Fellows Cemetery, Starkville, Oktibbeha County, Mississippi

Children

    Robert Allison (see below)

    William G. - d. young

    Elnora - b. 1836

        m. Dr. John W. Caldwell

        Children

            Joseph Lampkin Caldwell - b. July 23, 1863

                d. February 22, 1940

                bur. Odd Fellows Cemetery; Starkville, Oktibbeha County, Mississippi

    Cordelia Felix - b. Franklin County, Alabama; October 3, 1837

        m. Dr. Enoch Prince Connell (b. Robertson County, Tennessee; February 12, 1831 d. Starkville, Mississippi; September 14, 1896), son of John Tinsley Connell; March 15, 1860

        d. Starkville, Oktibbeha County, Mississippi; April 5, 1917

        Children

            John Allison - d. young

            Robert Tinsley - d. young

            Mary Kate - d. young

Annie - m. William Ward; Starkville, Mississippi; June 13, 1889

Julia Eleanor - d. young

Tommy - d. young

Enoch Prince - m. Grace Shearer

John Tinsley - m. Augusta Jones

Katherine "Kitty" - b. April 3, 1845

m. John C. Rand (b. March 25, 1840 d. October 23, 1918); Starkville, Oktibbeha County, Mississippi; August 2, 1869

Alexina - b. Mississippi; January 6, 1847

m. George Gillespie (1842-1926), son of Dr. W.C. Gillespie; Oktibbeha County, Mississippi; November 29, 1869

d. April 1, 1884

bur. Odd Fellows Cemetery, Starkville, Oktibbeha County, Mississippi

Children

Julia - b. 1877

m. Mississippi A&M President Hugh Critz (b. 1876)

d. 1947

Alice - b. 1870

d. 1873

bur. Associated Reform Presbyterian Cemetery, Starkville, Oktibbeha County, Mississippi

2 dau

Edwina (tw) - b. Mississippi; 1849

m. never

Martha - d. young

Josephine - d. young

Alexander - d. young

Robert Allison Lampkin II (tw)
>   b. Mississippi; 1849
>   m. Mary Elizabeth "Molly" Rand (1853-1932); Starkville,
>   Oktibbeha County, Mississippi; October 27, 1869
>   d. 1915
>   bur. Odd Fellows Cemetery, Starkville, Oktibbeha County,
>   Mississippi
>   Children
>   >   Joe - b.c. 1873
>   >   >   d. 1877
>   >   >   bur. Odd Fellows Cemetery, Starkville,
>   >   >   Oktibbeha County, Mississippi
>   >   Evans
>   >   >   Children
>   >   >   >   Mary Evans - m. A.B. Butts
>   >   Allee - m. _____ Bonner
>   >   Robert A. III - b. December 9, 1887
>   >   >   d. June 8, 1889
>   >   >   bur. Odd Fellows Cemetery; Starkville,
>   >   >   Oktibbeha County, Mississippi

The earliest member of this family found was William Lampkin. Although he was born in North Carolina, he was in Washington County, Tennessee for his marriage to Rosanna Woods and the 1809 birth of his son. William and Rosanna eventually settled in Madison County, Alabama where William died in 1822 and Rosanna in 1831. Madison County had been established in December 1808 out of Cherokee and Chickasaw lands.

Consequently, Robert Allison Lampkin, son of William and Rosanna followed the Tennessee to Alabama to Mississippi route with his parents and siblings. Although his family did not spend a lot of time in Franklin County, Alabama; one girl he met there made enough of an impression on Robert that after moving to Mississippi, he returned to claim Cemantha Rand as his wife.

The area where Cemantha Rand had been born in 1812 was still Cherokee and Chickasaw land at the time. Franklin County, which was named for Benjamin Franklin, did not become a county until February 6, 1818.

Meanwhile, Robert's sister Mary married Elijah Hogan who, along with Robert arrived in Oktibbeha County, Mississippi as soon as the Treaty of Dancing Rabbit was signed. Hogan and Lampkin became an important member of the new community of Boardtown (later, Starkville). In 1834 Robert Lampkin became Oktibbeha County's sheriff in the county's first election. There were only three voting precincts and 66 votes cast in the county in that election.

At one time or another, both Elijah and Robert I served as county supervisors, with Hogan becoming the first president of the board. Moreover, Hogan erected the Hogan Tavern which eventually became known as the Hogan-Lampkin Tavern.

Like many of the speculators who bought up the land cheap, and turned around and sold it at a profit, Lampkin considered the land he purchased as an investment. Eighty acres, including two springs, he purchased in 1834 became downtown Starkville. As a matter of fact, the county paid him

$10,000 for just twenty-five acres on a ridge on which the Oktibbeha County courthouse and jail were built.

Starkville's first jail was a log building built with no windows or doors. Prisoners were lowered into the jail through a hole in the ceiling. There were no escapes.

The board of police (supervisors), with Elijah Hogan as president, measured off lots sixty-six feet wide by one hundred sixty feet long. The lots were sold in at least two public auctions. Lots sold for as little as $12 to as much as $182.50 each.

In 1835, Robert Lampkin I deeded some of his land to the Methodist Church with the stipulation that if the church was moved, the land would revert to the Lampkin family. The site of that first frame Methodist Church building became the site of First Methodist Church of Starkville.

Lampkin also helped organize the county's first bank which, as was the custom, printed its own money. And it was that custom that brought on the Panic of 1837, and as a result, the Starkville Real Estate and Banking Company folded. But shareholders remained solvent.

The family continued to do well financially and were slave owners. In 1841, an "R.A. Lampkin" was shown as owning 160 additional acres in neighboring Choctaw County.

The Lampkin children grew up pampered. Robert Lampkin was able to give each of his children a house when they married - even when three of them married between August 2 and November 29, 1869.

As children, they had a governess and attended a private school in Alabama, probably for good reason. In his journal, Dr. Ashbel Green Simonton, a northerner, who taught in Starkville in the early 1850's wrote -

"Starkville never has had a good school for any considerable length of time, and I venture to prophecy it never will until a change comes over the spirit of its dream. To earn a reputation here as a teacher is impossible, and this attempt I consider ridiculous."
Simonton gave as the principal problem the fact that the people of Starkville cared "so little for the success of the school." And in another entry, he called his Starkville students as "a stupid, vulgar set of boys."

Robert's son Robert Lampkin II and his grandson Evans followed Lampkin into the banking business. Robert II organized Security State Bank for which Evans later worked. Robert Allison Lampkin III also served as an Oktibbeha County supervisor from 1888 to 1912 and was on the Board of Directors for Sanders Cotton Mill. His granddaughter married A.B. Butts, a Starkville lawyer who became chancellor of the University of Mississippi.

Lavender Family

In 1628 a Nathaniel Lavinder/Lavinder/Lavendar was granted a coat of arms. The family's motto was "God defend the Right" and their crest featured a

"demi-horse rampant colored with a garland of the flower lavinder."

But the Lavender/Lavandar name probably did not originate with either the color or the flower. The first English Lavender may have washed and bleached flax and wool, an occupation closely related to the Scotch-Irish wool and flax producers of Antrim County in Ulster Plantation (Northern Ireland).

Or they might have been members of the French de La Vinder family who left France after the revocation of the Edict of Nantes. Hill described the de La Vinders as

"Industrious, clannish, honest, and as a rule too liberal to amass great fortunes, distinguished for hospitality, and every one a model of politeness, and many brilliant in writing and oratory."

Although they originated in Normandy, two, Richard and William de La Vinder were ultimately found in Bedford and Hertford, England.

A legion of early Lavenders who might have been related to this family showed up in early Alabama. Mrs. Jane Lavender was a member of the Bethesda Presbyterian church in Picken's County in the 1820's.The 1830 Alabama Federal Census listed a number of Lavenders in the state, including Robert "Lavinder" of Pickens County; H.L., Hugh and Robert Lavender of Greene County; and Simon Lavender of Lowndes County, Alabama. *Annals of Northwest Alabama* reported that a Missouri Lavender of Pickens County lost her arm in a mill accident. She met and married Douglas Smith, an employee of her Uncle Andrew T. Bonds of Franklin County, Alabama. Missouri supposedly had brothers named Tommy and Jimmy Lavender.

The Robert and David Lavender Family

_____ Lavender

Children

William (see below)

Hugh - b. Antrim County, Ireland; November 11, 1754
m. Rebecca Smith (b. Ireland; 1759 d. by 1834);
South Carolina; 1777
r. Fairfield/Camden District, South Carolina
d. Greene County, Alabama; September, 1834
wll dtd. September 8, 1834
bur. Concord Cemetery, Concord, Greene
County, Alabama

Children

Sarah - m. Kinnard Bennet

Children

Hugh Lavender Bennett

Ruth - m. _____ Barbous/Barbour

Mary - m. _____ Torbert

Nancy - m. William McDaniel

Margaret

Hugh Levi - m. Jane/Jennie Hopper (d.
Greene County, Alabama); Greene
County, Alabama; December 12, 1824

Children

John David

Lucy

Robert S. ("Bobbin") - m1 Sara Strothers (b.
May 15, 1817 d. Alabama; May 3,
1854)

m2 Margaret Hodges (1815-1871)

Children

    H.E.   David

    Nancy G.

John L. - b. Fairfield/Camden District, South Carolina; July 1, 1780

    m. Rebecca Sant (1784-1860)

    d. Greene County, Alabama; March 31, 1861

William Lavender

b. prob Ireland; by 1769

m. _____ Smith?

Children

    David (see below)

    Robert "Robbin" - b. South Carolina; c. 1797

        m. Mary "Polly" Ann Gammill (b. South Carolina; c. 1799 d. Pickens County Alabama; c. December, 1890)

        r. Mantua, Greene County, Alabama; December 11, 1893

        wll pro - Greene County, Alabama; 1894

        Children

            Julia Ann Frances - b. South Carolina; c. 1821

                m. John Smith Lavender (see below)

                d. Greene County, Alabama; October, 1878

            Margaret - b. Alabama; c. 1827

                d. prob by 1893

William - b. Alabama; c. 1828

Eliza - b. Alabama; c. 1830

Hugh - b. Alabama; c. 1832

Sarah E. - b. Alabama; c. 1833

d. by 1893

Children

Rufus L - r. Boyce, Ellis County, Texas; 1893

Morgan E. - r. Boyce, Ellis County, Texas; 1893

Mary E. - m. C.S. Harris

r. Boyce, Ellis County, Texas; 1893

Anna E. - m. D.C. McMullin

r. Waxnatchie, Ellis County, Texas; 1893

James William Smith - b. South Carolina; c. 1803

m. Matilda (b. South Carolina; c. 1808)

d. by March, 1861

Children

Spencer	Dock
Lewis	Dolphus
Sarah	

David Lavender

m. Eleanor

Children

John Smith (see below)

Jemima

John Smith Lavender

    b. South Carolina; c. 1816-1818

    m. Julia Ann Frances, dau of Robert and Mary Ann Gammill Lavender (see above)

    r. Mantua, Greene County, Alabama

    d. Pickens or Greene County, Alabama; April 9, 1874

    wll pro - Greene County Alabama; 1878

    Children

        Mary E. - b.c. 1838

            m. William Hammitt

            r. Insane asylum; Tuscaloosa, Alabama; 1893

        Margaret A. - b. Alabama; c. 1841

            m1 David W. Story (b. Alabama; c. 1831, son of Robert and Martha Story

            m2 Elijah Bolton, son of James Bolton

            d. by 1894

            Children

                Harriet - m. Abner Brewer

James Story	Robert
Josephine	John
Luther	

        Ann E. - m. Morris McDaniel

            r. Holly Springs, Mississippi; 1893

        Indiana/Irene - b. Alabama; c. 1848

            d. by 1894

        Robert S. - b.c. 1851

            r. Ladonia, Fannin County, Texas; 1894

        Martha - m. John Beard

            r. Panola County, Mississippi; 1893

        Arabella - b.c. 1857

m. Webster Franklin

r. Ashville, St. Clair County, Alabama; 1893

Frances D. - b. 1858

m. C.M. Huson of Arkansas

r. Clarksville, Johnston County, Arkansas; 1893

Mahala "Muhala" Adaline - m. E.W. Odom

r. Harmony, Johnston County, Arkansas; 1893

Eliza "Milissa"

Revolutionary Soldiers in Alabama showed that Hugh Lavender of this genealogy was a dragoon in the South Carolina Militia. On February 10, 1834, he was a seventy-nine year old applicant for a $66.21 annual pension for his Revolutionary War service (number S10972).

In that document, Hugh gave a brief history of his life. He claimed to have been born near "Bollynaena" in County Antrim, Ireland and to have emigrated as a boy of seventeen to South Carolina in 1771.

Antrim was in Ulster, the northern province of Ireland. Ulster, known as "Ulaidh" to the Irish, was the northern most of the four Irish provinces. Three of its nine counties eventually became a part of the Republic of Ireland. Antrim was one of the six counties that became Northern Ireland.

Antrim, or the Irish "Aontriom", probably came from "Endrium" meaning "habitation on the water" from of its location on the water, with its view of Mull of Kintyre in Scotland. Because of its proximity, Antrim became an obvious point of entry for any number of invaders, including the Scottish.

But it became a stronghold of the dour Scotch-Irish after the British Parliament promised Protestant Lowland Scots a market for their flax and wool in exchange for moving to Ulster to act as a buffer between the British and the Catholic Irishmen.

For centuries, the English had tried unsuccessfully to subdue the Irish, in particular those from Ulster. All the provinces of Ireland shared a language, enormous poverty, and a hatred of the English. In 1595, the Irish rebelled against the English. But they were defeated by Lord Mountjoy who, in addition to defeating the Irish and their Gaelic society, also leveled their land of houses, food and cattle; opening the way for the formation of the Plantation of Ulster and the settlement of a presumed more British-friendly people.

It has been said that the Protestant Reformation had stopped its progression across Europe at the Irish shores. So in reality, the Scots were being used to kick the Catholics off their land and act as a buffer against those "heathens."

As might have been expected, the actual land did not go to the Scots who would be living and working on it. Instead, it went to the English and Scottish landlords who stayed at home and sent their tenants to the plantation. But they were already being pushed from Scotland by famine, epidemics, rebellions and grinding poverty; so the Lowlanders had little choice but to agree.

And while life in Ireland was good in the beginning, soon the same famine, epidemics and repression followed the Scots there. Still looking for a better life, many Scotch-Irish went on to the New World.

After leaving Ireland, Hugh Lavender settled on Wateree Creek in the Camden District, which became the Fairfield District of South Carolina in 1785. The area was settled by Scotch-Irish, English and French Hugenots. It was a center for the

"Regulators", a vigilante group which was organized to bring "law and order" to the wilderness and to give the settlers more control over their own lives, but which frequently meant turbulent times with the British. In fact, from October 1780 to January 1781, Cornwallis had headquarters in Fairfield.

During the American Revolution, Hugh Lavender volunteered and served under Col. John Winn and Capt. Robert Allison. He volunteered again and served under Capt. John Mullen in 1775 and Capt. Casey in 1776.

A John Lavender received a land grant dated September 12, 1821 in Greene County. He was probably the son of Hugh, who received his own land grant on February 18, 1825. In 1822, Hugh had removed to Greene County, Alabama. Then, according to Deed Book E of Greene County records, on February 26, 1833, Hugh Lavender gave a gift of land to Hugh L. Bennett, the son of Lavender's daughter Sarah Elizabeth and her husband Kinnard Bennett.

Hugh Lavender died in Greene County in a portion which would later become part of Hale County, Alabama. His will was dated September 8, 1834 and named his son Robert S. Lavender and his son-in-law Kinnard Bennet as the executors. Since no wife was named, she must have pre-deceased him.

Hugh's son Robert was nicknamed "Bobbin". But Hugh's brother William also had a son named Robert (b.c. 1797). He was nicknamed "Robbin". Both lived in Alabama at about the same time.

Actually William Lavender had at least three sons - David, Robert and, probably Smith. Since the Smith name was found in several generations, perhaps it was the maiden name of the wife of an early Lavender, such as William (b. by 1769). According to

Fairfield County Marriages 1775-1879 Implied in Fairfield County, South Carolina Probate Records, in 1848, David's daughter Jemima Lavender was the common law wife of Darling Hollis.

In 1850, a number of Lavenders - including William, John, Paul, Thomas, Walter and Wright - appeared in the Greene County, Alabama census. Other Lavenders were in Pickens County (see APPENDIX 3). Smith Lavender (b. c. 1803) had land adjoining Robert Lavender (b.c. 1797) in Pickens County. At the time of the census, Smith stated he had been born in South Carolina. The W.P. Lavender, who was named administrator of Smith's estate on March 21, 1861, was probably the same W.P. Lavender who succeeded John Story as post master at Mantua in Pickens County. He was still there in the 1855 Alabama State Census.

Also in the 1855 census of Pickens County, John Smith Lavender (b.c. 1816-1818) may have been the Smith Lavender who appeared with four males under 21, two males over 21, one female under 21 and one female over 21 in his family. However, the number of females and number of males under 21 should have been the reverse. His uncle Smith Lavinder (b. 1803) was still alive then.

Robert "Robbin" Lavender, son of William, was also born in South Carolina circa 1797. But by February 1, 1826, he was living on Section 13 in Pickens County, Alabama; not far from the John Story family. He and his wife "Polly" had at least eight children. One of them, his daughter Julie Ann, married Robbin's nephew John Smith Lavender, son of Robbin's brother David.

The executor of Robert's will was Joseph H. Lavender, who testified in an 1804 deposition

"I am acquainted with the lands and they are the same of which Robbin Lavender did seize and possessed. The quality of the land is fair, some good and some very poor; and is of the value of $2 per acre for the tract."

There were about two hundred acres in the tract of land which was in Mantua Beat (district).

Original settlers of Mantua had come from Spartenburg, South Carolina with William N. Morrow circa 1817. And, according to *Records of Pickens County*, the original name of Mantua/Montua was actually Lavender, probably named after this family. But the first Lavender found in Greene County was John and he did not receive a land grant until 1821.

When Robbin Lavender died, Mantua was in Picken's County. But before the estate was settled, the legislature had conveyed the land to Greene County.

The family of Robbin's daughter Julia Ann seemed to be plagued with misfortune. When Julia's husband John Smith Lavender died in Mantua in 1874, everything John had owned, including his land, was lost to the family for taxes. He was only fifty-eight years old at the time of death. By the time she was fifty-five years old, Julia and John's daughter Mary was widowed and a resident of an insane asylum in Tuscaloosa.

Their daughter Margaret married David Story. But he was killed during the Civil War, leaving the young widow alone with at least one small child. On September 19, 1867, she married neighbor Elijah Bolton. The wedding took place in her parents' Greene County, Alabama home. In 1870, Margaret and her new husband moved to Mississippi, where Margaret eventually died.

The Charles Lavender Family

Charles Lavender Jr.

> b. Amherst County, Virginia
>
> m. Lucinda Ballew (1766-1846); 1785
>
> r. North and South Carolina
>
> d. Edgefield District, South Carolina; May 5, 1802
>
> Children
>
>> Charles III (see below)
>>
>> Simeon - b.c. 1786
>>
>>> m. Mary McCrary
>>
>> Willis - b.c. 1790

Charles Lavender III

> b. Edgefield District, South Carolina; 1802
>
> m. Mariah Teresa Edwards (b. 1798)
>
> r. Jackson County, Georgia; 1853
>
> Children (7)
>
>> John Edgar (see below)

John Edgar Lavender

> b. Georgia; 1826
>
> m. Mary L. McMillan (1828-1920); Georgia; May, 1848
>
> r. Alabama before 1860
>
> d. Steens, Mississippi; 1916
>
> Children (7)
>
>> Charles William (see below)

Charles William Lavender

> b. Wilkinson County, Georgia; 1850

m. Anna Poe (b. Alabama; May 24, 1855 d. Mississippi; December 12, 1912), dau of Elbert and Matilda Cates Poe; c. 1877

d. Lackey, Monroe County, Mississippi; March 27, 1930

bur. New Prospect Cemetery, Lackey, Monroe County, Mississippi

Children

    Charles Poe - b. 1879

        d. 1881

    Perry John E. - b. 1881

        d. 1887

    Lena - m. Ernest Belden Neely

    Adeline - m. John L. Buck

    James O'Conner - m. Robbie Malone

    James Thomas - b. 1889

        m. Eulalie Halbert, dau of William Pinkney and Caroline Morris Halbert

    Gertrude

Members of this Lavender family were early Virginia settlers. According to Hill's History *of Henry County, Virginia*, the "Lavenders" of Virginia were descended from the de La Vinder family originally from Normandy. She described them as "wealthy and cultured". But their actual line of descent to Charles Lavender, Sr. of this genealogy has remained a mystery.

Charles Lavender Jr. served as a private in Col. Merriwether's Virginia Regiment during the Revolutionary War. He fought in the Battle of Brandywine and at the Siege of Yorktown. He also served as a guard of prisoners at Albemarle Barracks.

Charles Lavender appeared as the head of a household in the 1790 South Carolina census for Edgefield County. He was still there when he was struck by lightening and died on May 5, 1802.

Through the next generations, the family followed the usual migration west, moving from Amherst, Virginia; to North Carolina; to Edgefield District, South Carolina; to Wilkinson County, Georgia; to Alabama; and finally to Steens, Mississippi.

Lincecum Family

Pascal Linseycomb/Lincecum
    m. France
    d. Maryland
    Children
        Gideon I (see below)
        3 dau

Gideon Lincecum I
    b. France
    m. Miriam "Millay" Bowie (b.c. 1725 d. Putnam, Georgia; c.1813)
    d. betw. 1775-1783
    Children
        Hezekiah (see below)
        Edward/ Edmund - b. North Carolina; by 1769
            d. 1781 in Battle of Cowpens
        John - b. North Carolina; by 1769
            d. 1781 in Battle of Cowpens
        Sally - b. North Carolina; by 1769
            m. Tyre Kelly
            Children
                Asa - m. Malinda Nevels
        Dolly - b. North Carolina; by 1769
            m. Durbin
        Nancy - b. North Carolina; by 1769

Hezekiah Lincecum
    b. Warren County, Georgia, 1770

m1 Sally Strange

m2 Sally Hickman (b.c. 1777 d. May 28, 1848; Catahoula Parish, Louisiana), dau of William and Marie [H]ornbeck Hickman; c. 1791/2

d. near Columbus, Mississippi; March 4, 1839

Children

> Gideon - b. Wilkes or Warren County, Georgia; April 22, 1793
>
> > m. Sarah Bryan/Bryant (b. aft 1794 d.c. 1867), sis of Joseph Bryan; October 25, 1814
> >
> > d. Long Point, Washington County, Texas; November 28, 1873/74
> >
> > Children (13)
> >
> > > Emily - m. Daniel B. Moore; Tishomingo County, Mississippi; July 16, 1830
> > >
> > > Lycurgis/Lysurgis
> > >
> > > Lysander/Lisander - b. 1836
> > >
> > > > d. 1875
> > > >
> > > > bur. Burton Cemetery, Washington County, Texas
> > >
> > > Lucullus
> > >
> > > Leonida
> > >
> > > Leander
> > >
> > > Lyconyon
> > >
> > > Lucifer
> > >
> > > Sarah Matilda - m. L.L. Doran of Hempstead, Texas
> > >
> > > Lenora - d. aft 1895
> > >
> > > > m. prob. James Matson; Washington County, Texas; October 4, 1848

Mary - d. aft 1895

2 children - d. young

Grant - d. Dallas, Texas; c. 1862

   r. Catahoula Parish, Louisiana; 1850

Grabel/Gabriel - m. Willmouth

   d. Oktibbeha County, Mississippi; 1836

   wll dtd - November 9, 1836

   wll pro - Noxubee County, Mississippi; May 1, 1837

   Children

      ?Heyward/Haywood/Hairwood? - b.c. 1825

         m1 Mary A. Brown; Noxubee County, Mississippi; January 3, 1850

         m2 Elizabeth "Betsy" McIlwain (b. November 25, 1840 d. March 27, 1890 bur. Sanders Cemetery, Oktoc, Oktibbeha County, Mississippi); Oktibbeha County, Mississippi; January 21, 1873

         r. Oktibbeha County, Mississippi; 1850

         d. Noxubee County, Mississippi; April 9, 1900

         bur. Soule Chapel, Noxubee County, Mississippi

         Children

            Brooks

   Bartley C.

   Elizabeth - m. Jackson Huckaby; Noxubee County, Mississippi; April 23, 1854

Willmouth

Ducianne Amanda - r. Oktibbeha County, Mississippi; 1850

   m. Josiah B. Cole; Noxubee County, Mississippi; April 23, 1854

Grabel E.

Mary - m. Joseph Bryan/Bryant, bro of Sarah Bryan

Emily - m. _____ Moore

Garland R. - b. 1797

   m. Martha J. Moore; Lowndes County, Mississippi; November 1, 1836

   r. Caldwell, Texas, 1850

   d. 1853

Rezin Bowie - b.c. 1808

   d. Kentucky; 1835

Green - r. Arkansas; 1820 and 1830

Thornton

?Polly?

This is the history of three brothers - one who settled in Lowndes County, Mississippi and two who settled in Oktibbeha County, Mississippi. They were born Gideon, Grant, and Gabriel; sons of Hezekiah and Sally Linseycomb/Lincecum (see APPENDIX 4); grandsons of Gideon and Miriam Bowie Lincecum; and great grandsons of Pascal Lincecum.

Gideon II would later write that "Paschal" was the son of one

> "Linseycomb, an Englishman who was left by the British Army during the terrible wars of that period as an unexchanged prisoner of war."

After the war, Pascal's father supposedly remained in France and married.

Pascal Lincecum was a French Hugenot - a Protestant in a Catholic country - who refused to repudiate his religion. He also cherished republican principles so much that he took his family from Maryland. That love of freedom was something Pascal would pass on to future generations

Years later, when Gideon II (b. 1793) had reached adulthood, he wrote that his grandparents

> "were all Europeans - French, Scotch, English, Dutch. My father resulted from the conjugal union that took place between the French Huguenot Gideon Lincecum and the Scotch lassie Miriam ("Millays") Bowie - own aunt to the celebrated desperado, James Bowie, the originator of the Bowie knife. If glory and greatness consist in the amount of throat cutting performed, the Bowie knife was a greater invention than ... Napoleon Bonaparte."

But Pascal thought the Bowies were pretentious and was not pleased with Gideon's engagement. Meanwhile, according to Gideon Lincecum II, Miriam's brother

> "could not consent for his beautiful, young and highly accomplished sister to become the wife of a frog-eating Frenchman."

Since both set of parents objected, Gideon and Miriam eloped.

While they were living in North Carolina at least five children were born to them. Then after their move to Georgia, their son Hezekiah Lincecum was born in 1770 in what would become Wilkes County (in 1777) and then Warren County (1793), Georgia.

They were industrious people and the farm the Lincecums established did well. But at the time of Hezekiah's birth, the area was just untamed, fertile, piedmont land. Although traders and settlers were there as early as the 1750's, formal settlement and the boundary survey weren't begun until 1773. Those earliest settlers were English and Scotch-Irish going into an area with no towns and no government. And the neighbors were hostile. In January 1774, Creek Indians attacked the fort on the Little River and massacured seven settlers.

During the American Revolution, many backwoodsmen were fierce supporters of the rebels. But there also were militant loyalists active in those backwoods. Families were divided and brutality became the routine. But it wasn't until 1778-79, after the fall of Savannah and Augusta, that British troops arrived in the area in force.

Gideon and Miriam's eldest sons, Edward/Edmund and John were Tories during the American Revolutionary War. On April 10, 1779, both sons were under arrest in South Carolina. According to Wilkes County court records

"John Lyncecum - Confesses to this Court that he was aiding and assisting in the taking & delivering Capt. David Robinson to the British forces & Noted by some of the Members of this court as an attrocious Villian do Order him to Confinement till discharg'd by due Course of Law."

After adjourning, the court met again on April 12th, 1779 and those records included

"Edmund Lyncecum Confeses (sic) that he was with the Indians in arms against the United States & is

known to be an attrocious Villian the Court therefore
is of opinion that he be kept in Close Confinement."
Eventually they were released.

But the war which pitted brother against brother and father against son was especially vicious in South Carolina. The 1781 Battle of Cowpens was a victory for the patriots who had 12 killed and 61 wounded, which was comparatively light considering the cost to the British. They lost 110 killed, 830 wounded or captured, 800 muskets, 60 slaves, 100 horses and a large quantity of ammunition.

In his jouirnal, Gideon II merely reported that his uncles had been taken prisoner, but shot soon after the Battle of Cowpens, and never stated on which side they fought. However, because of their previous dealings with the British, it was apparent that John and Edmund Lincecum were two of the 110 killed on the British side. Further, that was even more likely considering that following the war, Miriam "never afterwards heard what went with" her sons, or their wives and children.

That was probably because during the war, John and Edmund's father Gideon Lincecum I served as captain of a company of rangers who protected the frontier areas from Muscogee Indians. At that time, the Muscogees were serving as mercenaries for the British. As payment, the British government agreed to give them a bottle of rum and $8.00 for each settler scalp the Mucogees took. Eventually Gideon was killed and scalped following an ambush by the Indians.

Then later during the war, Tories who had overrun the area, severely beat Gideon's widow with an iron ramrod in an attempt to get her to reveal where her money was. Her slaves fled and feeling alone and unsafe in her own home, Miriam joined a group of Georgians going into the Edgefield District of South Carolina. She remained there until peace came in 1783 and then returned to Wilkes County where she found her home and crops had been burned and livestock stolen by Tories.

Back in Wilkes County, Georgia, Miriam's youngest son Hezekiah was the only male Lincecum to survive the war. His son Gideon wrote that because of the unsettled nature of the country

"at the time (Hezekiah) was forming (his) character, it had been woefully misdirected."

Eventually he was persuaded to enlist and spent three years protecting the Georgia border country with Thomas Roberts, a charming, brash, highly educated deserter from the British army. Roberts became a fast friend of Hezekiah and Gideon wrote that Hezekiah Lincecum was "raised in the school of rebellion" and "graduated on ... battlefields."

After three years, a treaty of peace was signed with the Muscogees and Hezekiah returned home a real hellraiser. He could out fight, out swear and out drink anyone. His son Gideon Lincecum II would later describe Hezekiah as

"...a large powerful man, six feet high and weighing in the prime of his life 200 pounds. I saw him, when I was a little boy, lift a forge hammer at Byrd's Iron Works that weighed 596 pounds and hold it on his arms until a six-inch rule was set under it."

Hezekiah was fittingly feared by anyone who crossed him.

Eventually, Hezekiah joined the Baptist Church after hearing a Rev. Brantley preach. He threw himself into his new religion as unwaveringly as he did everything else he attempted. Soon Hezekiah began to preach and lead singing himself.

Also, sometime during this period according to tradition, Hezekiah Lincecum married one of his converts. But the young minister and his saintly wife were having problems and soon the teary eyed Sally returned to her parent's home. Apparently, no divorce was ever granted.

Although town folk were predicting Hezekiah would become a great minister, he soon got into trouble for baptizing a cat and was excommunicated. That put an end to his religious phase.

Next Hezekiah decided, as a grown man, to get an education. But while attending school, fellow student Sally Hickman caught his eye. Later Gideon would write that his mother

"originated from the union of the Englishman, William Hickman, and the Dutch lady, Marie [H]Ornbeck."

Like Hezekiah, Sally was the youngest of her family. She was unremarkable

"Except that she could outrun any body (sic); was handsom, healthy, energetic, ingenious, industrious, frugal."

They married circa 1791, when Sally was only fourteen years old and Hezekiah probably had not divorced his first wife. Gideon, their first child, was born in Warren County, Georgia, when Sally was barely sixteen years old. It was 1793, the same year that Warren was broken off from old Wilkes County.

Like many of the families who ended up settling in Mississippi, the Lincecum family had started out in the Carolinas, moved south to Georgia several times, and on to Alabama. But in between, they lived for a while in Abbeville District, South Carolina and also to the Pendleton District, South Carolina. Pendleton District was the area which later became Pickens,

Anderson and Oconee counties. Records showed that on January 23, 1805,

> "Hezekiah Linucum of Pendleton District ... sold to
> John P. Odell of same place ... for $250.00 ... 200 a.
> in Pendleton District, on Waters of 18 mile creek,
> waters of Savannah River."

The land had been sold to Hezekiah less than a year earlier on March 12, 1804.

The elder Lincecums lived a border life, moving further west each time Hezekiah became restless again, always waiting for each new group of Indian lands to open to settlement. After leaving Georgia, the Hezekiah Lincecum family headed for Tennessee, but almost immediately his mother became ill. Instead of continuing on to Tennessee, Hezekiah rented a house and farm on Calhoun Creek, Abbeville District, South Carolina. Another farm on the property housed Hezekiah's nephew Asa Kelly and his wife.

Next the family moved to Athens, Georgia where they raised good crops of cotton. Gideon wrote,

> "We all did our best to get the cotton out by
> Christmas. We succeeded and Father took it to the
> gin and got receipts for 4643 pounds, for which he got
> five cents a pound."

Despite his success, Hezekiah was a restless again and the family started out on their third attempt to get to Tennessee.

At the Savannah River, Hezekiah and a driver he had hired got roaring drunk as they waited for a horse to be shod. The drunken driver fell off the wagon, causing the team to go wild. When the wagon overturned. Hezekiah's mother and children were injured. But Gideon II's efforts probably saved his grandmother's life.

It was three weeks before the family was well enough to set out once more. Yet again, they did not make it to Tennessee, settling instead near Pendleton, South Carolina. Shortly, Hezekiah became restless again and took his family to land on the Oconee River below Athens, Georgia.

Hezekiah Lincecum could barely read and Sally was illiterate. The only school their children attended was a primitive one they attended for only five months. Their father paid $7 per child. So the brothers received most of their education from the Muscogee Indians in western Georgia. Their playmates were Indian children and their hunting tools were bows and arrows, and blow guns.

Hezekiah had been moving around so much that when land in the west opened, he was not entitled to lottery land. But Hezekiah still moved circa 1806 onto land on the Little River, later a part of Putnam County, Georgia, which was carved out of Baldwin County in 1807. Unfortunately the land had been drawn in the lottery by Thomas McLellan who did not want to give up the land or the cabin he had built there. After considerable bargaining, McLellan agreed to move, but it took every penny the Lincecum family could put together. And it was there that Miriam Bowie Lincecum died and was buried.

It was during those Putnam County days that Gideon II, at age 15, left home for three years after a disagreement with his father. He supported himself working for two area merchants. Moreover, one of them allowed Gideon to make the dry goods store's lumber room into a combination bedroom and library. As a sales agent for Mason Weems "Flying Library", Gideon Lincecum had

> "a library of $5000 worth of the best knowledge the
> world could boast."

Weems was so impressed with Gideon's efforts on his behalf, he gave Gideon a number of books in addition to his salary. The books included some medical books and Erasmus Darwin's *Zoonomia, or The Laws of Organic Life*, which would make a lasting influence on Gideon.

Twice during the War of 1812, Gideon Lincecum II volunteered for military service and, like his father, achieved the rank of colonel. He served as tax collector for Putnam County between his two tours of military service. In the 1813 Putnam County Tax Digest, his father "Hezekiah Linthieum" was listed as living in Capt. William Minton's district.

During his self-education, Gideon had read Benjamin Franklin's advice to marry young and declared that

> "This agreed perfectly with my semi-civilized
> humanity, and the influence of the controlling animal
> developments ... I did so, and thereby in course of
> time, demonstrated the fallacy of the Franklin theory
> ... I was utterly incompetent to the duties and
> responsibilities of domestic life. I, however, made out
> to worry through it without calling for help."

After his marriage to Sally Bryan/Bryant, Gideon II returned to his father's farm and worked it with his brothers.

At one point, Gideon claimed he left Putnam County when rich relatives of his wife called him poor and "cast little slurs at her and her poverty." Whatever the reason, in 1817, along with his father, Gideon Lincecum II and his family started out for the

Alabama Territory. His father got as far as the Ocmulgee River about 45 miles away and decided to stop. Consequently, Gideon stopped too and began to teach school there despite his own brief education. He charged $10 per student for a 9½ month term. He had forty-five pupils, fifteen of them grown men and five grown women.

The writings of Erasmus Darwin, grandfather of Charles Darwin, had a profound effect on Gideon creating in him an appreciation of nature and disgust with the imperfections of man. He educated himself, especially in the sciences, and eventually became a botanical or "still" physician, naturalist, teacher and explorer. He scorned the medical doctors and thought of their remedies as more harmful than helpful.

When more people began to move into the region, it was time for Hezekiah, his wife, eight children and their spouses, eight slaves, horses, wagons guns and dogs to move on. That move took them west to Tuscaloosa, a small settlement in the middle of the wilderness. The family left on March 10, 1818 for a trip which took six weeks to travel the five hundred miles through the Alabama Territory wilderness.

Gideon Lincecum II remained in a small clapboard house on the riverside of Tuscaloosa, while others in the family went farther down the Warrior River. He found life there expensive - $25 for a barrel of flour, with game and beef rare. Eventually the money he arrived with was gone, although he knew his skills would carry them through. During that time, he practiced medicine in Dr. Isbell's shop, kept a hotel, cut planks, among other odd jobs for eight months.

His work with a whipsaw operation came to an end when Tuscaloosa was threatened with an Indian attack. While priming his gun

"It exploded and burnt (him) nearly half in two ...; the explosion blew all the skin and some of the nails off (his) hands and burnt (his) face badly."

Although he was badly injured, Gideon still had a family to support. So he rented a billard table and earned money attending to it himself.

In November, 1818 Hezekiah returned to visit Gideon and to urge him to take a twelve day trip farther west of the Tombigbee River. Having nothing to keep him in Tuscaloosa, Gideon agreed to leave. And just three days later, all the Lincecums - father, sons and daughters, and spouses - moved again, with Gideon and his brother going ahead, hacking a road through the wilderness for the wagons. The women and children strolled alongside the wagons, collecting nuts, grapes and fall fruits.

They stopped near what would become Coumbus, Mississippi. At the time, Columbus was part of Monroe County, but the district later becames a portion of Lowndes County, Mississippi. Although they were part of the state of Mississippi, the Tombigbee River separated them from Indian land which divided them from the rest of the state, two hundred miles away. Gideon wrote that the area was the

"land of promise ... the wildest, least trodden and tomahawk marked"

country he had ever seen. At their first campfire in the area they heard "the panthers scream; the racoons complained; the owls came near and hooted awfully; and the wolves howled all night. The teals swarmed and the beavers slapped their tails delightfully."

Within a few days they had a clapboard house up along the Tombigbee River and Gideon and his brother Garland had cleared ground to plant corn.

Gideon Lincecum was listed as living in Columbus, Monroe County, in the 1820 census. There were ten in the family, including four males ages 19 to 26 and two males ages 26 to 45 years old. Since Gideon would have been approximately 27 years old at the time, the other males over 18 years of age were probably some of his brothers. Hezekiah also was listed in the Columbus 1820 census with another ten Lincecums listed in his family.

It was about that time that Gideon II befriended young Peter Pitchlynn, son of the Choctaw interpreter John Pitchlynn, Sr. Later, the younger Pitchlynn credited Gideon Licecum for his hunger for learning.

Gideon entered into a partnership with John Pitchlynn, Jr. and became manager of their storehouse and ferry. There he bartered for anything from beeswax to deer skins, from blowguns to hickory nuts. And quickly Gideon Lincecum became a man of substance.

According to an 1825 census, Gideon II, Hezekiah and an illegible notation that could have been Grabel Lincecum were in Monroe County, Mississippi. Gideon resided in Cotton Gin Port, Monroe County and then moved to a community ten miles east.

That community had actually begun around William Wall's sizeable plantation. In August, 1825, a road was built to connect the plantation with Cotton Gin Port. A post office was established in 1828 and it was named Wall's Tanyard. The post office was closed in 1852 and the town eventually disappeared.

On February 12, 1821, Gideon was appointed by the Mississippi legislature as Chief Justice of the quorum with power to appoint all other Monroe County officers necessary to organize a county. He wrote that it was difficult because everybody wanted an office.

As an busy civic leader, Gideon was appointed chairman of the school board and oversaw the building of a male and a female academy. He was also authorized to lay out and lease town lots for Possum Town (Columbus), Mississippi. Then from 1823 through 1827, Gideon held offices in the Columbus Masonic Lodge. He may also have been Possum Town's first postmaster.

But while living there, Dr. Gideon Lincecum signed up as physician on a 1835 expedition to Texas to determine its potential as a place to settle. Gideon ended up remaining for six months, studying and writing about the area's natural resources. His journal became an important source of information about Texas history.

On his way back from Texas, Gideon made a stop at Alexandria, Louisiana where cholera was raging. He hurried along, but at the Mississippi River he was joined by a man with a small boy riding behind him on his horse. Gideon wrote that the man

> "had lost $400,000 worth of negroes, and that his wife
> and all his children except the one with him had died.
> At several places along the river all the inhabitants

were dead and many unburied and the dogs were howling piteously in the yards."

After his trip, Gideon returned to Mississippi and set-up a practice in Wall's Tanyard where on March 16, 1838, he became the post master and renamed the town Electra in honor of his use of electricity in his treatment of patients.

In fact, Gideon Lincecum became a doctor of some rebute and patients converged on him for his "cure". People traveled as much as sixty miles to be treated by him. So many arrive that he first "prepared rooms for them," and then "erected a new office with rooms adjoing." But those rooms were soon occupied and he was forced to build a one hundred foot long hospital of sorts. He later complained that

> "The fame of this curative establishment was spread
> in all directions. And as a consequence was turning
> (his) house into a tavern and subjecting (his) family to
> all the inconveniences of such an establishment."

His cures were not all botanical or electrical. Convinced that medical books were written by northerners who did not understand Southern diseases, Gideon decided to seek out a Choctaw medicine man of great reputation to learn his methods of treating disease. Gideon was to pay the Indian doctor fifty cents a day for six weeks of lecture at an agreed upon place on the Noxubee River seventy miles from Gideon's home and one hundred thirty miles from the medicine man's home. The two lived off the earth and for those six weeks, Gideon learned everything the medicine man had to teach. At the end of the training, Gideon returned to his medical practice.

From that time on, he carried "old school medicines" in one saddle bag and a combination of botanic and Indian remedies in the other. He was willing to use whatever worked.

One newspaper article reported that when Samuel Greenwood of Monroe County "was in a very low state," his doctor,

> "Dr. Gid Lincecum played a fiddle and told tales by the dozen and never administered any medicine and thus the severity of Samuel's illness was lessened by his spirits becoming so exhilarated."

Through the years he was in the Alabama and Mississippi Territories, Gideon had become a lifelong friend of the Choctaws. In 1829 he organized a group of Choctaw ballplayers and took them on tour to perform exhibition games and Indian dances.

His Indian name was "Shappo tohoba," meaning "White Hat" because he was wearing one the first time the Indians saw him. Sometimes he was also called "Anumpatashula ebisuya" meaning "Interpreter's Nephew" in reference to his close friendship with John Pitchlynn. Gideon was sometime also referred to as "Hopigeh cheto" meaning "Big Leader" because he

> "conducted a party of 100 (Indians) out of a condition of starvation on (their) return from a failure in attempting to get some scalps from a large camp of Ooassashes (sic), west of the Mississippi."

Then, in January, 1841, Gideon left Electra and returned to Columbus. It took eleven wagons and a carriage to move everything. While living there he served as Worshipful Master of the Masons.

And his medical practice thrived there too. He claimed that during the nearly seven years he practiced in Columbus, he "lost no case of any kind of fever." And in his last year of practice there, he "treated 2236 cases, mostly fever." The last month he practiced in Columbus was September, 1847. He earned $1266 that month.

He watched the Columbus area change from woodland to thriving financial center. But by 1847, Gideon Lincecum had become appalled by what civilization had done to his family. His sons were drinking, his daughters were dancing, all his children were dressing lavishly, and they were spending an astonishing $3,000 to 5,000 a year.

> "Parties and dancing schools, shopping and 'charge
> it to Poppa' was all they seemed to care for. The
> entire community of young people were similar in their
> habits."

Afraid that they would end up marrying people just like themselves, Gideon and his wife loaded up their unmarried children and fled the confinements of civilization for the wilds of the Brazos River area in Washington County, Texas, which was originally part of Austin's Colony.

Texas had been part of Imperial Mexico when in 1821 Moses Austin traveled south to inspect the land for possible settlement. But Austin died before he was able to take his dream to fruition. However, his eldest son, Stephen F. Austin decided to carry on with the project. On December 23, 1821, Stephen F. Austin and three hundred followers entered Texas at Nacgdoches.

Austin obtained several grants from the Mexican-Spanish authorities. So in 1824, the first colony was confirmed at the

"San Antonio Crossing" at today's Bastrop, Texas. But the limits of the colony were not fixed until 1827. Then, in 1828, the Colony was greatly expanded. Austin's Colony had the mouth of the Brazos and Colorado Rivers on the south, included Fayette and Lavaca Counties to the west, Liberty and San Jacinto Counties to the east, and Brazos and Madison Counties, Texas to the north.

The sizeable "Municipality of Washington" was established in 1835 and just a short time later that area became Washington County. Large chunks of the county were later taken over by other counties.

The Lincecums settled near the center of the county. The town of Washington (also known as Washington-on-the-Brazos and Old Washington) was just to the northeast of where the Lincecums settled. The 1850 town of Washington was

> "Filled with large brick buildings and doing immense
> business, the prairie between there and Houston
> being almost impassable in consequence of mud,"

according to *Austin County Pioneers.*

The Lincecum family lived at Long Point, between the Burton and Gay Hill settlements. Gay Hill had its first settler circa 1834. At age seventy-five, Gideon II was still searching for the freedom the Lincecums had been looking for since the first Gideon left France with his father. Gideon II wrote

> "I was not formed by nature for any kind of
> government. If I had the choosing I would not have
> preferred an agricultural community. Nature intended
> me for the forests but dropped me in a locality that
> was soon overrun and cut down by a race of world
> spoilers.

In Texas, Gideon Lincecum became a prolific recorder of his scientific observations and a "pen-pal" of sorts with such luminaries as Charles Darwin. Darwin even sponsored the publication of some of Gideon's scientific papers.

Gideon soon left the medical work to his son, in particular Lusullus Lincecum, and became more of a naturalist himself. He loved ants and bees, making them almost pets, studying them and collecting data about them. He wrote that his bees were "all acquainted" with him and was even asked to donated collections to the Smithsonian.

Many of Gideon's scientific conclusions were biased at best. He readily admitted that his

> "observations and conclusions, be them right or wrong, (were) not trammelled by the sway of other minds."

In fact, according to *Science on the Texas Frontier*, one scientist suggested that Gideon Lincecum

> "had many peculiar notions about society, religion, and the genus homo generally, which he could not refrain from thrusting ... into the midst of his notes."

In Texas, Gideon maintained a home of his own, separate from his wife. In a letter to a colleague, Gideon explained why he maintained a separate residence and described his home as

> "a substantial little house composed entirely of red cedar, 40 feet from the main dwelling where the old lady resides; (she) having always, by turns, that gives pleasure to her, a noisy bustle of growing dears (grandchildren); book spoilers and paper scribblers. To get out of the way of these dear little pictures of health and devilment, the above named little house

was constructed. In this little house is my bed, books,
papers, writing instruments, copying press,
microscopes, cases of Entomological specimens ...;
hanging on the wall are all sorts of hats."

He wore no shoes in the summers. His meals were exact - 3
ounces of corn bread, a spoonful of butter and a cup of coffee
every breakfast. And he slept with all windows and doors open
so every breath he took was "a new one."

But Gideon Lincecum supported slavery and with the Civil
War, he supported the confederates. He built spinning wheels
and looms, while his wife Sarah and their daughters spun, wove
and knitted for the southern cause.

Sarah Lincecum preceded her husband in death.
Afterwards he wrote

"I can not look calmly upon the turned plate at the
table, nor the old empty chair on the left hand side of
the fireplace. Everything I see, minds me of my lost
one ... I am of no use here nohow."

Accordingly, Gideon busied himself with excursions into West
Texas and the Gulf shores.

But the settlers were beginning to arrive and Gideon
complained that

"society, villianous, *civilized* society, has gradually
thickened around me until there is no little, sacred,
untramped nook to which I might retire and hide
myself from the unholy gaze of intermedling
civilization. Hence I go to the wilds of the mountain
forests of Tuxapan."

Although his children tried to persuade him to not go to Mexico,
he did go for a short time and even had a ranch there.

But it was an excursion to East Texas where he and many of his party became quite ill with yellow fever which began to make him question a permanent move to Mexico. Then his fear that the United States intended to "possess themselves of Mexico" and that he "would have to move again," made Gideon give up the idea of moving althogether.

While in Texas, Gideon amassed a great wealth, most of which he lost during the Civil War. In 1866 he wrote

"When the war broke up, and I had time to look around, I found I had lost everything but the homestead It is the truth that I did not have a blanket, nor horse, no mule nor jackass left to my name, nor one single dollar."

Gideon Lincecum died in 1874. Sixty-two years after his death, a tombstone was placed near the statue of Stephen F. Austin in "Founders Row" of the Texas State Cemetery in Austin, Texas. Gideon's stone declared him a "Veteran of the War of 1812" and an "Internationally Famous Botanist."

In contrast, in 1830 his brother Grabel/Gabriel, who was living in the far southeastern section of Oktibbeha County, Mississippi, got into a dispute with a Choctaw. Unfortunately, the Indian was killed. Although in his history of the county, Judge Thomas B. Carroll called the killing "justifiable, or at least excusable," the Choctaws didn't see it that way. So with his own life in jeopardy, Grabel Lincecum packed up his wife and children and fled along Indian trails to Arkansas.

Later his problems with the Choctaws were settled, possibly through brother Gideon's intervention. And soon after his return to Oktibbeha County, Grabel Lincecum became a member of the first board of police (supervisors).

According to *Old Tuskaloosa Land Office Records*, on September 5, 1822, a "Gravel" Lincecum of Monroe County, Mississippi was awarded land in Sec26 T16 R17W. This might have been yet another son of Hezekiah. Or, I believe more likely, the cursive signature of Grabel/Gabriel was misread. The only other land granted to a Lincecum by the Tuscaloosa land office was given to "Grabel" Lincecum on December 11, 1822. That property was described as Sec26 T16 R17W in Monroe County.

Sometime between 1826 and 1832, he had built a bridge on the Robinson or Military Road across the Noxubee River on land he had purchased from Daniel Nail in the southern portion of Oktibbeha County. When Oktibbeha County was later organized, Lincecum was granted an annual appropriation of $500 from the county so county residents could cross the bridge for free. Others paid a fee of fifteen cents per adult, five cents per child, two cents per large animal and five cents per dozen of smaller animals. Traffic on the bridge was heavy with travelers moving from the Atlantic Coast states west. Families in covered wagons drawn by oxen, driving cattle and other livestock, had to cross that bridge for a fee.

This first toll bridge in the Choctaw Nation had an iron super-structure and wood plank flooring. When he first built it, Grabrel paid $500 for it. He sold it for $1,000, bought it again for $5,000, and finally, resold it for $20,000. Grabel sold at the right time because soon after that sale, use fell off and the price plummeted.

He also owned a mill on the Noxubee River that, after Grabrel's 1836 death, continued to be owned by members of the family. His will appeared in Noxubee County's Book A and was dated November 9, 1836. It was probated on May 1, 1837, so his death took place between those dates. One possible child was not mentioned in his will. According to a 1900 *Macon Beacon*, Heyward Lincecum, age 75 and a Mexican War veteran, died on April 9, 1900 leaving a son Brooks Lincecum and a sister Mrs. J.B. Cole. Supposedly Grabel had a grandson named Leo Cole. So was Heyward the son of Grabel? Both "Hairwood" and "Ducia A." Lincecum/Lincicum were in the Mississippi 1850 census as heads of households. On November 3, 1842, a Wilmouth Lincecum married James P. Haynes. Since Grabrel died in 1836, was this Grabel's wife or daughter Wilmouth.

The third brother was Grant Lincecum. After arriving in thie Mississippi area with his family, Grant became acquainted with Col. William Ward, the U.S. agent appointed to register land for those Choctaws who did not want to move to Indian territory in the west.

Ward, an alcoholic, purposely made it difficult for some and totally impossible for other Choctaws who wanted to register. And Grant Lincecum witnessed Ward's abuse of power.

Then, when Ward was about to leave the agency, Gabrel Lincecum purchased books and papers of Ward's. While going through them Gabrel discovered that Ward had not transferred the names of orphans onto land books.

Because of Ward's Choctaw land frauds, both Gabrel and Grant Lincecum gave depositions against Ward. It must have added to their anger that during his tenure Ward had allowed "houses of entertainment" to infiltrate the area, and thefts and robberies had become commonplace. People disappeared. Outlaw John Murrel and his gang operated in the Agency area.

Grant Lincecum had moved to Catahoula Parish, Louisiana by 1848, when his mother died there. She had gotten that far as she accompanied her son Gideon to Texas. Grant was still in Catahoula Parish in the 1850 census. Later he moved on to Dallas, Texas where he died. A Harmon Lincecum also lived in Catahoula during the 1850 census.

Another brother, Rezin Bowie Lincecum was part-owner of Lincecum, Barry & Co. in Columbus in 1835. He was supposedly residing in Tennessee in 1830, but died in 1835 in Kentucky while on his way from Mississippi to New York. His obituary appeared in an 1835 *Southern Argus Newspaper*, from Columbus, Mississippi. In it he was listed as a merchant from Columbus.

In 1823, a Garland R. Lincecum received a land patent in Leake County, Mississippi. After the Indian lands were opened to white settlement, many member of the family received land out of the Lowndes County, Mississippi land office. Lincecums listed in the records were

Name	Date	Sec.	Twp.	Range	No. of Acres
Garland R.	11/29/34	31	19N	18E	160.82
	10/17/34	5	18N	17E	82.48
	10/17/34	29	19N	18E	66.00
Hezekiah	10/18/28	30	17N	18W	78.31
	05/31/34	30	17N	18W	39.16
	12/17/31	31	17N	18W	79.37
	10/09/34	29	17N	18W	40.00
Regina" Bowie (Rezin)					
	07/26/31	31	17N	18W	39.70
	01/23/31	31	17N	18W	39.69

In December, 1828, Peter Pitchlynn wrote in his diary about meeting with "Uncle Edmund Folsom and his son Peter" and Garland Lincecum at the Choctaw Agency in the Fort Smith area of Arkansas. Edmund Folsom, actually Pitchlynn's great uncle, apparently had moved west with an earlier group. From the diary, Garland Lincecum was with them in Arkansas, possibly moving west with that earlier group of Indians.

However, unfortunately Pitchlynn's renewed acquaintance with Garland was not a good one. The December 11, 1828 entry in Pitchlynn's journal, he wrote

"Lincecum this morning got drunk and commenced a quarrel with me."

Garland Lincecum was in Calwell, Texas in 1850. Brother Green Lincecum was in Arkansas in 1820 and 1830. But these brothers did not have the influence on the Mississippi that their other three brothers did, although descendants of theirs remained in the state.

On April 26, 1861, an E. Pluribus Lincecum, age 24, enlisted in Company E of the 11th Mississippi Infantry Regiment. He was recruited out of Crawford (then Crawfordsville), in far southwestern Lowndes County, Mississippi, where Gideon had lived and just across the county border from Grabrel and Grant in Oktibbeha County. According to Confederate records, E. Pluribus died of "Thyphoid Pneumonia" at Harpers Ferry, Virginia, on June 7, 1861. E. Pluribus was probably the son of one of the Lincecum brothers of this genealogy.

And there is a grave for a Jane Lincecum, "d. Oct, 8, 1885 age 65 years" in Easter Cemetery, fifteen miles northeast of Aberdeen in Monroe County, Mississippi. But her relationship to this family has not been determined.

Mangum Family

John Mangum I

    b. pos Surry County, Virginia; c. 1672

    m. Frances Bennett; betw 1696-1700

    d. Isle of Wight County, Virginia; 1737

    Children

        John II (see below)

        William - b. Surry County, Virginia; 1706 - 1709

            m. Mary, pos dau of Job or John Person; c. 1730

            r. Edgecombe County, North Carolina; May, 1748

        wit deed 1748

        Children

            James - b. Albemarle Parrish, Surry County, Virginia; June 2, 1734

            Samuel

                Children

                    Joseph

            Joseph - b. 1747-1752

                r. Granville County, North Carolina

                Children

                    Josiah   Gray

                    Joseph Jr.   William

            William, Jr. - b. May 16, 1736

            Sarah - b. October 14, 1743

            Arthur - b. May 2, 1741

        James - b. 1706-1710

            m. Mary

            d. Sussex County, Virginia; c. 1794

wll dtd Sussex County, Virginia; November 29, 1782

Children

    Samuel - b. by 1738

    Lucy - b. July 26, 1741

    Absolom - b. Virginia; c. 1742

        r. Johnson County, North Carolina; 1769

        r. Granville County, North Carolina 1788

        d. by 1802

    James, Jr. - b. January 22, 1743/44

    John - b.c. 1745

Mary - b.c. 1710

    m. John Langston

Sarah - b. Surry County, Virginia; c. 1714

John Mangum II

    b. Albemarle, Virginia; c. 1710

    m. Olive "Savidge", dau of Robert Savage

    d. Surry County, Virginia; 1744

    Children

        John III (see below)

John Mangum III

    b. Surry County, Virginia; 1732

    m. Mary (b. 1734 d. by 1794)

    d. Newberry County, South Carolina; 1794

    Children

        John IV (see below)

William 1 - b. November 12, 1756

Lucy - b. November 20, 1758

Sarah - b. November 6, 1760

William 2 - b. 1765

    d. 1827

Lewis - b. 1768

Mary - b. 1769

John Mangum IV

    b. Mecklenburg County, North Carolina; January 19, 1763

    m. Rebecca Canida or Jemima Googins; South Carolina

    m. Ellen Bardsley or Elizabeth Murdock; South Carolina

    m. Rebecca Knowles (b. England; October 10, 1785 d. Winter Quarters, Nebraska; 1847); Warren County, Ohio; January 19, 1809

    d. Fulton, Itawamba County, Mississippi; March 23, 1843

    Children

        John V (see below)

        Cyrus - b. South Carolina; January 5, 1803

            m. Lucinda (b South Carolina; c. 1812)

            r. Texas

            d. aft 1850

            Children

David	Warren	Elizabeth
Nancy	Alabama	Samuel
Dily/Wiley	John	

        Jemima - b. Warren County, Ohio; September, 1809

            m. Samuel Jefferson Adair, son of Thomas Jefferson Adair

William - b. Giles County, Tennessee; December,
1811

m1 Sarah Adair (d. near Platte River, Nebraska;
July 3, 1852), dau of Thomas Jefferson Adair

m2 Delight Potter, dau of Arnold Potter

d. Circleville, Utah; February 26, 1886

Rebecca - b. Giles County, Tennessee; August 10,
1814

m. John Mosely Adair

d. Arizonia

Jennie - b. Maury County, Tennessee; July 14, 1824

m. Jedediah Brown

Lucinda - Pickens County, Alabama; July 20, 1826

m. James Richey (1821-1879), son of William
and Margaret Ann Adair Richey; Nauvoo,
Hancock County, Illinois; March 23, 1846

d. Arizonia, February 23, 1903

James - St. Clair, Alabama

m. Eliza Cook; Itawamba County, Mississippi;
June 1, 1842

?Joseph - b. Pickens County, Alabama

d. Iowa

John Mangum V

b. St. Clair County, Alabama; June 10, 1817

bpt. November 18, 1844

m1 Mary Ann Adair (b. Pickens County, Alabama; July 5,
1822 d. Kane County, Utah; May 9, 1892), dau of Thomas
and Rebecca Brown Adair; Noxubee County, Mississippi;
August 20, 1841

d. Alpine, Apache County, Arizonia; May 23, 1885

Children

> William Perry - b. Itawamba County, Mississippi; October, 1841
>
> d. betw 1846 and 1852
>
> Rebecca Francis - b. Itawamba County, Mississippi; October 10, 1843
>
> bpt. February, 1852
>
> m. Gabriel Reynolds; April, 1858
>
> d. Duncan, Greenlee County, Arizonia; April 13, 1928
>
> bur. Central Heights, Graham County, Arizonia; April 15, 1928
>
> Laney Ann - b. Chickasaw County, Mississippi; January 6, 1846
>
> d. November, 1846
>
> Martha Elizabeth - b. Pottawattomie County, Iowa; September 30, 1848

For the purpose of this genealogy, the "Mangum" spelling will be used. However, the name has been found as Mangum, Mingham, Mangom, Mangrum, Mangan, Mangham and a variety of other spellings which could be Welsh, English, Scotch or Irish in origin. One possible origin was Maningham, an English family whose motto was "Ad Finem fidelis" meaning "Faithful to the last." Furthermore, in England there were towns or villages named Mengham, Magham-Down and Mongeham, which could have become surnames for their citizens.

But the British Isles were not the only places of possible origin. The Netherlands had the surname Manger, Luxembourg had Mangin, France had Mangon, Ireland had Maughan and Wales had Mangolus. There were French Hugenots named Mangamis who fled to Wales and changed their named to Manngham.

The first member of the family in this genealogy was John Mangum, an early Virginia settler. Various sources have had his birthplace as England, Isle of Man, Ireland, Wales and Surry County, Virginia.

But whatever his birthplace, John I may have been the John "Mangom" on the Lawnes Creek Parrish list for of Surry County, Virginia in 1693 or the John "Manghan" on a different tax list for Surry County on June 10, 1694. Or he may have been the John Mangum who, in the *Douglas Register*, appeared as

"John, ye son of Daniel & Miriam Mangauhan was born ye 18 Feb. 1678/9 in Virginia."

The John Mangum of this genealogy was definitely in Virginia by his May 25, 1695 purchase of land from Richard Bennett, Sr. in Surry County, Virginia. There has been speculation that his wife Francis was a member of the Bennett family. They married between 1696 and 1700. At John's death, Frances Mangum became administrator of his estate.

In 1728 a John Mangum witnessed a will in Surry County, Virginia. This could not have been John I as that John was illiterate and used "x" or "+" iin place of a signature in earlier documents. So it may be assumed it was his son John Mangum II, who had been born circa 1710 in Albemarle, Virginia. John II died in 1744 and his widow, Olive was named administer of his estate.

Their son John Mangum III was born in 1732. That John moved his family to Mecklenburg County.

John Mangum IV (S16939) enlisted in the Newbury District, South Carolina during the Revolutionary War and served as a private from 1778 (age 15) through August 1782. He served in Colonel James Williams' Regiment, then with Colonel McRory, General Elijah Clark and Major Ford. According to some Mangum family lore, John IV may have been captured, but his life spared because his older brother was a Tory. It is true that there were several John and William Mangums and at least one of the William's was a Tory. But whether he was the brother of the John of this genealogy has not been proven.

After the war, John Mangum IV took a different route from most of the settlers going from North Carolina to Alabama. Circa 1805 John moved to Warren County (now Clinton), Ohio where he remained until 1815 when he moved to Tennessee and St. Clair County, Illinois or Alabama, depending upon the source. Then in 1823 or 1824, he moved to Pickens County, Alabama where he testified for John Wigginton's application for a Revolutionary War pension.

In the 1830 Federal census for Pickens County, Cyrus and John Mangum appeared on page 110. In 1830 Cyrus had been granted land in Sec27 T20 R15W in Pickens County. On September 23, 1834, a John Mangum received land in Sec22 T20 R15W near land given to Rebecca Adair. The Adair and Mangum families would be united in marriage in the next generation. A William Mangum received grants of land in the same township and range in 1835 and 1836. William, John and Cyrus Mangum's land grants were all north of Carrollton; and southwest of Reform, in Pickens County, Alabama. They were probably John IV (b. 1763) and his sons Cyrus (b. 1803) and William (b. 1811).

Then, in the 1850 Federal Census, C. Mangum was in the southern district of Pickens County, Alabama. He reported that he was born in South Carolina circa 1803. In 1803, John IV was forty years old and residing in South Carolina too. Was Cyrus his son or grandson?

So was Cyrus the first child of John IV as has commonly been accepted? If the children listed as John IV's (b. 1763) were in deed his, then John V was born when his father was 54 years old. Daughter Lucinda was born in 1826, when he was 63 years old.

According to Noxubee County, Mississippi records, John "Mangrum" V married Mary Ann Adair were married on August 20, 1841 by Probate Judge J.J. Beauchamp in Noxubee County. Interestingly, their son William Perry Mangum was born in October 1841, in Itawamba County, Mississippi.

Since Noxubee County, Mississippi bordered Pickens County, Alabama where Mary Ann was born, a marriage in Noxubee would not be surprising. There was a great deal of movement between the two counties. But the birth of a child two months later in a different county would be surprising and could explain the marriage in a different county.

Among other Itawamba County, Mississippi records was one for a Jane Mangum married George Crawford on June 8, 1841. It was while John V and Mary Ann were in Itawamba County that members of the family were baptized into the Mormon Church. Before moving west with the Mormons, a John Mangum moved to Chickasaw County, Mississippi by January 6, 1846 when his daughter Laney Ann was born.

There was a John "Mangrum" was living in T14 R8E of Attala County, Mississippi in the 1850 census, but he was not

John Mangum V of this genealogy since the family had left to travel west with the Mormons by then.

Although John Mangum IV had died before the trip, his third wife Rebecca Knowles Mangum made it to Winter Quarters, Iowa, before dying in 1847. Winter Quarters was in Pottawattomie County, just east of Omaha and the Missouri River. According to *The Encyclopedia of American West* many Mormons died there. The poor living conditions, the lack of supplies took a toll on the families. Many lived in tents well into the winter. But even when the seven hundred sod houses were completed, conditions were not that much better.

Brigham Young's first group left Winter Quarters in 1847. Many were so poor it was difficult for them to make the trip. In fact, in 1849 Young had to set up the Perpetual Emigrating Fund to help poor converts make the trip. Circa 1856, Young urged converts to walk using handcarts. And, finally, beginning in the 1860's volunteers left Utah each year to return to Nebraska to bring new settlers along the Mormon Trail.

The Mangums may have been among the poor because they were still in Pottawattomie County when John V and Mary Ann's daughter Martha Elizabeth Mangum was born on September 30, 1848. And John Mangum was listed in the 1850 census as living in District 21, Pottawattomie County, Iowa.

Whether they were helped by the Perpetual Fund or not, the Mangums did finally get to Utah. John Mangum V died in Arizonia in 1885, having followed the Mormons west. His wife Mary Ann died seven years later in Utah.

Meek/Meeks Family

As might be expected, the first person with the Meek/Meeks surname was probably humble and submissive. However, as the following genealogies demontrate, Meek certainly was not an appropriate term to describe some of the courage of family members with this surname.

They were probably initially Scottish or English, but may have taken refuge in Ulster. A Thomas Meek who may have fought against the Spanish Armada went to Ireland and raised at least five sons - Francis, Matthew, Arthur, James and Thomas. The genealogies of three Meek families included here took the same general route west follow.

The Robert and James Meek Family

Robert Meek
    b. Ireland; by 1726
    m. Jean Mitchell (d. York County, South Carolina; 1794-97), dau of Andrew and Jean Mitchell
    d. Cecil County, Maryland; 1767
    wll dtd Cecil County, Maryland; August 1, 1767
    wll pro October 10, 1767
    Children
        James (see below)
        Andrew - b. 1746
            m. Martha
        Rebecca - m. _____ Scott
        Jean - b. 1750
            m. John Hope; Union County, South Carolina
            d. Union County, South Carolina; August 21, 1817
        Moses - b. January 29, 1754
            m. Agnes Hope
            d. York District, South Carolina; December 23, 1815
        Adam - b. Cecil County, Maryland; 1760
            m. Nancy Ann Byers
            d. York District, South Carolina; January 26, 1807
        Mary
        Margaret
        Nancy

James Meek

> b. pos Cecil County, Maryland; c. 1758
>
> m. Susannah Byers (b. March 12, 1771 d. April 3, 1844 bur. Beersheba Cemetery), dau of Captain William and Elizabeth Walton Byers; York County, South Carolina; January 21, 1790
>
> d. Alabama; c. March 3, 1819
>
> bur. Col. Anderson's Plantation
>
> Children
>
> > Abner (see below)
> >
> > Adam - b.d. 1791
> >
> > Elizabeth - b. 1793
> >
> > > d. 1794
> >
> > Jean Mitchell - b.d. 1794
> >
> > Eli - b. October 14, 1797
> >
> > > m. Martha Louisa Starr
> >
> > "Cinthya" - b. August 18, 1800
> >
> > Permela - b. May 31, 1802
> >
> > Amzi - b. March 8, 1804
> >
> > > d. February 9, 1839
> >
> > Drucilla - b.d. 1806
> >
> > Lucinda - b. January 18, 1808
> >
> > > m. Cheterfield McKinney
> > >
> > > r. Holly Springs, Marshall County, Mississippi
> >
> > James Byers - b. March 1, 1810
> >
> > > d. Louisville, Mississippi
> >
> > Marion - b. May 28, 1813
> >
> > > September 22, 1825
> >
> > William Baldwin - b. March 7, 1815

m. Mary Moore McCorkle (b. November 29, 1814 d. March 24, 1846), dau of Joseph and Violet Mary Hanna McCorkle

d. March 24, 1846

Abner Meek

b. York County, South Carolina; December 11, 1795

m. Eliza Smith (b. South Carolina; June 30, 1801 d. November 1, 1873), dau of Robert and Ann McCaw Smith

r. Winston County, Mississippi; 1850

d. February 6, 1855

bur. Koscuisko City Cemetery, Attala County, Mississippi

Children

Frances Ann (see below)

Susan - b.c. 1831

Robert - b.c. 1834

Mary - b. August 25, 1834

d. York County, South Carolina; 1836

Sarah - b. 1835

d. York County, South Carolina; 1836

Nancy Jane - b. Mississippi; c. 1837

William Erwin - b. November 28, 1838

m. Ida Eugenia Potts

d. Attala County, Mississippi; July 6, 1883

Children

J.A. - b./d. 1874

Martha - b. August 10, 1842

John - b. February 4, 1844

d. Atlanta, Georgia; July 20, 1864

Cornelia - b.c. 1846

James Smith - d. Winston County, Mississippi

Frances Ann Meek
> b. York District, South Carolina; September 10, 1826/28
>
> m. Dr. Amzi Godden Garrigues (b. June 13, 1819; Morristown/Newark, New Jersey d. March 2, 1892; Louisville, Winston County, Mississippi), son of James and Elizabeth Godden Garrigues; December 1845
>
> d. July 14, 1901
>
> bur. Masonic Cemetery; Louisville, Winston County, Mississippi
>
> Children
>> Mary "Molly" Elizabeth Garrigues - b. October 2,1846
>>> m. Will Hammond of Koscuisko, Mississippi
>>>
>>> d. March 22, 1924
>>
>> Susan Caroline Garrigues - b. June 2,1848
>>> m. James W. White of Koscuisko, Mississippi
>>>
>>> d. April 12, 1887
>>>
>>> Children
>>>> James   Anne   Infant
>>
>> Henry Abner Garrigues - b. December, 1849
>>> m. never
>>>
>>> d. 1924
>>
>> James Meek Garrigues - b. d. 1852
>>
>> Elizabeth Godden Garrigues - b. April 24, 1853
>>> m. W.A. Tobe Comfort, son of David Samuel and Martha Caroline White Comfort; November 1, 1876
>>>
>>> d. March 2, 1920

bur. Kosciusko City Cemetery, Attala County,
Mississippi

Joseph Elmer Garrigues - b. 1855

    m. Gillie Hudson

Harriet "Hettie" Augusta Garrigues - b. August 28,
1857

    m. John Bunyan Brown

    r. Texas

    d. 1941

Nannie Makel Meek Garrigues - b. January 8, 1860

    m. James David or Jeff Comfort; January 2, 1887

    r. Memphis, Tennessee

    d. 1961

Gillie Cornelia Garrigues - b. November 21, 1862

    d. 1871, in accident

Robert F. Garrigues - d. young

Fannie Meek Garrigues - b. March 28, 1866

    m. Henry Clark Gage; Winston County,
Mississippi; November 13, 1888

    d. 1964

William Amzi Garrigues - b. November 6, 1868

    m. Sallie Hughes Jones; Winston County,
Mississippi; November 27, 1894

    d. 1956

Martha "Ida" Garrigues - b. November 13, 1870

    m. G.W. Edgar Bennett; Winston County,
Mississippi; November 2, 1890's

    d. 1960

2 children - d. young

There were Meeks who received land grants in Maryland as early as 1661. Those early Marylanders were a thought to be descendants of Guy Meek and may have been related to Adam Meek of this genealogy.

However, this Adam Meek was probably born in Ireland, But Meek was not a typically Irish name. The name however was among the Scotch-Irish of Northern Ireland. Whatever the origin, Adam's wanderlust guided him across the Atlantic to Maryland.

He was an adult by the time he received land patents on the Susquehanna River in Maryland in 1745 and 1747. His son Andrew was born in 1746. But when he died, Adam Meek had minor children, including James (b.c. 1758). So he was relatively young when he died in 1767. He named his wife Jean and his son Andrew who was just twenty-one years old as executors of his estate which was valued at over 460 British pounds, including 160 British pound for four slaves he had owned.

Adam also had held lands in Baltimore County, Maryland on the upper branches of Swan Creek and north of Deer Creek near the Pennsylvania River and a larger plantation in Cecil County, Maryland. But upon his death, Adam's widow took her children to York County, South Carolina. The reason for the move has never been uncovered. Perhaps she had family there. One Meek genealogist reported that at the time, a number of families were following highly regarded ministers to York County, South Carolina. Whatever the reason, Jean Meek and her children were in South Carolina by her purchase of land on Bullock's Creek in Camden District in 1777/78.

Adam and Jean's son James was probably born in Cecil County, Maryland, which had been settled before 1634. James Meek and his brother Adam inherited their farther's plantation in

Cecil County, but went with their mother to South Carolina. It was in York County, South Carolina, that James met Susannah, the daughter of Captain William and Elizabeth Byers. Captain Byers was a member of South Carolina's Second Provincial Congress in 1775-1776.

During the Revolutionary War, James joined Sumter's Command and, depending upon the source, may have served with his future father-in-law or brother-in-law. They were at the Battle of Kings Mountain and the August 18, 1780 defeat at Fishing Creek. James eventually reached the rank of Captain.

At one point James was captured by the Tories. But Sumter's men were tipped off by a Tory friend of James named John Swan as to where James was being taken. So when his captors stopped for dinner at a Tory home, James' fellow soldiers rescued him.

After the war, James became undersheriff of York County, South Carolina for his brother Adam Meek who was sheriff. When their mother died in 1794, Adam and James inherited her 275 acre farm.

Regardless, James seemed to have inherited his father's wanderlust and he set out alone for Alabama and Mississippi, possibly to look for land for his family. But James Meek disappeared in 1819 on that land purchasing trip. His body was eventually found in the Seneca River near Col Anderson's ferry.

Although, it was always suspected that he had been robbed and killed, he also may have accidentally drown while trying to ford the river. At first, he was buried on Col. Anderson's Plantation. But his tombstone was moved in 1959 to the Baptist Cemetery in Andersonville, South Carolina when a dam was being built which would flood the old plantation area.

The Meek family were slave owners. In fact, Abner owned 23 at his death. In one curious 1821 record

"Jeremiah Hunt, a poor boy of color, with the consent of his mother Elizabeth Hunt"

was apprenticed to Abner Meek until his 21st birthday on November 17, 1827. In return, Abner agreed to send Jeremiah "to an English school" and provide him with food and clothing.

Although some sources, including censuses and Abner's obituary indicated the family arrived in Mississippi circa 1838, in 1835 James Byers Meek supposedly joined "A . Meek" in a firm name Meek and Brother in Columbus, Mississippi. Eventually the firm "A. Meek and Brother" opened in Louisville, Winston County, Mississippi. Of course, the "A." Meek could have been Abner's brother Amzi. If that was so, Abner probably followed brothers Amzi and James.

But Abner Meek was in Winston County by 1838 when the court appointed him "overseer" of part of the DeKalb Road. And he did own land in the town of Louisville. Although Abner was listed in the Winston County census of 1850, he moved afterwards to Attala County, Mississippi.

Abner had married Eliza Smith circa 1823 in South Carolina. But the both died in Attala County. Their son John Meek died on duty in Atlanta during the Civil War.

Abner's daughter Frances Ann Meek married Amzi Godden Garrigues (see APPENDIX 5). Amzi Garrigues had worked in an apothecary shop circa 1833 to 1836 in New Jersey, when he decided to accompany his Uncle Amzi Godden who along with his wife intended to teach at the Female Academy in Louisville, Winston County, Mississippi. While in Louisville, Amzi worked in a drug store owned by James Meek before deciding to become a doctor.

Frances and Amzi were among the founders of Louisville's First Presbyterian Church built in 1845. Amzi was a trustee, while Frances Ann was the church's first organist. A James Meek donated the land, served as trustee and brought his slaves to help construct the church. After her uncle or brother James died, Frances inherited land seven miles southeast of Louisville.

The Dr. James Meek(s) Family

Dr. James Meek(s)

 m. Mary Wyche; November 15, 1815

 Children

  George Wyche (see below)

  John 1 - d. young

  Dr. William - r. Bay St. Louis, Mississippi

  James - r. Arkansas

  Robert - r. Kosciusko, Attala County, Mississippi

  John 2 - d. Gettysburg, Pennsylvania; 1863

  Ellen - m. McCormick

   r. Meredian, Mississippi

  Sarah - m. William/John McAtee

   r. Goodman, Mississippi

  Lydia - m. John Harmon

   r. Attala County, Mississippi

  Caroline - m. William White

   r. Camden, Mississippi

  Lucinda G.

  Susan - m. Rev. W.A. Ross

  Emma - d. age 16

George Wyche Meeks

 m. Sarah Ann Simmons (b. South Carolina; August 16, 1846 d. December 23, 1907)

 r. Pickens County, Alabama; 1841 and 1843

 bur. Goodman Cemetery, Holmes County, Mississippi

 Children

  William Edward (see below)

James Leonidus - r. Goodman, Mississippi

David Adolphus - m. Sallie Lou McCloud

    r. West Point, Clay County, Mississippi

L. Alonzo - m. Daisy Mabry; Attala County, Mississippi; January 31, 1900

Emma Lela - m. I.U. Donald

    r. Goodman, Mississippi

    d. June 28, 1909

George - m. Ida Williamson

    r. Covina, California

William Edward Meeks

    b. January 21, 1868

    m. Ella Elizabeth Hutchinson; Attala County, Mississippi; February 14, 1894

    r. Goodman, Holmes County, Mississippi

    d. October 11, 1952

    bur. Goodman Cemetery, Holmes County, Mississippi

    Children

        Nola - d. young

        Arthur Maurice - b. February 14, 1900

            m. Christine Buchanen, dau of James Walter and Estra Bays Buchanen, of Eupora, Webster County, Mississippi

            d. October 17, 1983

            bur. Eupora Cemetery, Webster County, Mississippi

            Children

                Walter Buchanen

        Corinne - b. 1902

d. 1905

Clifton - b. 1907

   d. 1925

   bur. Goodman Cemetery, Holmes County

Eleanor Lucille - m. Louis L. Long; Holmes County, Mississippi; December 26, 1918

   Children

      Dr. Eleanor Long

Edwena - m. William Lee Mallory of Earle, Arkansas

   Children

      Sara Ann

Gwendolyn - m. Harold P. Hammett of Lexington, Mississippi

   Children

Harold P.	Sandra
Gwenda Kellum	Fran
Laura Atkinson	Sara Lynn

Three Meeks brothers were among the one hundred sixteen immigrants who arrived in Georgia from England with General James Edward Oglethorpe. Oglethorpe intended to establish a buffer between the English to the North and the Spanish to the South and to increase trade in the region. The group arrived from England aboard the ship *Ann* and landed at Yamacraw Bluff, where in 1733 the group established the city of Savannah and the thirteenth colony which Oglethorpe named after King George.

One of those three Meeks brothers with Oglethorpe was the father of Dr. James Meeks. Not content to remain in one place, James moved first to Alabama and then to Attala County,

Mississippi, when the Choctaw land was opened to settlement in 1833.

Apparently, Dr. Meeks sons did not all move when he did. In 1841, a George W. Meek had an account in Peterson's Store in Pickensville, Pickens County, Alabama. Then on January 2, 1843, a George W. and a J.E. Meeks formed a partnership as "drapers and tailers" in Pickens County, Alabama. On April 3, 1841, George W. Meeks announced in the *Pickensville Register* that he was opening a tailor shop "in the house formerly occupied by Dr. McNee" of Pickensville.

But eventually George did move to Mississippi and during the Civil War, George was fighting with the 15th Mississippi Infantry. The 15th infantry was organized in Choctaw County, Mississippi in May 1861. They fought at Fishing Creek, Shiloh, Baton Rouge, Corinth, Vicksburg, Atlanta and Bentonville. And the toll was terrible. At just Fishing Creek, 44 members of the 15th Infantry's 854 men and officers were killed, 153 were wounded, and 29 were declared missing.

Later, George's son William Edward Meeks and William's wife ran a hotel in Goodman, Holmes County, Mississippi. Actually it was a large two-story home built by the McDermott family. A history of Goodman recounted that when a large man died in an upstairs bedroom of that hotel, they were forced to wrap him in sheets and lower him out a window rather than taking the body down the narrow staircase.

Actually William Meeks was involved in a number of enterprises. In addition to being a merchant, he also served as superintendent of the Methodist Sunday School for thirty-five years and mayor of Goodman, Mississippi for twenty-eight years.

The Samuel Mills Meek Family

Samuel Mills Meek I

 b. Laurens District, South Carolina; August 20, 1786

 m. Ann Arabella McDowell (b.c. 1799; South Carolina d.c. 1853; Tuscaloosa, Alabama)

 d. Tuscaloosa, Alabama; May 27, 1846

 bur. Greenwood Cemetery, Tuscaloosa, Alabama

 Children

  Alexander Beaufort - b. prob. South Carolina; July 17, 1814

   m1 Emma Slater Donaldson

   m2 Eliza Jane Cannon

   d. Columbus, Mississippi; November 1, 1865

   Children

    Caroline - b. Tuscaloosa, Alabama; c. 1830

    Samuel M. - b. Tuscaloosa, Alabama; c. 1831

    Henry F. - b. Tuscaloosa, Alabama; c. 1833

    Benjamin - b. Tuscaloosa, Alabama; c.1836

  Mary Alice - b.c. 1817

   d.c. 1821

   bur. Greenwood Cemetery, Tuscaloosa, Alabama

  ?Samuel

Samuel Meek of this genealogy was born in South Carolina; the son of an unnamed Revolutionary War soldier who supposedly had lost his leg at Cowpens. Samuel arrived in

Tuscaloosa from South Carolina circa 1819. He became a man of distinction - a doctor, who also ran a drug store in Tuscaloosa. He served as president of Alabama's State Medical board for twenty years. In addition, Samuel helped found the first Methodist Church in Tuscaloosa. And he married into a family of good repute, according to *Biographical and Historical Memoirs of Mississippi*. Samuel's wife Ann was the second cousin to Gov. McDowell of Virginia.

His son Alexander Meek was one of the University of Alabama's earliest students. He became a lawyer and judge and even the editor of the *Mobile Register*. Several sources claimed that Alexander served as Secretary of the Treasury in the Polk administration. However, the Secretary of the Treasury at that time was Robert J. Walker of Mississippi, who was appointed in 1845. He died and was buried in Columbus, Mississippi.

A Samuel Meek, possibly the son of Samuel I or probably the son of Alexander, also graduated from the University of Alabama and went on to be politically active. Right after college Samuel II went to teach for two years in Oktibbeha County, Mississippi followed by one year at Odd Fellow's Collegiate High School in Columbus. He was admitted to the bar in 1854 and became an active Democrat in Columbus. Eventually he became district attorney (1858 and 1862) and ran for Congress.

During the Civil War, Samuel Meek II enlisted as a private but advanced to the rank of lieutenant-colonel for the Confederate Army in the West. He fought in campaigns from Bowling Green to Vicksburg.

After the war, his success as a criminal lawyer lead to an unsuccessful attempt to become a congressman in Mississippi's

First District in 1880. However, he continued to be a highly regarded lawyer.

Supposedly, Nathan Bedford Forest, a confederate general and the father of the Ku Klux Klan, left his field glasses at his death to this Samuel Meek. The glasses were said to orginally have belonged to Louis Napoleon.

Pitchlynn Family

Isaac Pitchlynn

    b. England

    d. Choctaw Nation, Mississippi

    Children

        John (see below)

John Pitchlynn (Major)

    b. South Carolina; c. 1765

    m1 Rhoda Folsom (d. 1805; Choctaw Nation, Mississippi), dau of Ebenezer Folsom and an Indian woman; early 1780's

    m2 Sophia Folsom (d. Choctaw Nation West; 1870), sister of Chief David Folsom, dau of Nathaniel Folsom, cousin of Rhoda Folsom Pitchlynn

    d. by May 1835

    bur. Waverly, Mississippi

    Children by Rhoda

        James - b. Plymouth, Choctaw Nation, Mississippi

            m. Chickasaw woman

            d. by 1835

            Children

                Alexander - b. Chickasaw Nation, Mississippi

        John Jr. - b. Plymouth, Choctaw Nation, Mississippi; July 12, 1792

            d. by 1835

        Joseph C. - b. Plymouth, Choctaw Nation, Mississippi

            d. by 1835

Children by Sophia

    Peter (see below)

    Silas - b. Choctaw Nation, Mississippi

    Mary - b. Choctaw Nation, Mississippi

        m. Samuel Garland/Gardner

        d. Choctaw Nation West

    Rhoda - b. Choctaw Nation, Mississippi

        m. Calvin Howell

        d. Choctaw Nation West

    Thomas - b. Choctaw Nation, Mississippi

        d. Choctaw Nation West

    Eliza - b. Choctaw Nation, Mississippi

        m. William R. Harris; Lowndes County, Mississippi; November 27, 1835

        d. Choctaw Nation West

        Children

Henry	Frances	Evelina
Joseph	Caroline	Kesiah
Edward		

    Elizabeth - b. Choctaw Nation, Mississippi

        m. Lorenzo G. Harris; Lowndes County, Mississippi; November 4, 1836

        d. Choctaw Nation West

        Children

Priscilla	Virginia	Fredona
John	Sarah	Frederetta

    Keziah - b. Choctaw Nation, Mississippi

        d. Choctaw Nation West

Peter Pitchlynn (Chief)

    b. Hush-ook-wa on the Noxubee River, Mississippi; January 30, 1804/06

    m1 Rhoda Folsom (d. March, 1844; Wheelock Mission, Oklahoma), dau of Nathaniel Folsom, half-aunt of Peter Pitchlynn

    m2 Carolyn Eckloff Lombardi, wid; Washington D.C.; October 21, 1869

    r. Apukshunnubbee District, Eagle County, Oklahoma; 1855

    d. Washington, D.C.; January 17, 1881

    bur. Congressional Cemetery, Washington, D.C.; February 21, 1881

    Children by Rhoda

        Lavina - b. Choctaw Nation, Mississippi; 1825

            m. Richard Harkins, 1846

        Malvina - b. Choctaw Nation, Mississippi; April 7, 1828

            m. Loring S.W. Folsom, first cousin of Malvina; c. 1851

        Lycurgis - b. Choctaw Territory, Mississippi; July, 1830

            m. Mary J. _____ of New Orleans, Louisiana; 1858

            r. Apukshunnubbee District, Eagle County, Oklahoma; 1855

        infant - b. & d. 1832

        Leonidas - b. Choctaw Nation West; c. 1835

            m. Sophia Harris, first cousin of Leonidas; April 1856

            r. Red River County, Texas; 1850

            d. early 1860's

        Peter Jr. - b. Choctaw Nation West

m. _____ of Arkansas; 1859

d. early 1860's

Rhoda - b. Choctaw Nation West

m1 John Arnold (marriage annulled); c. 1862

m2 _____ Kennedy; 1873

Israel - b. Choctaw Nation West; c. 1843

d.c. 1846

Children by Carolyn

Sampson - b. Washington, D.C.; November, 1857

d. young

Tommy - Washington, D.C.; 1859

Edward Everette - Washington, D.C.; 1860

Sophia - b. Choctaw Nation West; 1864

Lee - Washington, D.C.; 1866

r. Washington, D.C.

One suggested beginning for the Pitchlynn family name was that the first Pitchlynn had worked with pitch in King's Lynn, England. John Pitchlynn's name took on a number of spellings after he went to Mississippi. On a 1784 document, he was John Peachland. In a 1792 document, the Spanish referred to him as Jean Pchiline. By the 1800's he was signing his name as Pitchlynn, while others still spelled it Peachland or Pitchlyn. One of his daughter's marriage license had the name as Pitchlym.

How John Pitchlynn came to be living in Mississippi also has had several explanations. Baird claimed that John was born between 1750 and 1756 aboard a ship off the island of St. Thomas and that his father Isaac was a Tory merchant. If the birthdates given were correct, John would have been between

36 and 42 years old when only the second of his eleven children was born.

Several sources have reported that Isaac Pitchlynn was a British trader who died in the Choctaw Nation, leaving his son John in the care of the Indians. At the time, the Choctaw lands were divided into three districts in central Mississippi. Then in 1763, after the French and Indian War, France was forced to abandon the American West , opening the way for British traders and a few intrepid settlers. Perhaps Isaac was among them.

But John's friend George Gaines, the United States Factor at Fort St. Stephens, who first met John Pitchlynn in 1804 reported that Pitchlynn was born circa 1765 in South Carolina, the son of a British officer in the commissary department. According to Gaines, during the Revolutionary War, the father and son were traveling from Natchez to Georgia when they were "necessarily detained" in the Choctaw Nation. And like other sources, Gaines reported that the father died while they were there, leaving the boy in the care of the Choctaws.

In the unpublished speech given at the dedication of a government marker at John Pitchlynn's grave, C.L. Wood reported that Pitchlynn's father died of fever in "Choctaw Country" when the boy was only nine years old. If it was during the Revolutionary War as Gaines claimed, John would have had to have been at least ten years old.

Confusing the matter even more, Baird listed John's father Isaac as a resident of John's house when it was damaged by fire in 1804. That was the year that Gaines met John, so if Isaac were still alive at that time, Gaines should have known it.

It was most likely that John was left as an adolescent in the care of the Choctaws, after his father's death in the territory and that John elected to remain among the Indians. The Choctaws lived, in towns in log cabins with dirt floors and smoke holes in their roofs. They were particulary good farmers. Planting and harvesting was done communally and they raised beans, potatoes, pumpkins and melons.

Choctaws were well-liked throughout the South and a sort of "Pidgin" Choctaw became the trade language used by many tribes and traders. They moved freely with other people and mixed-blood Choctaws frequently held degrees of power.

After the American Revolution, ownership of the Gulf Coast was in dispute between Spain and the United States. So John acted as interpreter in the efforts of the United States to gain trading dominance over the Choctaws. So by 1786 John was the Choctaw Nation's official interrpreter. He had become very close to both the Choctaw and Chickasaw Indians and had become nearly flawless in both their languages. He remained the government's official interrpreter until the Indians removal west.

Yet in 1792, the Spanish considered Pitchlynn a threat to Spanish interest. In the early 1790's, the Spanish began to realize they were losing control over the Mississippi/Tombigbee River regions. De la Villebeuvre called for the arrest of Pitchlynn in an attempt to solidify Spanish control. But de la Villebeuvre had some problems with that and on September 12, 1792, he wrote that "Jean Pchiline" lived

"Near the Chickasaw road away from other villages
but with six Indian huts in his vicinity to help him."

With that much help, John Pitchlynn could not be arrested.

Although Gaines described John as a "natural gentleman" who was "strikingly handsome denoting mildness and firmness of purpose."

The Spanish considered him a threat because John encouraged the adoption of Indian treaties with the Americans. And, according to Baird, Pitchlynn "concurred in the land cession provisions". He received no compensation for his work with the United States government from 1786 on, even though territorial Governor William Claiborne interceded on his behalf in 1802 after Pitchlynn served as a "trouble shooter" for the territory.

Although the Treaty of 1805 did provide $2500 for him, there was a question as to whether he ever received the money. And yet, Pitchlynn continued to work on the behalf of the government.

Pitchlynn married twice. Both wives were members of the Folsom family, which had originated in the area by three possible brothers - Nathaniel, Ebenezer and Israel. Israel Folsom died in 1784, leaving three children Edmund, Abigail and Sarah.

John's first wife Rhoda was the daughter of Ebenezer Folsom. Sophia, John's second wife, was sister of Choctaw Chief David Folsom and one of twenty-five children of Nathaniel Folsom.

The Pitchlynns and the Folsoms were just two of a number of half blood families and traders in Choctaw Nation of the Mississippi Territory by the War of 1812. The Leflore family was another highly regarded mixed blood family living in the Choctaw Nation at the time. Louis and Michael Leflore were the early settlers of that family.

John's first known home was on the Noxubee River near present day Macon in Noxubee County, Mississippi. In 1804, a friend of Pitchlynn's named James Tyrrel turned in John Kincaid into the Indian Agent for giving taffy to a Choctaw hunter. In retaliation, Pitchlynn's storehouse was blown up, destroying nearly two thousand deerskins belonging to Tyrrel. Although Pitchlynn's nearby home was heavily damaged, none of the eleven people staying in the home were injured. Pitchlynn arrested those responsible parties and turned them in at Choctaw Agency.

Circa 1806, John Pitchlynn moved his residence to Plymouth Bluff, which Gaines described as being on the Tombigbee River just south of "Okatibbee" (Tibbee) Creek.

> "This was in part the dividing line between the
> Choctaws and Chickasaws and took its name from a
> great battle fought upon it at the Ford near the mouth
> and hence was called fighting water."

The community became the first settlement of any significance in the area and soon became known locally as Pitchlynn's or Peachland.

While there, Pitchlynn became more involved in trading with the Indians and moving goods for other traders and trappers. He worked with George Gaines, the Virginian who headed the trading post (called a factory) at Ft. St. Stephens on the lower Tombigbee. Pitchlynn and Gaines would ship goods overland from the Tennessee River to the Tombigbee River where they would be loaded on boats and shipped to St. Stephens.

By 1813, the route from the Natchez Trace to the docks at Pitchlynn's had been made passable for wagons and named Gaines' Trace. A southern route from Pitchlynn's to Ft. St. Stephens was opened between 1814 and 1817 and named St. Stephen's Trace. But the opening of these roads did more than ease the overland shipment of goods and reduce the Pitchlynn family's isolation. As more whites passed through, it also separated them somewhat from Choctaw society.

Pitchlynn owned huge herds of cattle he grazed on prairie lands. He also grew cotton and corn and owned the slaves and equipment of a typical early southern plantation. In fact, C.L. Wood described Pitchlynn's Plymouth Bluff residence as a

"Dwelling house and council house joined by a large two story addition which gave, in all, eleven rooms. The house was built of logs and unpainted with long galleries on three sides, was situated in a shady grove surrounded on all sides by the open treeless prairie."

In the Spring of 1811, Shawnee orator and chief Tecumseh met with nearly every tribe in the Mississippi Territory in an effort to unite them against the white intruders. His hatred for the whites was evident when he met with the Choctaws and Chickasaws in an attempt to form an alliance with their tribes. Although Tecumseh's argument's had appeal, the arguement of Chief Pushmataha on behalf of the U.S. government prevailed. And when Tecumseh began quoting from the Bible, Pitchlynn returned with his own Biblical quotes until Tecumseh left without gaining the support he had hoped to obtain. Later Choctaw Chief Pushmataha reported

"You know Tecumseh. He is a bad man. He came through our Nation, but we did not turn our heads."

For the son of a British officer or a Tory, John Pitchlynn was surprisingly supportive of the United States government. During the War of 1812, Pitchlynn enlisted six hundred Choctaw warriors to fight on the side of the Americans. Meanwhile he persuaded the territorial governor to arm and clothe them and kept the Americans advised of Creek movements. The Creeks were siding with the British. The Choctaws, with Pitchlynn as interpreter, proceeded to the Creek Nation early in 1814. Their destination was a village forty miles north of the mouth of Black Warrior River. Depending upon the source, they either found it already destroyed by Davy Crockett's men or they found the village empty and burned it themselves.

During the war a number of full or part Indians received commissions. For instance, Pushmataha and Hummingbird became Lieutenant Colonels, Louis Leflore became a Major and John Pitchlynn Jr. was a First Lieutenant. But even though John Sr. was called Major for the rest of his life, he may not have actually obtained the rank during the war.

In 1818, Pitchlynn was approached to help Rev. Cyrus Kingsbury locate a mission in the region. The site selected became Mayhew Mission in northwest Lowndes County. Then in March, 1820, John Pitchlynn Jr. and his brother Joseph talked the southern District of the Choctaw Nation into helping support the mission school at Mayhew.

Sometime by the mid-1820's, John Pitchlynn, Sr. had moved his family to a house on the Robinson Road, west of the Tombigbee River and quite near the inn opened by Chief David Folsom. It was probably the same area where on February 7, 1835, the Columbus, Mississippi *Southern Argus Newspaper* reported there were lots for sale. The paper described the location as

> "West Port, heretofore known as Pitchlyn's Bluff - on west side of River Bigbee, one and a half miles west of Columbus."

Shortly after that move, John joined Robert Jemison of Tuscaloosa in operating a stage line.

He remained there until 1834 when old age forced him to live with his grandson Alexander in the old Chickasaw territory, west of Columbus. He lived near Waverly, two miles north of Plymouth near the eventual Lowndes-Clay County border. Waverly was never actually incorporated as a town. But its placement just north of Tibbe Creek and on the west bank of the Tombigbee River made it an important settlement, which eventually had a post office, store and railroad stop. Waverly was near the prairie, but not a part of it. Instead, it was in the uplands along the Tombigbee bank. At Waverly, John Pitchlynn engaged in farming and he owned a number of slaves.

The move to Waverly had been precipitated by the removal of the Indians, including a number of his children, to the west. The decision whether John should sell his assets and leave was a difficult one. He was very family-oriented and showered his children with money and property. When his sons died, John took their families into his home. When the Treaty of Dancing Rabbit (see APPENDIX 8) split his family, John was heartbroken. After they left, he was lonely and finally wrote to his son Peter begging him to return to Mississippi.

John Pitchlynn, Sr. died soon after the letter was written and was buried in a field at Waverly, south of where Waverly mansion would eventually be built by George Hampton Young . Young had purchased the land from Alexander Pitchlynn on March 1, 1836.

John Pitchlynn's will was executed in Columbus, Lowndes County, Mississippi, and he named sons Peter and Thomas and son-in-law Samuel Garland as executors. His estate was valued at $35,000, most of which was composed of his sixty-six slaves.

After John's death, Alexander sold the land and moved west like other members of his family. John's widow Sophia also moved west but returned occasionally to take care of his grave. Upon her last visit she may have disinterred his remains and taken them with her.

The idea of moving entire tribes of Indians into the wilderness of the west probably began with Andrew Jackson's arrival in the territory during the War of 1812. He later arrived as an emmissary of the U.S. government and went on to push for the relocation of the Choctaws to lands in the west that were unoccupied by whites.

Several times during 1818 and 1819, James Pitchlynn personally wrote to Andrew Jackson offering his services in negotiating a land cession and move west. However, when the Federal government sent General Jackson to direct the completion of the Military Road, it became quickly evident that Pushmataha and Mushulatubbe were against leaving and talks collapsed.

But when Jackson returned in 1820 and tribal leaders again fought the idea, Jackson tried some unconventional tactics. After a number of threats and bribe's, including $500 to Jackson's interpreter John Pitchlynn and $75 to James Pitchlynn, the Treaty of Doak's Stand was signed on October 18, 1820. The Treaty of Dancing Rabbit and notorious "Trail of Tears" soon followed. It was sold to the Indians as an attempt to maintain tribal integrity, but in reality it was a way to get as much Indian land as they could for as cheap as possible.

According to land records, a number of Pitchlynns received sizeable land patents, including

Jack	24	19N	17E	127 acres
	25	19N	17E	595.76 acres
John	28	19N	17E	644.28 acres
	30	19N	17E	506.03 acres
	28	19N	17E	644.28 acres
John Sr.	34	19N	17E	643.12 acres
Peter	32	18N	16E	638.84 acres
	20	19N	17E	638.44 acres
Silas	27	19N	17E	637.36 acres
Thomas	21	19n	17E	641.48 acres

All three of John's sons by his first wife Rhoda - not just James - became politically active and all died before their father. James and John Jr. enlisted with the American Forces during the War of 1812. John Pitchlynn, Jr. served as a first lieutenant and quartermaster in the Choctaw Battalion in 1814 and 1815.

However, John Jr. had some major problems as described by Gideon Lincecum. Lincecum had been appointed by the legislature to lay out the town of Columbus, Mississippi, to set up school there and to appoint city officials. After those duties were completed, Lincecum wrote that he

"Immediately went over the river and entered into partnership with John Pitchlynn, Jr., a half-breed Choctaw ... (Pitchlynn) was a highly educated man and a very clever fellow, but a most incorrigible drunkard. "

That, however, made no difference in their business dealings. Lincecum made sure that John Pitchlynn, Jr. was to have nothing to do with the management of the business. And a thriving business it was.

> "Pitchlynn had a pretty good storehouse at the ferry landing opposite Columbus, and four or five thousand dollars' worth of goods. (Lincecum) had about the same amount"

Pitchlynn's residence was two miles from the store, a situation Gideon Lincecum found favorable to their business;

> "for (Pitchlynn) was, when drunk, so abusive, and so often drunk, that he was not popular with the Indians."

Pitchlynn's problem with alcohol would be his undoing when he killed his half-brother Silas in a drunken brawl and escaped the Choctaw Territory for Cotton Gin Port in Chickasaw Territory. John Pitchlynn, Jr. was killed while there, and according to some sources, with the encouragement of his step-mother, Sila's mother.

While traders and missionaries visiting the Pitchlynn parents' home discovered a piece of "white civilization" in the middle of Indian territory, Peter Pitchlynn was christened Hatchoc-tuck-nee (Snapping Turtle) by the Indians. And although he was the son of a well-to-do white trader, Peter was raised as a Choctaw. So while his father John Sr. sympathized with the whites, Peter's chief allegiance was to the Choctaws, even though he was only one-quarter Indian.

Peter became great friends with the same Gideon Lincecum who thought so little of Peter's brother John. In fact, Peter Pitchlynn credited Lincecum with awakening his passion for learning. He wrote to Lincecum

> "Twas then you came and took me by the hand and led me by your council to the source of knowledge."

Then at age fourteen, Peter's parents entered him in a nearby school. Later he attended several schools in Tennessee, but never for very long.

In the 1820's, Peter was elected as an officer of the Choctaws and served as a sort of policeman, judge and jury. He helped form a local police force and curbed the trade in whiskey. It would be just the first of many important positions Peter would hold.

In July 1827, Peter went to Transylvania University in Kentucky. But by the next February, Peter was at Choctaw Academy in Kentucky, where he lasted only three months. His protest over the filth and disrepair at that school brought a response from the Academy director, Col. Richard Johnson who in 1836 would become Vice President of the United States. The resulting negative publicity probably sped up the eventual closure of the Academy.

Peter Pitchlynn married his mother's half-sister. Unlike many Choctaws of the time, his marriage was monogamous. They settled two miles south of today's Artesia, Mississippi and began raising hogs, cattle and crops.

During negotiations concerning the possible move west, Peter Pitchlynn at times seved as a Choctaw representative. And unlike his father, even when the tribe was offerred one million dollars, Peter Pitchlynn steadfastly opposed it.

There was so much opposition among the Indians, the government organized an excursion to the proposed new Indian lands in an effort to encourage the wary Choctaw and Chickasaws, and the belligerent Creeks to make the move. And Peter Pitchlynn was chosen to go along on the expedition.

Thirteen Chickasaws, six Choctaws, four Creeks, several white men serving as interpreters, and a few black slaves made up the company. Rev. Isaac McCoy, a Baptist missionary for the Potawatomi, led the expedition, but Army Capt. George Kennedy was in actual command. In his journal of the trip, Pitchlynn wrote of their September 26, 1828 departure -

> "When we made our departure from our country we knew not what would be the result - whether we should again return to it, or be left to moulder in a foreign land, unburied and unlamented ... There was before us an extensive, and unknown region, which we were to enter, our road laid through nations that were rude and that loved war, particularly that of the Washashees, with whom we have been for the last forty years upon the bitterest terms of enmity."

The expedition proceeded to Memphis where the Choctaws connected with the Chickasaw delegation and took a steamboat to St. Louis. There the delegation met with General Clark whom the Choctaws had met before and a group of Sioux whom Pitchlynn described as a "poor and miserable race."

Their travels took them to a meeting with "the Great Prophet of the Shawanoes, brother of Tecumseh" . The Prophet was a Shawnee medicine man named Tenskwatwa ("Open Door") who

> "Spoke some length of time on the subject of the ignorance of the Indians in general ... He then spoke of the great wisdom of the President of the United States ... Knowing these things to be true, he said that he had given up his own opinion on things respecting the interest of his nation and that he looked to the

Great Father, the President ... and that he obeyed him
in all things like an obedient child, and recommended
that we should do the same".

The expedition stayed with the Shawnees for five days.

Then in late November the group toured the land between
Kansas and the Osage Indians. But Pitchlynn was not impressed
with the prospect of settling on that land. On November 27th he
wrote that

"All I can say of that portion of the world is that it is
good for nothing and never will be, for it is all prairie
and nothing but rock and gravel. A tree in that country
is a perfect curiousity. The buffalo is still three
hundred miles west of that country, and as to deer we
never saw none at all, nor any kind of game whatever
... Notwithstanding that these things are all true, the
white people with us have been presumptuous
enough to tell us that it is a fine country."

And after meeting the Indians already there, Pitchlynn wrote
that their "manners and action (were) wild in the extreme."

Upon his return to Mississippi, Pitchlynn was elected chief
of the Northeast District and aligned himself against the move.
But late in 1831, it became apparent that four thousand
Choctaws would indeed have to make the five hundred mile
journey carrying everything they owned with them.

Peter purchased more slaves before traveling west to
Indian Territory. And then in 1832, he sold his two section
allotment of land, just south of today's Artesia in Lowndes
County, along with fifty head of cattle, other livestock and a full
corn crib to Booth Malone for $6000 and the cancellation of a
$12,000 note. But since Peter did not receive the actual patent

until 1839, he held out turning it over to Malone until Malone paid another $3000.

Pitchlynn began the move west leading a group of five hundred out of Mississippi. But possibly at Memphis, his family left the larger group. They chose to travel alone, fearing diseases like cholera that had decimated other groups of Indians from the Five Civilized Tribes who were being removed from their Southern homelands.

They were supposed to go through Little Rock, but due to mis-communication, the ended up in the Arkansas Post with nearly two thousand other Choctaws who suffered through a blizzard with little food, clothing or shelter.

They arrived at Skullyville on November 1, 1832, and settled on six hundred acres of land in nearby New Hope in the Arkansas River area. The Arkansas River was about a quarter of a mile wide in the area they would settle, with sandy banks and bottom. However, on the 1828 trip, Pitchlynn had not been impressed with that part of Arkansas and had written

"Soon after crossing (the Arkansas River) we entered the prairie where the wind blew intolerably high - the country was rolling, and at a distance to our left we saw high hills covered with timber in places. The soil in some places was middlin good. This country is too scarce of timber to be inviting ... The Choctaw (assigned) lands are generally poor and unfit for cultivation, no springs."

Soon after settling there, the Arkansas River flooded his crop and killed most of Peter's livestock. Then, during August and September 1833, six hundred people in the area died of "fever."

Peter began looking for a better place to locate. He found a good agricultural area and many of those who had gone west with David Folsom and the Mayhew missionaries in the Mountain Fork River area. So in 1834, he settled his family near today's Eagletown, Oklahoma.

But his diary made clear his feelings about the others out on the frontier with him. He did not see the whites as competition for the land. Instead, he saw them as fellow victims of the "hostile" Indian tribes. However, later in Pitchlynn's life, white encroachment worsened and eventually Indian land was decreased in size to make way for white settlers.

Circa 1838, Peter moved further south, to the Wheelock Mission area near today's Tom, Oklahoma, where with the help of his son Leonidas, Peter tried to build a prospersous plantation. But the cotton crop of 1856 bottomed out and only brought the family $2500.

In addition, he invested his money unwisely. In 1841 the family had only four slaves. But an 1866 census indicated 135 freedmen who had belonged to Peter Pitchlynn. Peter found that feeding and clothing all those people ate into his profits. The only time Peter saw a profit with slavery was when he was able to hire them out to others.

Although he was a financial catastrophe, Peter Pichlynn was more successful politically. In 1838, Peter wrote the rough draft of the Choctaw Nation constitution which was ultimately adopted. By 1845, he had already made three trips to Washington, D.C., although some of his dealings during those years were on the shady side.

Because of Peter's political aspirations he spent long periods of time away from home which took a terrible toll on his family. His wife was fragile and, after Israel's birth in 1843, Rhoda never fully recovered. She died in March 1844.

Even though his children were motherless, Peter did not remain at home. And, just a year after Rhoda's death, he farmed his children out to various relatives and missionaries. His uncle Israel Folsom wrote to him that

> "I am truely astonished of the course you have taken in leaving your little children to be absent from them several months."

Actually, Peter was gone two years that time searching for new opportunities and becoming more well-known.

In fact, during Charles Dickens' visit to America, he met Peter Pitchlynn on board a steamboat and later wrote about Peter in his *American Notes*. Obviously, Peter had neglected to tell Dickens that he was only one-quarter Indian, for Dickens was surprised to find that Peter

> "... spoke English perfectly well, though he had not begun to learn the language, he told me, until he was a young man grown. He had read many books; and Scott's poetry appeared to have left a strong impression on his mind: especially the opening of *The Lady of the Lake* ...

> "He told me that he had been away from his home, west of the Mississippi, seventeen months: and was now returning. He had been chiefly at Washington on some negotiations pending between his Tribe and the government: which were not settled yet [he said in a melancholy way], and he feared never would be: for what could a few poor Indians do against such well-skilled men of business as the

whites? He had no love for Washington; tired of towns and cities very soon; and longed for the Forest and the Prairie.

"I asked him what he thought of Congress? He answered, with a smile, that it wanted dignity, in an Indian's eyes.

"He would very much like, he said to see England before he died; and spoke with much interest about the great things to be seen there. When I told him of that chamber in the British Museum wherein are preserved household memorials of a race that ceased to be, thousands of years ago, he was very attentive, and it was not hard to see that he had a reference in his mind to the gradual fading away of his own people."

In 1853, Peter Pitchlynn, Dickson Lewis, Israel Folsom and Samuel Garland were elected as delegates to Washington. And despite Charles Dicken's assertion that Peter despised Washington, D.C., he spent twenty-five years there serving as a representative of the Choctaw Nation.

When the Civil War broke out, as principal chief of the Choctaws, Pitchlynn even met with President Lincoln to discuss the tribes' status. It was decided that the tribe would remain neutral. But despite the agreement, a majority of the Choctaws joined the Confederacy and Pitchlynn owned more than one hundred slaves himself.

In Washington, Peter met Carolyn Eckloff Lombardi, a widow, who he took as his "common law" wife. It wasn't until 1869, after the birth of five children and a serious illness, that Peter finally married Carolyn.

While in Washington, the Choctaws paid few of Peter's expenses and his plantation quit making money. So the family was in constant financial trouble. When Peter died in 1881, the family was too destitute to bury him. The rites were presided over by Albert Pike at Washington's Masonic Temple, but the body had to be stored until after Peter Folsom was able to petition the government to allow Pitchlynn's burial in the Congressional Cemetery. Burial took place there on February 21, 1881.

Meanwhile his children still back in the Choctaw Nation paid dearly for his inattention. One teacher wrote that son Lycurgis was

"of good abilities and perhaps the best scholar of them all but utterly destitute of stability or principle."

In addition, Lycurgis was an alcoholic, as was his younger brother Leonidas. Eventually both brothers were convicted of assault and battery after Lycurgis shot off a man's finger.

After managing his father's farm, Leonidas went on to manage his own farm in 1859 and Peter Jr. took over managing his father's farm. But Peter Pitchlynn, Jr. also had problems with his temper and in 1860 he killed his Uncle Lorenzo Harris in a disagreement over a blacksmith.

Because of their father's influence none of Peter Pitchlynn's sons were seriously punished for their crimes. But all died young. Peter Jr. and Leonidas were killed during the Civil War. Lycurgis died of fever in 1866.

Even relationships were problems for Peter Sr.'s children. Malvina and Leonideas Pitchlynn both married their first cousins. Leonidas and Rhoda both had to elope. Peter Sr. was so upset over his daughter Rhoda's marriage to John Arnold that he had tribal courts annul the marriage.

But his daughter Malvina probably had the harshes life of all of Peter's children. Many of Malvina's children died young. Then she witnessed her husband's murder and, later watched one of her daughters slowly go insane.

Richey Family

Robert Richey
> b. South Carolina
>
> m. Rebecca Belton
>
> d. Pickens County, Alabama; 1858
>
> Children
>> William (see below)
>>
>> David - b. South Carolina; c. 1805
>>> m. _____ Didama?
>>>
>>> r. Pickens County, Alabama
>>>
>>> Children

John	Jane	Clark
Caroline	Susan	Nancy
Robert	Richard	Leona

William Richey
> b. Laurens, South Carolina; February 1, 1796
>
> m. Margaret Ann Adair (b. Laurens, South Carolina; c. 1804; d.c. 1850), dau of Thomas Jefferson and Rebecca Brown Adair; Pickens County, Alabama; February 10, 1820
>
> d. Parowan, Iron County, Utah; 1879
>
> Children
>> James - b. Pickens County, Alabama; August 13, 1821
>>> m. Lucinda Mangum; Nauvoo, Hancock County, Illinois; March 23/28, 1846
>>>
>>> m2 & 3

Joseph - b. near Pickensville, Pickens County, Alabama; November 10, 1825

Rebecca Sarah - b. near Pickensville, Pickens County, Alabama; December 7, 1828

Emily Melissa - b. Pickens County, Alabama; March 12, 1830/1

m. Solomon Cowles Case; May 12, 1847

m2 & 3

John Belton - b. Noxubee County, Mississippi; February 17, 1833

Martha Ann (tw) - Noxubee County, Mississippi; December 30, 1837

d. Nauvoo, Hancock County, Illinois; 1845

Eliza Jane (tw) - b. Noxubee County, Mississippi; December 30 1837

m. John Milton Adair

d. Lincoln County, Nevada; May, 1908

William Belton - b. Pickensville, Pickens County, Alabama; May, 1840

m. Johanna Marie Hougaard; Manti Sanpete, Utah; August 26, 1868

Robert - b. Noxubee County, Mississippi; October 5, 1842

d. Nauvoo, Hancock County, Illinois; 1845

Benjamin W.

Like "Ritchie", the name Richey was used as a deminuative form of Richard and probably the originator of this Richey family took his surname for that reason. This particular family may have been Scotch-Irish in origin.

A number of Richeys resided in the Lauren and Abbeville County areas of South Carolina. But one of them, Joe Richey, went to Arkansas and became an outlaw.

Robert Richey of this genealogy also was born in South Carolina. And like Joe Richey, he was drawn west. But that was where the similarities ended.

Robert Richey may have been related to the Robert Richey/Ritchey who was born circa 1754 in Abbeville, South Carolina. According to individual records of the Church of Jesus Christ of the Latter-Day Saints (LDS or Mormon Church), that Robert was the son of James and Margaret Caldwell Richey. Although the two Roberts may have been related, the son of James and Margaret was probably not the Robert of this genealogy as he would have been 104 years old at his death.

The earliest records found for the Robert Richey of this genealogy were land records in which Robert and his son William received several parcels of land in T22 R16W in Pickens County, Alabama between 1825 and 1833. A David Richey also received land in T22 R16W in 1833. According to census records, David was born circa 1805 in South Carolina. So David was the probable son of Robert, brother of William of this genealogy. But unlike William, David Richey was still residing in Pickens County at the time of the 1850 Federal census.

In addition to David, other Richeys lived in Pickens County. A John was there in 1830 and a George and James were there in 1850. On September 8, 1858, a same John Richey was named administrator of Robert Richey's estate in Pickens County. So he was probably Robert's son, brother or nephew.

Although it was William's son James who converted the Adair, Carson and Mangum families to the Church of Jesus

Christ of the Latter-Day Saints, the entire Richey family became members as part of a nationwide movement of religious revivalism. Circa 1820, when he was just fourteen years old, Joseph Smith of Palmyra, New York claimed to have begun having visions. In 1830, he established the Church of Christ in Fayette, New York, with himself as President and "Prophet". The religion's startling growth and "close-knit" society led to suspicion and persecution of them.

Soon the church's name was changed and the church headquarters was moved to Ohio, with another Mormon settlement situated in Missouri. But persecution followed and in Missouri, Mormon leaders were arrested, sentenced to death, but allowed to escape.

The Mormon Church, formally known as the Church of Jesus Christ of the Latter-Day Saints, was a Christian religion founded on the principle that Christianity was corrupt and that it was important to restore the true Christian doctrine. Soon, Mormon missionaries spread out to disseminate the word.

By 1839, they were fleeing Missouri and Ohio because of animosity they felt from non-Mormon residents who feared the economic competition and Mormon bloc voting. They settled along the Mississippi River at Commerce, Illinois which they renamed Nauvoo and were given permission to form a militia to protect themselves. In the early 1840's, the Mississippi Richeys migrated to Nauvoo, Illinois in order to join the majority of church members already there.

Nauvoo had been a wilderness when the Mormons had arrived, but they soon turned from a disease-ridden swamp area into a healthier, more industrious town. By 1844, the Nauvoo settlement had a population reaching 11,000, with another 4,000 Mormons in the surrounding area.

The cleanup of Nauvoo, Hancock County, Illinois was not totally complete when an outbreak of measles killed three of William and Margaret Ann Richey's children in in 1845. Robert was three, Martha Ann was eight and Rebecca Ann was seventeen years old.

Despite the improvement they had brought to the area, resentment by non-members intensified due to the Mormon practice of polygomy and the power of Joseph Smith. After Smith and his brother were imprisoned in Carthage, Illinois; the brothers were forcibly taken from the jail and assassinated by a mob in 1844.

After Smith's death, Brigham Young successfully led the Mormons from Illinois to the new Mormon settlement on the Great Salt Lake in Utah. They left Nauvoo in 1846. Along the way Young ordered the building of temporary settlements so that groups that followed would find crops and cabins for shelter.

Upon arrival in Utah, groups of Mormons began fanning out across the territory. Soon, more than three hundred other settlements were established across the west. And William Richey's children were among those who moved out from Salt Lake City, locating themselves in a number of Mormon settlements.

Although polygamy was openly practiced by only ten to twenty percent of the Mormons, in the 1850's the federal government sent an army to enforce compliance of laws outlawing it. More judicial and legislative efforts persisted until 1890 when church President Wilford Woodruff issued a manifesto which in effect ended polygamy.

Sellers Family

James Sellers I

    m. Mary Gulledge, dau of Mortimer Frederick and Hannah Gulledge

    d. Monticello, Georgia; early 1830's

    Children

        Thomas George (see below)

Thomas George Sellers

    b. Cheraw, Chesterfield County, South Carolina; August 27, 1831

    m1 Mary Elizabeth Crenshaw (b. Alabama; October 29, 1836 d. Starkville, Mississippi; November 28, 1870) circa 1857

    m2 Sarah/Sallie Washington Crenshaw (b. January 30, 1844 d. Texas; 1931); 1870

    d. Starkville, Oktibbeha County, Mississippi; March 11, 1899

    bur. Oddfellows Cemetery; Starkville, Oktibbeha County, Mississippi

    Children by Mary Elizabeth

        William Alson - b. Oktibbeha County, Mississippi; October 24, 1858

            m. Carrie Rogers

            d. aft 1935

            Children

                1 son - d. young

        James Freeman - b. Oktibbeha County, Mississippi; June 1, 1862

Children
> James Freeman, Jr.   Erle Dees
>
> William Roy   Mark Ashley
>
> Tom Fort   Abbot Mannie

Salanna Dessimine "Dessie" - b. Oktibbeha County, Mississippi; December 13, 1868

m. Walter Compere Lattimore; Oktibbeha County, Mississippi; December 30, 1890

d. 1906

Children
> Joe Blunt   John Lee
>
> Sellers   Walter C.
>
> William Freeman

George Eaton

Mary Thomas

Carson Fuller

1 other child

Children by Sarah Washington

Annie Lee - b. Oktibbeha County, Mississippi; August 5, 1872

Sallie Graves "Pet" - b. Oktibbeha County, Mississippi; September 18, 1874

d. aft 1974

Hattie Sue - b. Oktibbeha County, Mississippi; August 5, 1876

d. March 24, 1878

Ada Curry - b. Oktibbeha County, Mississippi; July 27, 1879

m. W.C. Lattimore

Children (0)

Mary Crenshaw - b. Oktibbeha County, Mississippi;
November 19, 1882

Robert Pearson (tw) - b. Oktibbeha County,
Mississippi; August 30, 1884

m. Susie Smith

Children

Suzanne

Robert Jr.

Elva Gulledge (tw) - b. Oktibbeha County, Mississippi;
August 30, 1884

Children (0)

Thomas Geroge Jr. - b. Oktibbeha County,
Mississippi; September 22, 1886

Children (0)

Lucy Skinner - d. young

Sellers were found in Derbyshire and Nottinghamshire, England. According to Barton Griffin, at least one Sellers family migrated from France to England during the late sixteenth century. And some of the spellings above did seem to have a French flavor.

The Sellars/Sellers name could have originated with the French "sellier", meaning "saddler." Or it could have stemmed from the German "seilers" meaning "ropers". Or the Sellers name could have been of Scotch, Irish or English origin, coming from "seller" or "cellar".

The name Sellere appeared in a 1086 Latin document. Osbert de Sallor was in Derbyshire, England circa 1180 and Richard de Solers was there circa 1200. Other early spellings included Cellier, Sellow, de Cellar, Scellars, Cellers, de Sallowe, Sellars and even Zeller.

America had a number of early Sellers settlers. There was a Benjamin Sellers in Edgecombe County, North Carolina. And although no son named James was listed in Benjamin's 1761 will, his children still living at home were not named individually. And James could also have been Benjamin's grandson. At least several of Benjamin's descendants; including William Sellars of Baker, later Mitchell, County; moved to Georgia and on to Alabama.

There also were Samuel and George Sellers, English Quakers who went to Pennsylvania. A William Sellers who settled in North Carolina also had a son Benjamin whose descendants settled Marion County, South Carolina. And another of William's sons removed to Louisiana and Texas.

James and Thomas George Sellers of this genealogy may or may not have been descendants of that William and Benjamin. Or they may have been related to John Robert Sellers, Sr. who was born in 1814 in the Chesterfield area of South Carolina. Like James Sellers of this genealogy, John Robert took his family to Georgia from Chesterfield.

According to James Freeman Sellers, shortly after the birth of Thomas George Sellers in 1831, Thomas' father James I moved his young family from South Carolina to Monticello, Georgia, where James I soon died of typhoid fever. But a newpaper biography written by James' sister-in-law, Caroline Gulledge Hale, reported that James I died a short time before his son's birth.

Whichever was correct, after James' death, his widow Mary returned to her father's home and allowed Thomas to be raised by his grandparents, Mortimer Frederick and Hannah Gulledge (see APPENDIX 6) of Cheraw, Chesterfield County, South Carolina.

The area was named for the Cheraw Indians, along with the and Pee Dee Indians, were members of the Eastern Sioux. The Cheraw Indians were at their most powerful circa 1650. But after being decimated by disease probably brought by early European adventurers, the Cheraw joined with the Cahaba Indian Nation.

The first westerners in the region were Welsh Baptists who came from Pennsylvania and Delaware and settled along the Greater Pee Dee River. Scotch-Irish, English, French Hugenots and Germans followed.

The community of Cheraw was settled circa 1748 and in 1750 was one of only six settlements in South Carolina shown on English maps. It actually was the large Cheraw District until 1785 when is was divided into three counties. The town of Cheraw found itself in Chesterfield County, which, depending upon the source, was named for either Lord Chesterfield or for the Virginia homeplace of some early Cheraw District settlers.

But while Thomas Sellers was still quite young, the family left Cheraw and moved to eastern Tennessee. Instead of attending a formal school, Thomas was tutored by his young Aunt Caroline Gulledge and she prepared him well for college.

He was sixteen years old when the family moved again, this time to Madison County, Alabama. At seventeen (1848), Thomas attended a camp meeting conducted by the Cumberland Presbyterians. He professed his faith at that meeting and joined the Baptist Church near his home in Enon. Later that year he moved to Huntsville and then to New Market, Alabama, where he joined the New Market Baptist Church.

After much encouragement, in 1851 he entered Union University in Murfreesboro, Tennessee to study for the ministry. He graduated with honors and, in all, earned three degrees - an A.B. in 1856, an A.M. in 1859, and a D.D. in 1880.

In 1856, Thomas became the preacher for the Baptist Church in Athens, Alabama. Although he remained there for only about a year, it was in Athens that Thomas met Mary Elizabeth Crenshaw, a student at Mary Sharp College, who was to become his bride. They fully intended to become foreign missionaries after their marriage. But that never happened.

Instead, Starkville, in Oktibbeha County, Mississippi, became their permanent home in 1857. And with the exception of two years during the Civil War and twelve years spent with the Starkville Female Institute, Dr. Thomas Sellers continued as pastor of the Baptist Church until his death in 1899.

Sellers probably had his "hands full" in Starkville. Little could have changed between his arrival in 1857, and 1854 when Dr. Ashbel Green Simonton wrote in his journal -

"The fact is, there is more wickedness and vulgarity in these little towns than enough, and Starkville though famed for its sobriety and morality is little better then the rest of them.

"Loaferism abounds here among old and young. Planters come in day after day and sit in the back rooms or in front of the stores, and talk hour after hour in foolish if not improper conversation. I have been astonished at the indolent habits of many men of the highest standing, who leaving their overseers to attend to the 'hands', come to town to roll marbles or pitch dollars - not once or twice, but habitually. When such an example is set by parents the character of the boys may be guessed at."

Thomas and Mary Sellers had three children who grew to adulthood. Two other children died in accidents, two others of natural causes. Their second son, James Freeman Sellers, was born in 1862 as his father was marching to the Second Battle of Manassas.

During the Civil War, Lt. Thomas Sellers served with Company L of the 48th Mississippi. Actually the 48th was organized in Fredricksburg, Virginia, in November 1862. But Mississippi's 2nd Infantry which had disbanded that summer formed the nucleus.

In addition to the Second Battle of Manassas, the 48th fought with the Army of Northern Virginia at Fredericksburg, Cold Harbor, Gettysburg, Petersburg and Appomattox. At the surrender, the 48th had only eleven officers and eighty-seven men left.

It may have been the hardships of the War, the deaths of her children, childbirth, or delicate health that caused Mary Sellers' death. Whatever the cause, Mary died on November 28, 1870 at the young age of thirty-four years and twenty days. She was buried on a small cemetery at Starkville Baptist Church.

Later a Sunday School addition was built over the graves of Mary, four of her children, and two of Thomas' children by his second wife. When the congregation decided to build the addition, they wrote to Thomas' widow Sarah, who also was Mary's sister, and asked permission to use the land where her sister, nephews, nieces and daughters were buried. According to another daughter's remembrances, Sarah considered the building to be a fitting monument for her family.

Sarah Crenshaw had originally arrived in Starkville before the Civil War to attend the girls academy there and to live with her brother-in-law and sister, Thomas and Mary Sellers. But when the Civil War broke out, Sarah was forced to leave the school.

Mary died in November, 1870 and, according to family records, her sister Sarah married Thomas before the end of 1870. There was no record of their marriage in Mississippi. And while many courthouse records were destroyed in the Oktibbeha County Courthouse fire of 1875, the marriage records were among the few records to survive. Perhaps Thomas and Sarah were married in her parents' home in Alabama.

Before the War, when the belief was not very popular in the area, Dr. Sellers was openly opposed to slavery and succession. But when Mississippi seceded from the Union, Thomas joined the confederate army as a soldier, not as chaplin. But when the war ended, Thomas took the oath of allegience and worked hard to make Reconstruction as peaceable as possible in Starkville.

Before emancipation, slaves attended church with their masters. But after the war the Baptist Church in Starkville separated into two churches divided along racial lines. Some of his former slave parishioners petitioned Dr. Sellers to pastor in one of their churches on Sunday afternoons.

During Reconstruction Dr. Sellers was principal and teacher at a boys school in Starkville. Then in the 1870's, he erected the Starkville Institute for Girls. For several years he served as both church pastor and institute president. And even after his resignation from First Baptist Church, Sellers continued to pastor at several county churches.

Although he served as pastor in Starkville for much of the time between 1857 and 1899, Judge Thomas Battle Carroll in his history of Oktibbeha County, reported that Thomas also preached at Salem Baptist as well from just after the Civil War until the 1890's. He also occaissionally preached at the Union Church and school building in Black Jack community. During those years, Dr. Sellers also took turns with other Starkville ministers at preaching to students at Mississippi State Agricultural and Mechanical College (later Mississippi State University).

For twenty years, Thomas Sellers ran the two-story frame Female Institute as both a boarding and day school. He recruited his own teacher, his Aunt Carolina Hale, as one of the Institutes first teachers. Many girls would never have had an advanced education if it were not for Dr. Seller's Institute. After the Civil War, southern colleges were exclusively for males. The Institute allowed young women graduates to receive Southern teaching certificates and attend graduate courses in Northern universities. Seller's salary as principal was $50 a month in 1891. The school term was only seven months long.

But after the state established a women's college in neighboring Lowndes County, the need for a private college was eliminated. So in 1892 Dr. Sellers sold it to the city of Starkville for $3000. The city used the building as a public school and a school continued to occupy that piece of land in Starkville.

Thomas taught his children himself. He was able to teach Latin, Greek, science, geography and mathematics. His son James Freeman did so well on his college entrance exams, he was admitted as a junior.

Circa 1892, the Baptist Church in Starkville was again without a minister. So he returned to pastor that congregation until his death in 1899. In all, he was the minister for the church eventually named the First Baptist Church of Starkville for thirty-one years.

According to his obituary in the Starkville newspaper, Seller's death followed a "long and painful illness". His Aunt Caroline wrote that he had suffered "for over a year" before his death. He was only sixty-eight years old.

His funeral took place at eleven o'clock in the morning, Sunday, March 12, 1899 at his church. Services at all other churches in Starkville were suspended and the entire city gathered in one final tribute to Dr. Thomas Sellers. A number of ministers and the president of the college eulogized him at the service.

His widow Sarah and many of Thomas' children went to live in Texas after his death.

Starnes Family

Jacob Starnes
>
> b. North Carolina; April 5, 1796
>
> m. Jennie/Jane Russell (b. South Carolina; February 14, 1802 d. by 1850) Mecklenburg County, North Carolina; May 21/31, 1821
>
> r. Choctaw County, Mississippi; 1850
>
> bur. Starnes Cemetery, Webster County, Mississippi
>
> Children
>
>> James R. (see below)
>>
>> Joseph W. - b. North Carolina; April 12, 1822
>>
>>> m. Sarah Agnes Holland (b. Pickens County, Alabama; February 13, 1822 d. Choctaw County, Mississippi; February 6, 1905), dau of Charles Miller and Dicy Childress Holland; Choctaw County, Mississippi; by 1850
>>>
>>> d. April 13, 1908
>>>
>>> bur. New Hope Cemetery; Webster, Mississippi
>>>
>>> wll dtd March 22, 1895
>>>
>>> Children
>>>
>>>> Mary - b. Choctaw County, Mississippi
>>>>
>>>>> m. _____ Williams
>>>>
>>>> Jane - m. Elijah Williams; Choctaw County, Mississippi
>>>>
>>>> Children
>>>>
>>>>> Mary Bell
>>>>>
>>>>> Joseph Argus
>>>>
>>>> Henry H. - b. Choctaw County, Mississippi; 1848

m. Jennie (b. Georgia; 1851)

d. 1925

bur. New Hope Cemetery, Webster County, Mississippi

Children

    Thomas W.

    Henry O.

David Russell (tw) - b. Choctaw County, Mississippi; February 3, 1850

    m. Mattie A Perkins; Oktibbeha County, Mississippi; October 11, 1871

    d. March 30, 1919

    bur. New Hope Cemetery, Webster County, Mississippi

    Children

        Thaddeus

        William

W.R. (tw) - b. Choctaw County, Mississippi; February 3, 1850

    d. September 22, 1875

John V. - b. Choctaw County, Mississippi; 1854

    d. February 16, 1816

Lewellen - b. Choctaw County, Mississippi; September 14, 1856

    d. October 13, 1861

Roxie A. - b. Choctaw County, Mississippi; c.1860

Joseph Jackson - b. Choctaw County, Mississippi; c.1863

Nancy - b. Choctaw County, Mississippi; c. 1865

    m. _____ Head

Charles M. - b. Choctaw County, Mississippi; December 22, 1867

    m. Susie Langston; Webster County, Mississippi; October 27, 1896

    d. March 7, 1912

    bur. New Hope Cemetery, Webster County, Mississippi

son - d. as infant

Mary - b. March 16, 1824

    m. George H. Holland (b. Pickens County, Alabama; June, 1819 d. Jackson, Mississippi; February 16, 1875), son of Charles Miller and Dicy Childress Holland; Oktibbeha County, Mississippi; c.1847

    d. Webster County, Mississippi; February 12, 1860

    bur. New Hope Cemetery, Webster County, Mississippi

John - b. April 11, 1826

    m. Mary ___; Mecklenburg, North Carolina; August 14, 1851

    bur. Starnes Cemetery, Webster County, Mississippi

Mollie - b. January 5, 1832

Margaret - b. Mississippi; September 1, 1834

Jackson - b. Mississippi; June, 1836

William - b. Mississippi; June, 1839

m. Mary E.F. (b. Alabama; c.1841)

Children

    Thomas R. - b. Mississippi; 1865

Thomas - b. Mississippi; October 17, 1841

Phillip - b. Mississippi; June 5, 1844

    m. Ann Wheary

    d. Choctaw County, Mississippi; October, 1870

    bur. Starnes Cemetery, Webster County, Mississippi

    Children

        Cicero

Major/Magar James R. Starnes

    b. Alabama; September 5, 1829

    m1 Flora (b. Alabama; May 31, 1836 d. Webster County, Mississippi; October 17, 1875); Webster County, Mississippi

    m2 S.J. McClure; Webster County, Mississippi; November 15, 1876

    bur. Starnes Cemetery, Webster County, Mississippi

    Children

        Sarah Jones - b. Choctaw County, Mississippi; July 26, 1855

        Sophia A. - b. Choctaw County, Mississippi; January 7, 1857

        m. E.B. Johnson; November 26, 1878

        d. Ackerman, Choctaw County, Mississippi; March 3, 1899

        bur. Mt. Nebo Graveyard, Choctaw County, Mississippi

Children (7)

Louis Walter - b. Choctaw County, Mississippi; October 27, 1858

Jennie/Mary - b. Choctaw County, Mississippi;October 22, 1860

m. C. C. Crow; Webster County, Mississippi; August 19, 1878

George A. - b. Choctaw County, Mississippi; October 23, 1862

d. July 24, 1883

bur. New Hope Cemetery; Webster County, Mississippi

James Russell - b. Choctaw County, Mississippi; November 16, 1864

Margaret Della - b. Choctaw County, Mississippi; November 26, 1866

Jacob - b. Choctaw County, Mississippi; October 25, 1868

Columbia "Laurie" - b. Choctaw County, Mississippi; November 29, 1870

m. Thomas E. Ballard (b. South Carolina; September 17, 1855 d. Lamar County, Texas; February 22, 1924), son of Hiram and Sarah Twitty Ballard; Webster County, Mississippi; January 29, 1888/89

d. Dallas County, Texas; July 22, 1945

bur. Forest Hill Cemetery, Lamar County, Texas

Children

Lillie	Sam
Annie Lee	Earnest

James Ray   Thelma/Velma

Ona   Mary/Margaret

Dora - b. Choctaw or Webster County, Mississippi;
     May 18, 1873

     m. J.M. Lewis; Webster County, Mississippi;
     January 6, 1892

Cassie - b. Choctaw or Webster County, Mississippi;
     August 22, 1874

Mary/Viola - b. Choctaw or Webster County,
     Mississippi; April 9, 1880

Nick - b. Choctaw or Webster County, Mississippi;
     September 23, 1882

A variety of meanings have been given to the Starnes/Starns name. It could have meant "severe", "austre" or "someone residing at the sign of the stars."

The Starnes of this family may have been members of that "Stearns" family, who C.W. Starnes referred to as people with "evangelical zeal." The first member of the New England Stearns was Charles Stearn who arrived in Massachusetts with the Winthrop Fleet. His great grandson Shubel Stearns III was a minister of the "New Light" and took his family first to Connecticut, and then through the Shenandoah Valley of Virginia into North Carolina in 1754. Although his wife Sarah and he had no children, Shubel Stearns III lead his sisters Rebecca, Elizabeth, Martha; his brothers Peter, Ebenezer; and their families on the journey.

Mecklenburg County, North Carolina was where the Starnes family of this genealogy settled. In 1790 Mecklenburg contained several who could have been Jacob's (b. 1796) father, including any of the "free white males over 16" listed below -

Names	Free white males over 16	Free white males under 16	Free white females
Widow Starns	1	2	3
Conrad Starns	1	3	5
Charles Starns	1	1	1
Frederick Starns	1		3
David Starns	1	3	1

After the "Regulators" became active there, much of the North Carolina branch of that Stearns family went into South Carolina circa 1771 and eventually farther west, many settling in Arkansas. But by the time they had a arrived in South Carolina, they were spelling their name "Starns."

Another suggested pedigree for Jacob Starnes of this genealogy included him as a son of Revolutionary War soldiers George Starnes who was buried in Jones Valley, Alabama or Nicholas Starnes who died in Jefferson County, Alabama. Nicholas Starnes had been born in Cecil County, Maryland, but had travel to Washington County, Virginia by his enlistment in the war.

Like those possible antecedents, Jacob Starnes was one of those restless beings who moved west as land opened for settlement. Although he was supposedly from South Carolina, the 1850 census listed North Carolina as his birthplace and he married Jane in Mecklenburg, North Carolina. Tunis Hood was bondsman and Isaac Alexander was the witness at their wedding. Then two years later, on February 8, 1823, Jacob was bondsman when Reuben Starnes and Mary Hood were married.

Several children were born to Jacob and Jane in Mecklenburg. But their son James was born in Alabama, so Jacob had moved again by 1829. Then, when Indian land opened, the family moved again and Jacob appeared on the 1835 tax list for Choctaw County, Mississippi. In 1844 both Jacob and his son Joseph appeared on the Choctaw County tax list. In the 1850 census, Jacob and his family were still living in Choctaw County and Jacob owned one slave.

But everything was not going well for the family. In 1868, some of Jacob's land had to be sold for taxes. Then Jacob's youngest son Phillip was crushed to death under a wagon in 1870. He was only twenty-five years old and left an infant son named Cicero. His young widow remarried J.P. Thorton.

In 1870, Jacob was living on T20 R10 in an area of Bellfontaine, Choctaw County, which would become part of Webster County, Mississippi. Jacob was seventy-five years old. His son William's family was living with him, as was twenty-two year old Henry H. Starnes who was probably Jacob's grandson by his son Joseph. A twenty-eight-year-old domestic servant named Sarah Jones was living with the group also. No female in the family unit could read or write.

On January 3, 1872, Jacob sold a piece of Choctaw County land for $193.13 to J.L. Hardy. But after that he did not appear in any public records.

Many of Jacob's children settled in the New Hope community, five miles northwest of Mathiston and three miles south of Clarkson in Webster County. The original New Hope Presbyterian Church was established by Presbyterian missionaries circa 1819 on land later patented to Jacob's son Joseph who eventually gave the church forty acres of his land.

Settlers were attracted by the wealth of game and the fertile soil. But soon farmhouses dotted the wooded hills and the nearby community of Starnes sprouted up circa 1840. Joseph Starnes operated a sawmill there and owned most of the surrounding land. Joseph's house was built from pine milled at his own sawmill. The land around the house was cleared by slaves. In addition to the sawmill, the community had flour, cotton gin and grist mills as well as a blacksmith shop, stores and a post office.

His son James' name has, at times, been preceeded by "Major" and "Magar". The reason for that name or title has remained unclear. He certainly did not reach the rank of major during the Civil War. The name "Magar" was of German origin. And not surprisingly, Mary Starnes; in an article in Curtis Publishing's *The History of Webster County*, reported that Jacob and James were born in Germany, removed to Holland and went to England before immigrating to the States. However, census records consistently indicated that Jacob and James were born in the United States.

James enlisted in company B of the 31st Mississippi Infantry in March 1862. Although the 31st was garrisoned at Vicksburg, they also fought at Baton rouge, Jackson and Atlanta. Of the 215 men from the 31st who fought at Peach Tree Creek, 76% were killed or wounded. By December 1864, only 86 men were left fit for duty. James was discharged April 1865 having reached the rank of lieutenant.

His son George Starnes was born seven months after he enlisted. Interestingly, James must not have been away from home during the entire time of his enlistment as he had a child named James Russell Starnes born on November 16, 1864.

In 1870 James, his wife Flora and eight children were living on T21 R10 near Bellfontaine. According to mortality schedules, in April of that year, their son Jacob J. died of "Erysepelas" - a severe streptococcal inflammation of the skin, accompanied by sore limbs, sore throat and tender glands.

By the 1880 census, Bellefontaine was a part of Webster County and nine children were living in the Starnes household. In addition to the family, a thirty-five year old "Mack McLure" was living with the family and working as a farm hand. McLure was probably a relative of James second wife.

On November 15, 1876, a J.R. Starnes had married an "S.J. McClure". James' first wife Flora had died on October 17, 1875, and was buried in Ebenezer Cemetery in Webster County.

There was a six year period between the birth of James' daughter Cassie (b. 1874) and his daughter Viola/Mary (b. 1880). His second wife produced James' last two children.

Webster County Cemetery Records from 1966 reported that the Starnes Cemetery was eight miles east of Walthall and badly neglected. Buried there was

"Jacob Starnes, a pioneer citizen, father, grandfather, great grandfather and great-great grandfather of the large family of Starnes, many of whom survive today. His wife and three sons Phillip, John and Major, along with others are buried there."

Many of James' children left Mississippi to continue west. Others settled in Lafayette, Choctaw, Clay and Oktibbeha Counties, Mississippi in addition to Webster County. James' daughter, Mrs. E.B. Johnson, died in 1857 at the age of forty-two, after a bout of measles turned into a deadly case of pneumonia.

One curiosity remained. One of James' daughters was named Sarah Jones Starnes (born 1855). In the 1870 census, James' father Jacob Starnes had a twenty-eight-year-old domestic servant named Sarah Jones (b.c. 1842). It would have been unlikely to name a child after a 13-year-old future domestic servant, but apparently she was. There must have been more to the relationship.

Stevens Family

Isham Stevens
> m. Winifred Smith
> Children
> > Hardy (see below)

Hardy Stevens
> b. Raleigh, Wake County, North Carolina; May 15, 1805
> m Elizabeth Myatt (b. Wake County, North Carolina; March 14, 1805 d. Lowndes County, Mississippi; August 18, 1885), dau of Alexander and Patsy Walton Myatt, Sr.; Pickens County, Alabama; c. 1830
> d. Columbus, Lowndes County, Mississippi; March 14, 1889
> bur. Friendship Cemetery, Columbus, Lowndes County, Mississippi
> Children
> > Joseph Henry (see below)
> > Mary C. - b. Alabama; c. 1831
> > > m Charles H. Hooks (d. by 1850); , Lowndes County, Mississippi; February 23, 1847
> > > d. by 1891
> > > bur. Friendship Cemetery, Lowndes County, Mississippi
> > > Children
> > > > Elizabeth - b.c. 1847
> > > > d. by 1859
> > Martha A. - b.c. 1833

m. John M. Taylor; Lowndes County, Mississippi;
July 27, 1854

r. Kentucky; c. 1891

James Alfred - b. Columbus, Lowndes County,
Mississippi; July 14, 1840

m1 & 2 ?

m3 Mary F. Crowder; Texas; July 15, 1885

d. Texas; December 21, 1922

John Alexander - b. Columbus, Lowndes County,
Mississippi; September 16, 1842

m. Fannie Gibson (1847-1910), dau of William
W. Gibson; Oktibbeha County, Mississippi;
November 15, 1866

d. Lumberton, Clay County, Mississippi;
November 4, 1909

Elizabeth - b. Columbus, Lowndes County,
Mississippi; c. 1844

m. W.S. Palmer; Columbus, Lowndes County,
Mississippi; November 30, 1874

d. aft 1891

Mariah - b. Columbus, Lowndes County, Mississippi;
c. 1846

d. by 1860 census

Fannie E. - b. Columbus, Lowndes County,
Mississippi; c. 1847

m. Joseph Cobb; Columbus, Lowndes County,
Mississippi; November 28, 1866

d. aft 1923

Joseph Henry Stevens

b. Columbus, Lowndes County, Mississippi; January, 1838

m. Ophelia Wallace (b. Lebanon, Tennessee); Columbus, Lowndes County, Mississippi; 1869

d. Columbus, Lowndes County, Mississippi; March 23, 1914

bur. Friendship Cemetery, Columbus, Lowndes County, Mississippi

Children

    Alice May "Allie" - b.c. 1869

        d. by May, 1938

    L.W.

In Scotland "stephen" meant "honor". By the Middle Ages, the name "Stephen" had belonged to the first Christian martyr, ten popes, one English king and several European rulers. So it was fitting that the name should be chosen as a surname.

A Hardy "Stephens" was named as bondsman for the December 1813 wedding of Marten Mann and Sally Holmes in Wake County, North Carolina. But since the Hardy Stevens of this genealogy was born in 1805, the bondsman was more likely an uncle or grandfather.

And although the Hardy Stevens of this genealogy was born in Raleigh, Wake County, North Carolina in 1805, it was circa 1830 that he went to Pickens County, Alabama and swept Elizabeth Myatt off her feet. She was the daughter of Alexander (b. Johnson County, North Carolina; 1760) and Patsy Walton Myatt. Elizabeth's grandfather was John Myatt (Miot) who was probably born in Staffordshire, England in 1726, but married Elizabeth Allen in Johnson County, North Carolina in 1743.

Hardy and Elizabeth Stevens moved to Columbus, Lowndes County, Mississippi, in the early 1830's and were there for the 1850 Federal Census. There were a number of Stevens families in Lowndes County which could have been related to Hardy. At the time he was forty-five years old and had been born in North Carolina. North Carolina was also the birthplace given for Edward (age forty). John G. Stevens (age forty-two) was born in South Carolina. Either, but in particular Edward, who was living in Columbus, could have been Hardy's brother.

While there, Hardy became a prominent citizen in Columbus' early years. Although Hardy had been raised as a planter, in Columbus he learned to be a carpenter and built several of Columbus' antebellum homes. He worked throughout Lowndes County and built an antebellum home in Artesia, Lowndes County and the Lodi bridge south of Columbus.

In the 1850 census, Hardy owned six slaves and had real estate valued at $2000. By standards of the time, he would have been considered rather successful.

His success was probably due to the fact that he was a popular figure in the area and was considered to be honest and hard working. And that was probably also the reason he became president of the Lowndes County Board of Supervisors. In addition, through the years he was a member of the school system's Board of Trustees, a city alderman and a member of the Masons.

His wife Elizabeth also was active. In fact, she was a founding member of Columbus' First Christian Church. And, although she was basically uneducated, Elizabeth appeared to be exceptionally intelligent.

The Civil War must have been a terrible time for Hardy and Elizabeth. All three of their sons fought for the Confederacy. Joseph Henry and John Alexander served with the 14th Mississippi Infantry, which was on the front lines for most of the war. Joseph served as a private of Company K of the 14th Mississippi except for a short period of time in which he was assigned to Company H of the 35th Mississippi and acted as the clerk in a court martial. The 35th Mississippi fought in many of the same battles as the 14th Mississippi.

The 14th Mississippi, also know as Beauregard Rifles, was organized with 1034 men from Lowndes and neighboring counties. The 650 men remaining in the 14th at Fort Donelson, Tennessee in February 1862 were exchanged and went on to fight at Coffeeville. At Vicksburg they were captured and exchanged again. Although the 14th went on to fight at Atlanta and Bentonville, by the surrender, the 14th Mississippi had only 40 men and no officers left.

Joseph Henry Stevens became deputy probate clerk for Lowndes County when he was only sixteen years old and worked as a clerk in a mercantile business. Then after the war, he served as the county's circuit clerk and a member of the Columbus Board of Aldermen, in addition to holding various other offices. In the late 1880's, Joseph Henry Stevens made a plat and index of land in Lowndes County. Between and after his civic responsibilities, Stevens engaged in merchandizing and was an active member of the Knight Templars and the Odd Fellows.

Story Family

George Storey
>b. Pennsylvania; 1725
>m1 Nancy Cantor
>d. 1805
>bur. Fairforest Cemetery, Fairforest, South Carolina
>Children
>>James (see below)
>>Anthony - b. 1746
>>>m. Sarah Farris
>>>d. 1783
>>>Children

George	Edward	Henry
Anthony	Thomas	Robert

>>George - b. 1751
>>>m. Susie Elder
>>>Child
>>>>Andrew
>>Henry M. - b. Newberry, South Carolina; June 21,1757
>>>m. Elizabeth Cunningham
>>>d. Greene County, Alabama; March 19, 1836
>>>Children

William W.	Henry M.	James

>>John - m. Nancy McIlwain
>>>d. 1790's
>>Margaret - m. _____ Elder

James Story
>b. Spartanburg, South Carolina; June 22, 1764

m1 Catherine Cunningham (November 3, 1768-June 27, 1811)

m2 Margaret White (d. aft 1826)

d. Greene County, Alabama; October 23, 1826

Children

> Robert (see below)
>
> John - b. Spartenburg, South Carolina; September 29, 1789
>> m. Jane (1810-1890); July 13, 1826
>>
>> d. 1862
>>
>> Children
>>
>>| | |
>>|---|---|
>>| James | Jacob Wilson |
>>| Charles L. | George Washington |
>>| James Cephas | Andrew Jackson |
>>| William Nelson | Henry Jasper |
>>| Sarah Ann | Samuel Hempstead |
>
> Elizabeth - b. January 10, 1792
>> m. _____ Morrow
>
> Margaret - b. Spartanburg, South Carolina; July 9, 1793
>> m. David Morrow (May 27, 1791-November 17, 1843
>>
>> d. 1870
>>
>> Children
>>
>>| | |
>>|---|---|
>>| Catherine | Samuel |
>>| Nancy | James |
>>| Andrew | Elizabeth Jane |
>>| David | Anthony |
>
> Hannah - b. December 20, 1798
>> d. August 13, 1825

Mary - b. 1800

    d. 1803

Anthony L. - b. September 30, 1803

    d. November 9, 1855

Samuel Wilson - b. July 18, 1805

    d. February 25, 1865

    r. Mobile, Alabama

Henry - b. November 7, 1807

    m1 Jane White (May 10, 1813-September 16, 1862); Greene County, Alabama; February 11. 1833

    m2 Eliza A. Stone (1845-1890); February 14, 1866

    d. August 16, 1871

James Jr. - b. June 14, 1809

    d. September 22, 1840

Robert Story

    b. South Carolina; c. 1795

    m. Martha Smith (d.c. 1838); Greene County, Alabama; May 10, 1824

    d. aft 1850

    Children

        David (see below)

        Sandford/Sandipher/Sandifer Smith - b. Alabama; October 8, 1825

            m. Nancy Jane (1835-1887)

            d. October 4, 1885

            bur. Greene County, Alabama

            Children

Eliza	Everett
Rufus	Martha
Mary	Drucilla
Robert W.	Megonville

Sebron/Cebron/Seaborn - Alabama; c. 1828

Robert Cunningham II - Alabama; October 1, 1830

>m. Sarah (b.c. 1840)

>d. June 11, 1895

>Children

>>Robert III - b.c. 1859

Elizabeth - b. Alabama; c. 1833

>m. _____ Johnson

William C. - b. Alabama; 1837

>m. Eleanor (b. Alabama; c. 1833) and/or Sarah
>Frances

>Children

>>Joel T. - b. Alabama; c. 1859

Margaret

A.L.

Mary

David W. Story

>b. Alabama; prob c. 1831

>m. Margaret A. Lavender (b.c. 1842), dau of John Smith
>and Julia Ann Frances Lavender

>d. by October 28, 1863

>Children

>>James - b. Pickens County, Alabama; December 5,
>>1861

>>>r. Celina, Collin County, Texas; 1893

Actually the Story/Storey/Storrey name was in the New World as far back as the Mayflower when one appeared on the ship's manifest. A John Story, trader from Lancaster County, Pennsylvania, and his brother Thomas Story roamed as far as South Carolina for their business ventures. In 1745, they were in the Augusta County, Virginia, where they were allured by the productivity of the region, which spurred such swift settlment that by 1738 the area had divided off from Orange County and had become Augusta County. It was named for Augusta, Princess of Wales, the mother of King George III. The original county of Augusta was bordered by the Mississippi River to the west, the blue Ridge Mountains to the sourth and extended for two hundred forty miles to the north. It became a refuge and stronghold for Scotch-Irish Presbyterians.

And the compilers of *The Family Storey* believed the family of this genealogy was of Scotch-Irish descent. So there is a possiblity either John or Thomas was the father of George of this genealogy and that the family was of Scoth-Irish origin.

Actually the term "Scotch-Irish" was an American term given to a group of people who began as lowlander Scots, constantly fighting off the English to the South and the Highlanders to the north. Scottish leadership was in shambles. Between 1400 and 1625, five Scottish Kings were minors with regents and no Scottish King had kept the English out since 1300. Furthermore, because remnants of the old feudal system remained, lowlanders were forced to work other men's land. With so insecure a life, they learned to live a temporary existence. So they were the perfect choice when the British

Parliament decided Protestants needed to be sent to Ulster (Northern Ireland) in an attempt to subdue the Catholic Irish and dilute the population with Presbyterian Scots.

But Ulster had a reputation for being religiously moderate at that time, so the move was attractive to the lowlanders. And their industries prospered in their adopted homeland.

Although they managed to life peaceably with the Irish, they kept their own customs and religion. Marriages between Scottish settlers and Irish were rare. Although they were known as Ulstermen, the Scots did not intermingle with the local citizenry. So the term Scoth-Irish did not refer to a group developed by the marriage of two groups. Instead, they were Scots through and through who fled to Ireland, but remained Scots wherever they went.

But life was not to remain calm. Eventually drought destroyed their flax crops and feed for their sheep. And in a further effort to control the Irish, the British took repressive measures against the competiting Irish linen and wool industries, which had a direct and negative effect on the Scots living there. Then in the 1700's, religious persecution began again. When William and Mary took the British throne, Scottish Presbyterians were forced to pay tithes to the Church of England.

Pushed by famine, epidemics, rebellions and the enclosure movement, many Scotch-Irish felt it necessary to leave Ireland for the New World. Between 1717 and 1780, two hundred fifty thousand people fled Ireland for the New World. In 1717 alone, five thousand Ulstermen left. Extended families, whole congregations, entire villages of Scotch-Irish Presbyterians left.

They were an independent group who came to the dolonies for a variety of religious and economic reasons. But unlike other groups, the Scotch-Irish did not arrive indentured to anyone. They paid their own way, even if they had to sell everything they owned to do it.

Many Scotch-Irish went first to Philidelphia, because Penn's settlements had the reputation of tolerance. But although they were pulled by the promise of fertile land, they found they weren't welcome when they arrived in the port of Philadelphia. From there, wagon routes through the Great Valley of Pennsylvania took them west until they were blocked by mountains, then down the Shanandoah Valley and into North Carolina. In fact many of Augusta County, Virginia's earliest settlers stopped briefly in Pennsylvania before moving south to Virginia.

Other Scotch-Irish who landed in Charleston ended up in the back hills of the Carolinas and Georgia, unlike their Scottish cousins who settled along the more populated eastern shore. The Scotch-Irish found themselves well-matched to frontier life, because land was cheap and the cost of raising a large family was afforable.

But again, because they had settled beyond the peripheries of civilization, they found themselves becoming a buffer colony between the settled colonies along the Atlantic seaboard and the Indians to the West. They also found themselves in territory populated by Indians who were not so dissimilar from themselves. Both had patriartical-warrior societies that liked weapons, horses and mock battles. And as might have been predicted, already having displaced the Irish in their homeland, made displacing the Indian a natural step.

In Scotland they had herded animals, living by the seasons. They ran sheep, swine and cattle through the woods, rounded them up once a year and drove them to market. This they continued in the New World.

They were described by Gwathney as a "hardy race of men" who were "jealous of their liberties, self-reliant and brave" who were uninfluenced by established government and church." They were stereotyped as large, uncouth people who loved their whisky.

George Story was born in 1725 in Chester, Lancaster or York County, Pennsylvania, and married Nancy Cantor circa 1745. According to *History of the Presbyterian Church of South Carolina*, he was in

"the district of Union, on the waters of a large creek by
the same name which falls into Tyger river, a branch
of Broad River in South Carolina"

The history reported that he was from one of "seven or eight families" who had emigrated from Pennsylvania. However, members of his family apparently stopped in Augusta County, Virginia for a while.

On November 10, 1752, George Story received a grant of land in Fairforest, North Carolina. That area later became a portion of the 96th District of South Carolina and, finally, Spartanburg County, South Carolina. George was a charter member of the Fairforest Presbyterian Church.

On December 23, 1771, George "Storrey" received another grant of two hundred acres, first surveyed for him in 1767. The land was described as

"Situate in Craven County on a Branch of Fair Forrest,
waters of Broad River."

According to W.M. Story, George's home was burned during the Revolutionary War. In order to protect those left behind when the young men went to war, he then built a fort on his land. Although he never served himself, George has been accepted by the DAR as a Revolutionary War soldier because of Story's Fort.

He died in 1805 and was buried in Fairforest Cemetery. Bequests in George's will were both odd and indicative of the time. Daughter Margaret and son Henry received only one slave each. Son Geoge received

"a negro girl named Fanny also one negro boy named Derre which is to remain with his mother until he is three years old"

and all of George's clothing.

The largest legacies went to Nancy Story and James Story. Daughter-in-law Nancy, widow of John, received a slave named Leath for ten years. After that Leath was to be sold and the money devided among Nancy's children. She also received a small parcel of land and her eldest son received three pounds. All of Nancy's children were to be educated.

Although he was the youngest son, James received the largest bequest in George's will. While James received one slave and 247 acres of land, heirs of George's eldest son Anthony received only $2.

George's son Henry served as a sergeant in the South Carolina militia during the Revolutionary War. In 1776, he enlisted in Newbery, South Carolina under Captain Robert Faris and continued to serve under a variety of officers until the end of the War. He began to receive Revolutionary War pension #S32537 of $120 per year when he was seventy-nine years old.

But by that time, he had left South Carolina. In December 1817, Henry Story moved his family to Alabama. At first he lived on Canoe Creek, a branch of the Coosa River. Then in October, 1820, he supposedly moved to Greene County, Alabama. However, in his Revolutionary War pension, Henry reported that he had moved to Green County in 1833.

But his brother James Story received federal land in Green County on October 3, 1825 and was in Greene County's Will Book A for 1826. Because of his youth (b. 1764), James was the only one of George Story's sons who did not fight in the Revolutionary War. After his first wife's death in 1811, James married Margaret White. He moved his family to Greene County between 1818 and 1823.

With his 1826 death James left his wife three slaves, four cows, a mare with her saddle and bridle, the kitchen furniture, a trunk, spinning wheel, small cupboard, one bedroom furniture and "sufficient provisions for one year." After her death, the slaves and their children were to be divided among James' children.

Children John, Elizabeth, Margaret and Robert received only slaves in the will. Anthony, James and A.L. received land and/or money. Son John and son-in-law David Morrow (husband of Margaret) were named executors.

A number of Storys who may have been related to the Storys of this genealogy (see APPENDIX 7), lived in the western Alabama region between the 1820's and 1840's. For instance, a James Storey received land in Township 22 Range 57 on March 14, 1828 on April 13, 1830. William W. Storey, Allen W. Story, Basdol Story, and Elias/Elsie/Eprey Story also owned land in Pickens County. An Allen Story also owned land in Tuscaloosa County. Then on July 20, 1822 an Arthur Story received 80 acres of land on Sec18 T18 R16W in Greene County.

And according to the 1850 Pickens County census, a Henry M. Story was born circa 1797 in South Carolina. That Henry would have been James' son, Robert's brother. Then records indicated that on August 6, 1849, Henry M. Story and Robert M. Story were both among the voters in the Yorkville Precinct of Pickens County. That Henry Story married Jane White in February 1833 in Greene County, Alabama

James' son John Story was a farmer, store owner, postmaster and possibly a doctor in Alabama. He received a land deed for Sec 24 of Pickens County on March 22, 1826 for land not far from land deeded to Robert Lavender. Later, Robert Lavender's daughter would marry a Story boy. But before that, John Story served as a Justice of the Peace in Pickens County. In 1851, he was postmaster at Mantua, Pickens County, Alabama. In fact, John showed up in the 1830, 1840, and 1850 Pickens County census. The 1850 census indicated he was born circa 1788 in South Carolina. Robert Story of this genealogy was born in the same state just seven years later. So the John Story in Pickens County probably was the one who was Robert's brother.

Although James Story's son Robert was born in Spartanburg, South Carolina in 1795, he showed up in Tuscaloosa, Alabama land records as early as 1825, when he received 160 acres in R18 R17 and 80 acres in T22 R14.

Robert's wife Martha died in Alabama circa 1838, possibly in childbirth. The 1840 census showed Robert as the sole adult with one boy and one girl under the age of 5, three boys and one girl age 5 to 10, and two boys and one girl age 10 to 15. But in the 1850 census he appeared with only six children. Three children from the 1840 census were missing. The girl age 10 to 15 in 1840 could have married by 1850. But the youngest girl and a boy aged 5 to 10 in 1840 were missing from the 1850 census. All of Robert's children were born in Alabama.

On August 6, 1849, Robert N. Story was listed as a voter in Pickens County. In the 1855 state census, Robert's family had three slaves. Robert Story served as a petit juror in Pickens in October, 1860. Then in 1866, "Bob" and "Sanford", who were probably Robert and Sandifer, appeared as heads of families in Pickens County. The G.C. and Baily Story families also lived in Pickens County.

In all, Robert Story had five sons who grew to adulthood. All of them served in the Civil War. William, Robert and David served in Company B of the 42nd Alabama. In fact, confederate military records showed R.C. Storey enlisted on March 28, 1862 at Olney, Alabama. The May 16, 1862 muster roll indicated Story was at Columbus, Mississippi.

According to confederate records, David W. Story enlisted on March 12, 1862 in Olney, Alabama. The 42nd Infantry Regiment was actually organized in May, 1862 in Columbus, Mississippi, although a number of the men came from the 2nd Alabama, as might have been the case with David. The 42nd was assigned to Tupelo, Mississippi, but fought at the Battle of Corinth where they lost 50% of their 700 men. They were captured during the seige, exchanged and reorganized at Vicksburg.

David Story was captured at Vicksburg on July 4, 1863. Although he lived to sign surrender papers when Vicksburg fell in July 1863, he never returned to Pickens County. And October

28, 1863 Confederate records indicated he had died. His place of burial remained unidentified.

After David's death, the 42nd Infantry went on to fight at Chattanooga and Atlanta. By the Battle of Chattanooga in December 1863, they were down to 311 men and 247 weapons. And more died before the surrender in 1865.

David's widow Margaret Lavender Story remarried and, with her children and her new husband, moved to Mississippi. David's son James Story was residing in Collen County, Texas in 1893.

Other Storys lived in Pickens County who were of the time of Robert Story's children. An A.J. Story was a private in the Calhoun Guards from Pickens in 1861. And an H.W. Story was a private in the Pickensville Blues. Three Storys - E. (1824-1900), S.M. (1819-1893), and William T. (1847-1877) - were buried in Big Creek Cemetery in Pickens County. A newspaper article reported that on July 4, 1860, a Mrs. Story lived near Mt. Taber Church in Pickens. And finally, a Mrs. Samuel M. Story died of paralysis "on January 30, 1900, in Pickensville in Pickens County.

Walser Family

Casper/Jasper/Gasper Walser
    b. prob Bern, Switzerland;
    m. Margaretha
    d. Rowan County, North Carolina; c. 1785
    est inv Rowan County, North Carolina; 1786
    Children
        Martin (see below)
        Frederick - b. Pennsylvania; December 25, 1760
            m. Margaretha Earnest/Ernest
            r. Rowan County, North Carolina; 1800
            d. December 24, 1837
            Children

Brittain	Henry	Jane
Elizabeth	George	Thomas
John	David	Mary

        John - b. Pennsylvania; c. 1770
            m. Lucy Doty
            d. Rowan County, North Carolina; c. 1794
            Children
                Susanna - b. March 15, 1792
                    m. Isaac Adams
        Phillip - b. Pensylvania; April 15, 1771
            m. Christianna Arrowood; March 17, 1795
            r. Rowan County, North Carolina; 1800
            wll pro Rowan County, North Carolina; 1813
        Jacob - b. Pennsylvania; May 1773
            m. Margaret Slaget/Slagel; December 30, 1793
            r. Rowan County, North Carolina; 1800

Children

  3 sons   4 dau

Martin Walser

 b. Pennsylvania; 1758

 m. Francis Lee (d. by 1804)

 wll pro - Rowan County, North Carolina; 1804

 Children

  David (see below)

  Catherine

  Margaretha/Margaret - r. Putnam County, Georgia by

   1810

  Squire Preston - m. Elizabeth Wagner

   r. Morgan County, Georgia

   d. 1846

   Children

    Caswell John Martin Mary Jane

    Daniel Elvira   Solomon

    John

  Solomon

  John

David Walser

 b. North Carolina; betw 1784 and 1798

 m. Elizabeth "Betsy" Darden (b. Georgia; December 3, 1788 d.c. 1848); c. 1812

 d. Tuscaloosa, Alabama; betw 1830 and 1855

 Children

  George Washington (see below)

Martha Burch - m. John P. Robertson, son of Loddick
and Nancy Robertson of Virginia; Tuscaloosa
County, Alabama; November 29, 1838
Children
William G. - b. Tuscaloosa, Alabama;
September 25, 1839
m. Sarah Gardner, dau of James and
Rebecca Cureton Gardner
Mary Ann - m. James W. Henry; Tuscaloosa County,
Alabama; September 18, 1834
Elizabeth - d. young
Margaret - m. Andrew Jackson Jones; Tuscaloosa
County, Alabama; August 28, 1841
Carolina - m. W. Frank Jones; Tuscaloosa County,
Alabama; January 17, 1848
David Casper - d. young
Rebecca Jane - m. William W. "Buck" Kyle;
Tuscaloosa County, Alabama January 17, 1848
Samuel Lemuel - d. young

George Washington Walser I
b. Wilkes County, Georgia; February 8, 1818
m1 Mary Ann Darden (b. North Carolina c. 1823);
Tuscaloosa County , Alabama; September 28 or 29, 1841
m2 _____ Canty
m3 Sarah Jane Blaylock (b. Mississippi; February, 1850 d.
Texas; 1912); Colfax County, Mississippi; September 28,
1873
d. Montague, Texas; June 2 or 23, 1902
bur. Smyrna Cemetery, Montague, Texas

Children

> David - b. Alabama; c. 1842
>
> John Thomas - b. Alabama; c. 1844
>> d. Civil War
>
> Samuel Lafayette - b. Alabama; c. 1847
>> m. Martha Mae Cornelia "Matt" Ingram
>
> James Jefferies/Jefferson - b. Oktibbeha County, Mississippi; October 22, 1851
>> m. Sarah Jane "Sally" Ingram, dau of William Timothy and Mary Grimsley Ingram; Van Buren, Arkansas; April 11, 1873
>>
>> d. Jones County, Texas; March 2, 1914
>>
>> Children
>>> George Washington II - b. Searcy, Arkansas; September 13, 1877
>
> Rufus B. - Oktibbeha County, Mississippi; c. 1853
>
> Francis Lee "Fannie" - b. Mississippi; c. 1858
>> m. James J. White
>
> George T. - b. Mississippi; June, 1870
>> m1 Bula Trottman
>>
>> m2 Myrtle Livingston
>
> Andrew Martin - b. Fayetteville, Arkansas; June 28, 1873
>> m. Ida Lee Allen; Montagne, Texas; March 26, 1889
>>
>> Children
>>> Lillian
>
> Cephus A. "Cea" - b.c. 1875
>> m. Eva Allen; July 16, 1899
>
> Mary "Betty" - b. Texas; c. 1879

m. Benjamin Franklin Coats; Montagne County,
Texas; July 16, 1899

Albert Leroy - b. Texas; July, 1883
retarded

Oscar T. and/or Tim - b. Texas; 1887

Frederick Lee - b. Texas, September, 1891
m. never married

J____ - b. Texas; February, 1891 or 1896

?Ruth/Rusha

?Anna - d. young

Richard Walser reported the Walser / Walcer / Walcher / Waltzer / Wasser family was from Valais in southwest Switzerland. But they moved to Graubunden and St. Gallen in eastern Switzerland and took the name Valaisian, which became Walliser and, eventually, Walser. Some members of the family moved to Austria - to an area in the northern Alps they named Kleines Walsertal (Little Walser Valley) - and others moved in Liechtenstein and Italy.

Casper / Gasper / Jasper Walser was probably born in Bern, Switzerland, but arrived in Pennsylvania from Rotterdam, Holland aboard the *Albany* on December 2, 1749, and took the "oaths to the Government". He married Margaretha after his arrival.

Casper appeared on the Linn Township, Northampton County, Pennsylvania tax list for the year 1762. By 1767 he had sheep, cattle, mills and land - wooded and cleared - and he was a member of the Albany Township, Berks County, Pennsylvania Luthern Church. He was still in Pennsylvania in 1774.

But on February 8, 1775, "Gasper Walser" received two hundred eighty-six acres of land on Reedy Branch (later, Dyker's Creek), North Carolina. And by 1778, he had assets worth seven hundred forty-five pound, quite well-off for the time. He applied for another three hundred thirty-five acres on Dyker's Creek in 1780 and eight acres, including an island in the Yadkin River, in 1784.

Casper died in Rowan County (later, Davidson County) circa 1785. His son Martin Walser and an Edward Williams were named executors. It took a while to divide Casper's land. In 1794, son Jacob received fifty acres, son Frederick received ninety-five acres and granddaughter Susanna received fifty-seven acres.

Rowan County had been formed in 1753 out of Anson County, North Carolina and named for acting-governor Matthew Rowan. The county originally included the entire northwestern section of North Carolina. But much of its territory was given over to Davidson (1822), Davie, Surry, Burke, Wilkes, and Iredell Counties.

Two of Casper's sons, Frederick and Martin "Walsor" appeared living on adjoining property in the 1790 Rowan County census. Frederick had two white males over 16 years of age, one white male under 16 and two white females in his family. Martin had one white male over 16 years of age and three females. Neither brother owned any slaves.

Casper's sons Frederick, Jacob and Phillip were listed as living in Rowan County in 1800. Although Martin may have left Rowan County, North Carolina by then, his will was proven there in 1804.

According to Richard Walser, Martin did not fight in the Revolutionary War since he was needed on the farm. In fact, his brother Frederick, who served as a minuteman patrolling the Yadkin River Valley, was the only one of Casper's sons who did fight in the war.

David was probably the David Walser who, according to Tuscaloosa land records, received land on Sec 33 T21 R9W in Jefferson County, Alabama on July 27, 1822. On February 22, 1822, a David "Walsen" had received land in Sec 35 T18 R5W in Jefferson County. David "Walsen" was probably David Walser. Jefferson and Tuscaloosa Counties were on the direct route from Georgia to Mississippi. Jefferson had been formed out of Blount County in 1819, with Birmingham, Alabama as the county seat.

David married Elizabeth Darden, probably the daughter of Lemuel and Rebecca Weaver Darden or George Washington and Elizabeth Strosier Darden. David's will was filed in Tuscaloosa County, Alabama Wills: 1821-1855, Book 1, page 206. He died after the 1830 census, since David Walser was listed in Tuscaloosa County at the time. His family consisted of

Females	Age	Males
2	0-5	
1	5-10	
1	10-15	1
1	15-20	
	20-30	
1	30-40	1
	40-50	1

In 1830, the family also had a male slave aged 10 through 24 years.

David's son George Washington Walser (b. 1818) would have been four years old when his father claimed his Alabama land. In the 1830 census George was listed as the only male age 10 through 15 in the family.

After George's first marriage and the birth of some of his children, he moved his family west to Mississippi circa 1848, before continuing on to Arkansas circa 1873 and to Texas by 1879. Using 1860 census information, apparently the move to Mississippi was made between the 1847 birth of George's son Samuel and the 1851 birth of his son James.

During the Civil War, George Walser joined Company E, Third Battalion of the Mississippi State Troopers on October 16, 1862. He was made a sergeant on May 1, 1863. Capt. James Ervin was the commander of the troopers which was made up primarily of middle-aged, married men from Oktibbeha County, Mississippi. Most were farmers and many had grown sons already fighting for the Confederacy.

At Vicksburg, the state troopers were first assigned to guard the riverfront. But after becoming trapped at Vicksburg, they were put under Confederate command and were sent to the trenches. During the long seige, a number of the troopers were killed, wounded or died of disease. George Washington Walser was captured at Vicksburg when Lt. Gen. John Pemberton surrendered the city to Ulysses S.Grant. After parole, the troopers were sent to Columbus, Mississippi, from where George was sent home to Oktibbeha County, Mississippi.

Interestingly, a Martha Walcer, a black woman born in Africa circa 1820, was listed as living in Oktibbeha County in the 1870 census. Since many slaves took their master's surname upon emancipation, she very well could have belonged to David at one time.

Weeks Family

Michael Weeks
>b. Virginia; October 22, 1768
>
>m. Isabella Sharp (1778-1850's)
>
>d. 1850's
>
>bur. Neshoba County, Mississippi
>
>Children
>>William Thomas (see below)
>>
>>David - d. Winston County, Mississippi
>>
>>Hiram - d. Winston County, Mississippi
>>
>>James Grigsby
>>
>>Solomon
>>
>>Emily - m. Myres
>>
>>Louiza

William Thomas Weeks
>m. Margaret Fulcher
>
>d. Oktibbeha County, Mississippi; 1834
>
>Children
>>Hiram Sharp (see below)

Hiram Sharp Weeks
>b. McMinn County, Tennessee; January 11, 1828
>
>m. Sarah Jane Johnston (b.c. 1830; Kentucky d. February 10, 1906), dau of John Johnston; Winton County, Mississippi; March 15, 1849
>
>d. Winston County, Mississippi; January 21, 1910
>
>bur. Bethel Methodist Cemetery, Oktibbeha County, Mississippi

Children

Mary Frances

Cornela Ann - b. Mississippi; April 17, 1851

    m. never

    d. Mississippi; August 3, 1932

    bur. Bethel Methodist Cemetery, Oktibbeha County, Mississippi

Sarah Florence - b. Mississippi; c. 1853

    m. Wallace

Ellen Louisas Elizabeth - b.c. 1854

Rachel - b. Mississippi; March 22, 1856

    m. Frederic T. Bagwell (September 5, 1858- May 24, 1921); December 23, 1875

    d. April 17, 1954

    bur. Poplar Flats Cemetery, Winston County, Mississippi

Margaret Emma - b. Mississippi; c. 1858

    m. Davis

Jessie William - b. Mississippi; c. 1860

Hiram Bragg - b. Mississippi; January, 1862

    m. M.L. _____ (1886-1904)

    d. June 17, 1950

    bur. Bethel Cemetery, Oktibbeha County, Mississippi

Martha Jane - b. Mississippi; ;January, 1865

    m. never

    d. September 21, 1890

    bur. Bethel Cemetery, Oktibbeha County, Mississippi

Osmond Darius - b. Mississippi; c. 1867

Lucy - b. Mississippi; September 13, 1869

    m. Chandler

    d. October 26, 1933

    bur. Bethel Cemetery, Oktibbeha County, Mississippi

Willis Riley - b. Mississippi; November 17, 1874

    m. Mattie Louvenia Israel

    d. September 4, 1957

    bur. Bethel Cemetery, Oktibbeha County, Mississippi

Viola

    The Weeks/Weekes/Weks/Weaks/Wykes/Wickes surname may have evolved from the family's place of residence - possibly a dairy farm. Sir Richard Weekes of Honeychurch, Devonshire and Williams Weekes of Tavistock had a coats of arms confirmed on them. William Weekes adopted the motto "God's beloved are in want of nothing." The Weeks of Sussex bore the same arms, but their two mottos were "Virtue is a way of life" and "Undertake and Persevere."

    Many American Weeks descended from George Weeks (b.c. 1603) of Devonshire England and his wife Jane Clapp, daughter of William and Johana Channon Clapp. Others descended from Roger Wykes of Bendon, Axmouth circa 1636.

    The Weeks name appeared early in Southern colonial records. John Weeks (b. 1617) left Gravesend, England on board the *Primrose* sailing for Virginia in 1635. A Thomas Weeks took the oath required to sail to the New World in 1634. A William was involved in a legal case concerning the Lost Colony in Virginia. A John settled south of the mouth of the

James River. Albemarle, Virginia, even had a town named Weeksville.

Priest reported that a Samuel Weeks; a Bristol, England merchant; was working with Roger Weeks of Charleston, South Carolina. In fact, they may have been members of the Weeks family which had a network of trade between England and the colonies of Maryland, Virginia and South Carolina during the 1600's and 1700's. The Weeks family of this genealogy may have been descended from any of the above.

Michael Weeks, his wife Isabella Sharp and their children were the travelers west in this Weeks family. Michael and Isabella were both born in Virginia. As they migrated west, the family lived in Warren County, Georgia; Perry County, Alabama; McMinn County, Tennessee; and finally, Winston County, Mississippi in the early 1830's. Most of the moves were overland, although the trip from Tennessee was made via a flatbed boat down the Tennessee, Ohio, and Mississippi Rivers and then up the Yazoo River.

For the final leg of the trip after the Indian land opened, the Weeks family moved up the Robinson Road to what would become northeastern Winston County, Mississippi when it was officially organized in December 1833. But when the Weeks family traveled it, the Robinson Road was an early Indian trail.

Eventually the Robinson Road became a primary means of travel from Birmingham, Alabama, southwest to Jackson, Mississippi. Indian agencies and inns were constructed along the route traveled by so many of those early pioneers.

Although most of Michael's children remained in the Winston/Oktibbeha/Clay counties area, in 1848, Isabella and he had moved to near their daughter Emily Myres in Neshoba

County, Mississippi. Their son William Thomas Weeks married Margaret Fulcher and had several children. They followed the elder Weeks and were residents of McMinn County, Tennessee when their son Hiram was born in 1828 and of Mississippi circa 1830.

William and Margaret's sons Hiram and David Weeks were both on an 1844 Choctaw County, Mississippi tax list. In 1841, David was a trustee of the Bethlehem Church there. His grandfather Michael had been one of the charter members in 1835.

During the Civil War, Hiram Sharp Weeks served as a private in Company D, 37th Regiment, Mississippi Infantry, C.S.A. It was a regiment made up of local men who organized in the Spring of 1862. Most of their early fighting was done in Mississippi and they were in Vicksburg when it fell. Hiram was wounded at the Battle of Corinth, but was on active duty in Greensboro, North Carolina when the war ended in April 1865.

Hiram's wife Sarah Jane Johnston Weeks had her own Civil War battle. When Union troops raided Winston County in 1863, they raided the Weeks farm. Sarah Jane locked her saddle horse in the smokehouse to keep it out of their hands. The raiders demanded the horse, but Sarah wouldn't give them the key. When one tried to breakdown the door, Sarah cut his hand with a butcher knife and the raiders gave up.

In 1870, the Weeks family had a personal property and real estate worth of $1765 and resided on Township 16, Range 12. But Hiram Weeks owned land in both Oktibbeha and Winston Counties.

1860 Federal Census - Itawamba County, Mississippi

Verona P.O.

1784 1784 Carson	John H.	42	M	Farmer	TN
	Eliza S.	42	F		TN
	Margaret	18	F	Teacher	MS
	Emily P	16	F		MS
	Amanda	14	F		MS
	Sarah R.	11	F		MS
	Robert N.	8	M		MS
	Fances	6	F		MS

Plantersville P.O.

1832 1832 Carson	Alfred F.	50	M	Farmer	TN
	Virginia	35	F		AL
	Warren	15	M		MS
	Henry	13	M		MS
	Louisa	11	F		MS
	Harper	1	M		MS
Lona	Nancy	17	F		MS

1860 Federal Census - Oktibbeha County, Mississippi

428	367	Duke William C.	38	farmer	2400	1650	AL
		Mary	28				MS
		James	10				MS
		Pleasant	8				MS
		Martha	6				MS
		Rufus	4				MS
		Mary	1				MS
	?Meredith	John	25	farm labor			AL

"Extr est H.J. Morris"

531	455	Duke John	36	farmer		1800	AL
		_ulin	29				AL
		Pleasant	9				MS
		Thomas	4				MS
	?Meredith	Nancy	15				AL
	Smith	Wm E.	62		400	800	VA

534	457	Meredith					
		David	28	farmer		2000	AL
		Martha	26				SC
		Duke John					

"Guadian for W.J. Meredith"

535	458	Duke Pleasant	62	farmer		600	TN
		Martha	62				GA
		Rufus	26	labor			AL
		Mary	23				AL

541	461	Duke Mathew	31	farmer	800	1500	AL
		Milly	21				AL
		Pricilla	2				MS
		Eliza	1				MS

546	466	Duke Pleasant	29	farmer	AL
		Sarah	29		TN
		Martha	6		MS
		Nancy	4		MS
		Mary	2		MS
		Clurinda	8/12		MS

599	518	Bolles			
		George	26	farmer	Ger
		Sarah	24		AL
		Sarah	8/12		MS
		Duke Elijah	27	physician	AL

Lavenders in the Pickens County, Alabama Federal Census

Ellender Lavender
>   1840   0001200   0001101

>   1850   family no. 1381   November 20
>   Ellender   56 years old $1450   SC
>   William   38   farmer   SC
>   Mary A.   34   AL

Hugh Lavender
>   1850   family no. 1380   November 20
>   Hugh   33 $700   farmer   SC
>   Eliza 27   AL

JJ Lavender
>   1850   family no. 1479   November 26
>   JJ   30   farmer   SC
>   Sarah   23   AL
>   Tabitha   3   AL
>   Sarah   2/12   AL

John S. Lavender
>   1840   0000100   1001000

>   1850   family no. 1377 November 20
>   John S.   34 $250   farmer   SC
>   India/Julia 29   SC
>   Mary E.   12   AL
>   Irene J.   2   AL
>   Margaret   9   AL

BF Garwell/ Gamell	27		carpenter	AL

Robert Lavender

    1840   10123001 0013010

    1850   family no. 1387   November 20

Robert	53	$1200 farmer	SC
Mary	51		SC
William	22		AL
Margaret	23		AL
Hugh	18		AL
Eliza	20		AL
Sarah	23		AL

Ruth Lavender

    1850 family no. 1382   November 20

Ruth	30	$1000	SC
Morgan	10		AL
Lavinia	5		AL
John	3		AL
Robert Anna (female)	1		AL

Smith Lavender

    1840   1200120 2010010

    1850   family no. 1386   November 20

Smith	47	$2000 farmer	SC
Matilda	42		SC
Spencer	15		AL
Lewis	13		AL
Sarah J.	8		AL
Dock	6		AL
Dolphus	4		AL
George McJunkin	43	wheelwright	SC

Marriages of Other Possibly Related Lincecums in Mississippi

Lincecum First Name	Married	Spouse's First Name	Surname	Date	County
O.B.		E.M.	Alston	1895	Noxubee
Wilmoth		James P.	Haynes	1842	Noxubee
Hayward		Betsy	McIlwain	1873	Oktibbeha
H.H.		M.E.	Perkins	1869	Oktibbeha
Ducea		Josiah B.	Cole	1854	Noxubee
Wilmoth		James	Haynes	1842	Noxubee
Florena		Robert	Swann	1854	Noxubee
Elizabeth		Jackson	Huckaby	1847	Noxubee
Richard		Amanda	Beard	1875	Lowndes
H.H.		Mary A.	Brown	1850	Noxubee
Marcella		John G.	Nordike	1846	Noxubee

Garrigues Family

Jean de la Garrigue
> b. France
> m. Maria de la Sussan
> Children
>> Henri (see below)

Henri De La Garrigues
> m. Rosanna Rosequet; France
> Children
>> Matthieu (see below)

Matthieu Garriques
> b. Mazamet or Perigold, France; 1675
> m. Susanna de la Roquet (1676-1743 or 1760); The Hague, Netherlands; May 28, 1702
> d. Philadelphia, Pennsylvania; September 6, 1726
> Children
>> Jacob Garrigues (see below)

Jacob Garrigues, Sr.
> b. Perigold, France; 1716
> m. Sarah (1720-1777), 1741
> d. Rockaway or Morristown, New Jersey; May 11, 1798
> Children
>> Jacob Jr. (see below)

Jacob Garrigues, Jr.
> b. 1752/3

m. Mary Calvey (1751-1824), dau of Robert McCalvey / McKelvey / Calvey

d. 1830

Children

    James

James Garrigues

    b. 1783

    m. Elizabeth Godden (1791-1870), dau of Joseph Godden; 1811

    d. 1847

    Children

        Dr. Amzi Godden Garriques (see Meek family)

The Garrigues' name was probably from "garric" in an old French dialect meaning "an oak." That probable origin was indicated in the coat of arms which contained five silver oak trees. But the name could also have come from locations in France named Le Jarrigue in Sanze-Vauasas and Limolong.

Early Garriques of this genealogy were French Huguenots who left the religious persecution of France for the religious freedom of the New World. Jacob Garriques, Sr. settled in New Jersey. His son Jacob Jr. served as a forgeman in the Revolutionary War.

Crenshaw / Martin Ancestors

Freeman Crenshaw
> b. 1776
> m. Elizabeth Martin (b. 1776)
> d. 1853
> Children
>> Dr. George Washington
>> William - m. Elva Ann
>>> Children
>>>> Mary Elizabeth - m. Thomas George Sellers
>>>> Sarah Washington - m. Thomas George Sellers
>>>> Ada - m. _____ Coffee

Gulledge Ancestors

Mortimer Frederick Gulledge
> m. Hannah
> Children
>> Mary - m1 James Sellers
>>> m2 _____ Wilson
>>> Children by James
>>>> Thomas George
>>> Children by _____ Wilson

Alex	Morris	Harriet
Ann	Joe	Lawson

>> Caroline - m. _____ Hale
>>> Children
>>>> Carrie Sue

Possibly Related Story Families
in Pickens County, Alabama 1850 Census Records

1720   Story

Basdol	51	farmer	1500	GA
Elizabeth	53			GA
Bailey	16			AL
Victoria	19			AL
"H.E.B.W.E"				

1718   Story

D.W.	41	farmer	500	GA
Nancy A.	17			AL

1719   Story

Eprey	41		1200	GA
B.F.	16			AL
Andrew	7			AL
Georgiann M.	9			AL
Malinda	4			AL

1038   Story

Henry M.	53	farmer	1200	SC
Jane	54			SC
Mary	21			AL
Margaret	19			AL
Wilson	18			AL
Marinda	16			AL
Artimissa	13			AL
McVay D.E.	21	farmer		TN

1412   Story

Henry	43	farmer	800	SC

		Name	Age	Occupation	Value	State
		Jane	35			SC
		Margaret	16			AL
		John	14			AL
		James W.	11			AL
		Sarah J.	9			AL
		Thomas W.	10			AL
		Henry A.	4			AL
		Martha	2			AL
1385	Story					
		John	62	farmer	4800	SC
		Jane	39			SC
		James	23			AL
		Jacob	21			AL
		George W.	18			AL
		John C.	14			AL
		Wm N.	12			AL
		Henry J.	8			AL
		Sarah A.	5			AL
		F.H.	4			AL
1705	Story					
		Walter	30	farmer	800	GA
		Martha	26			AL
		Mary A.	9			AL
		Drucilla	7			AL
		Bud	1/12			AL
		Josephine	5			AL
		Louise	3			AL

Below are relevant (but sometimes convoluted because of its use of pronouns) excerpts from the Treaty of Dancing Rabbit:

> A treaty of perpetual friendship, cession and limits, entered into by John Eaton and John Coffee, for and in behalf of the Government of the United States, and the Mingos, Chiefs, Captains and Warriors of the Choctaw Nation, begun and held at Dancing Rabbit Creek, on the fifteenth of September, in the year eighteen hundred and thirty.
>
> Whereas the General Assembly of the State of Mississippi has extended the laws of said State to persons and property within the chartered limits of the same, the President of the United States has said that he cannot protect the Choctaw people from the operation of these laws in peace with the United States and the State of Mississippi they have determined to sell their lands east of the Mississippi and have accordingly agreed to the following articles of treaty...
>
> **Article II** : The United States ... shall cause to be conveyed to the Choctaw Nation a tract of country west of the Mississippi River, in fee simple to them and their descendants, to inure to them while they shall exist as a nation and live on it, beginning near Fort Smith where the Arkansas boundary crosses the Arkansas River, running thence to the source of trhe Canadian fork; if in the limits of the United States, or to those limits; thence due south to Red River, and down Red River to the west boundary of the Territory of Arkansas; thence north along that line to the beginning.
>
> **Article III**: In consideration ..., the Choctaw nation of Indians consent and hereby cede to the United States, the

entire country they own and possess, east of the Mississippi River, early as practicable, and will so arrange their removal, that as many as possible of their people not exceeding one half of the whole number, shall depart during the falls of 1831 and 1832; the residue to follow during the succeeding fall of 1833; a better opportunity in this manner will be afforded the Government, to extend to them the facilities and comforts which it is desirable should be extended in conveying them in their new homes.

Article V: ... No war shall be undertaken or prosecuted by said Choctaw Nation but by declaration made in full Council, and to be approved by the U.S. unless it be in self defense against an open rebellion or against an enemy marching into their country, in which cases they shall defend, until the U.S. are advised thereof.

Article VII: All acts of violence committed upon persons and property of the people of the Choctaw Nation ... shall be referred to some authorized Agent by him to be referred to the President of the U.S. who shall examine in such cases...

Article XII: All intruders shall be removed from the Choctaw Nation and kept without it. Private property to be always respected and on no occasion taken for public purposes without just compensation being made therefor to the rightful owner ...

Article XIV: Each Choctaw head of a family being desirous to remain and become a citizen of the States, shall be permitted to do so, by signifying his intention to the Agent within six months from the ratification of this Treaty, and he or she shall thereupon shall (sic) be entitled to a reservation of one section of six hundred and forty acres of land, oto be bounded by sectional lines of survey; in like manner shall be entitled to one half that quantity for each unmarried child which is living with him over ten years of age; and a quarter section to each child as may be under ten years of age...

Article XV: To each of the Chiefs in the Choctaw Nation (to wit) Greenwood Leflore, Nutackachie, and Mushulatubbe there is granted a reservation of four sections of land ... Also to the three principal Chiefs and to their successors in office there shall be paid two hundred and fifty dollars annually while they shall continue in their respective offices, except to Mushulatubbe, who as he has an annuity of one hundred and fifty dollars under a former treaty, shall receive only the additional sum of one hundred dollars...

Article XVI: In wagons; and with steam boats as may be found necessary - the U.S. agree to remove the Indians to their new homes at their expense and under the care of discreet and careful persons, who will be kind and brotherly to them. They agree to furnish them with ample corn and beef, or pork for themselves and families for twelve months after reaching their new homes...

Article XIX: To Colonel David Fulsom (sic) four sections of which two shall include his present improvement, and two may be located elsewhere, on unoccupied, unimproved land ... To I. Garland, Colonel Robert Cole, Tuppanahomer, John Pytchlynn (Pitchlynn), Charles Juzan, Johokebetubbe, Eaychahobia, Ofehoma, two sections, each to include their improvements, and to be bounded by sectional lines ...

Article XXIII: The Chiefs of the Choctaws who have suggested that their people are in a state of rapid advancement in education and refinement, and have expressed a solcitude (sic) that they might have the privilege of a Delegate on the floor of the House of Representastives extended to them. The Commissioners do not feel that they can under a treaty stipulation accede to the request, but at their desire, present it in the Treaty, that Congress may consider of, and decide the application.

...at Dancing Rabbit creek, this 27th day of September, eighteen and thirty.

Among the numerous signers of the treaty were the following. The spelling was as it appeared on the treaty.

Jno. H Eaton	Jon. Coffee
Greenwood Leflore	Mushulatubbe
Nittucachee	John Garland
Jacob Folsom	John. Pitchlynn, Jr.
David Folsom	Isaac Folsom
Mingo hoomah	P.P. Pitchlynn
Silas D. Pitchlynn	Thomas Leflore Robert
Folsom	

The treaty was signed in the presence of -

E. Breathitt, secretary to the Commission,

William Ward, agent for Choctaws,

John Pitchlynn, United States interpreter,

M. Mackey, United States interpreter,

Geo. S. Gaines, of Alabama

among others. Then the next day, a supplement to the treary was drawn up which gave Peter and "Jack" Pitchlynn two additional sections of land because the chiefs "desire(d) that they might be provided for." As for the other children of John Pitchlynn, the supplement noted that

John Pitchlynn has long and faithfully served the nation in character of U. States Interpreter, he has acted, in addition to what has been done for him there shall be granted to two of his children, (to wit) Silas Pitchlynn, and Thomas Pitchlynn one section of land each, to adjoin the location of their father: likewise to James Madison and Peter sons of Mushulatubbee one section of land each to include the old house and improvement where their father

formerly lived on the old military road adjoining a large
Prerarie (sic).

In the supplement, land was given to Allen Glover and George S.
Gaines who were licensed traders in the Choctaw Nation to help
defray the nine thousand dollars owed to them by members of the
tribe. Another land grant was also given to

John Donly of Alabama who has several Choctaw
grandchildren, and who for twenty years has carried the
mail through the Choctaw Nation ...

Literature Cited

Achee, Benjamin E., and Margery Wright. *Index to Compiled Service Records: Alabama Units - Creek War - 1836-1837.* 2 Vols. Shreveport, Louisiana: 1971.

Adair History and Genealogy. Los Angeles: N.p., 1924.

Adair, Shirley Brown. *Robert Adair (1770-1845): An Adair Family History.* Rockwell, Texas: N.p., 1995.

Alabama Early Settlers 1816: Alabama Counties - Mississippi Territory. Hanceville, Alabama: Briarwood Press, 1983.

Baird, W. David. *Peter Pitchlyn: Chief of the Choctaws.* Norman, Oklahoma: University of Oklahoma Press, 1972.

Barefield, Marilyn Davis. *Researching in Alabama: A Genealogical Guide.* Easley, South Carolina: Southern Historical Press, 1987.

Barefield, Marilyn Davis, and Carr Byron Barefield, comps. *Pickens County, Alabama 1841-1861.* Easley, South Carolina: Southern Historical Press, 1984.

Barkesdale, James Kerry, comp. *Some of the Descendants of Hugh Lavender.* Tuscasloosa, Alabama: N.p., 1994.

Biographical and Historical Memoirs of Mississippi. 2 Vols. Spartenburg, South Carolina: Reprint Company, 1978.

Blaikie, Alexander. *Family History.* Unpublished: 1921.

Bla(y)lock Genealogy News. Ripley, Oklahoma: CBG Associates, 1987.

Bowman, Myreline Daily. *The Blalocks and Related Families.* Atlanta, Texas: Bowman, 1977.

Brandenberger, Evelyn Duke. *The Duke Family*. U.S.A: Brandenberger, 1979.

Brewer, W. *Alabama: Her History, Resources, War Record, and Public Men: From 1540 to 1872*. Tuscaloosa: Willo Publishing Company, 1964.

Burkhalter, Lois Wood. *Gideon Lincecum 1793-1874: A Biography*. Austin: University of Texas Press, n.d.

Carroll, Thomas Battle. *Historical Sketches of Oktibbeha County*. Gulfport, Mississippi: Dixie Press, 1931.

Carter, Clarence Edwin, ed. *The Territorial Papers of the United States, Volume VI*. The Territory of Mississippi. Washington, D.C.: Government Printing Office, 1938.

Clanahan, James F. *The History of Pickens County, Alabama 1540-1920*. Clanahan Publication. Carrollton, Alabama. n.d.

Clark, Meribah. *The James and Eliza Ritchey Family, 1700-1976*. Astoria, Illinois: Stevens Pub. Co., 1976.

Clay, Mary Harrison. "Gideon Lincecum, Southern Pioneer, 1793-1874." Master's thesis, Mississippi State College (Mississippi State University), 1953.

Clay County History Book Committee. *History of Clay County, Mississippi*. Curtis Media, 1988.

Coleman, J.P. *Choctaw County Chronicles: A History of Choctaw Co., Mississippi 1830-1978*. Nashville: Benson Printing Co., 1974.

Crute, Joseph H., Jr. *Units of the Confederate States Army*. Midlothian, Virginia: Derwent Books, 1987.

Dabbs, Miriam Adair. *Andrew Pickens Adair: His Ancestors and Descendants.* Cleveland, Mississippi: Underwood Printing, 1985.

Davis, Arthur. *Dakota Branches of the Sellers Family.* N.p., n.d.

Davis, Robert Scott, Jr. *The Wilkes County Papers 1773-1833.* Easley, South Carolina: Southern Historical Press, 1979.

1833-1983: 150 Years in Oktibbeha County. Starkville, Mississippi: Starkville Daily News, 1983.

Elliott, Carl, comp. *Annals of Northeast Alabama.* 3 Vols. Tuscaloosa: N.p. 1958-1965.

Family Records: Mississippi Revolutionary Soldiers. Mississippi Society, Daughters of the American Revolution, 1953-6.

Gandrud, Pauline Jones, comp. *Alabama Soldiers: Revolutionary, War of 1812, and Indian Wars.* N.p., 1975.

Genealogy News of the Blalock-Blaylock Clans. Ripley, Oklahoma: Greenwood Publications, 1980-1987.

Gonzales, John Edmond, ed. *A Mississippi Reader: Selected Articles from "The Journal of Mississippi History."* Jackson: Mississippi Historical Society, 1980.

Goodman, Mississippi: Holmes County 1856-1986. Goodman, Mississippi: Magnolia Club, 1986.

Green, Ben A. *A History of Tuscaloosa. Alabama 1816-1949.* University, Alabama: Confederate Publishing, 1949.

Griffin, Barton M. *The Sellers Family.* N.p., 1987.

Hill, Judith Parks America. *A History of Henry County, Virginia with Biographical Sketches of the Most Prominent Citizens and*

Genealogical History of Half a Hundred of Its Oldest Families.
Baltimore: Regional Publishing Company, 1976.

Holcombe, Brent, comp. *Marriages of Mecklenburg County,
North Carolina: 1783-1868.* Baltimore: Genealogical Publishing
Company, 1981.

_____. *Spartenburgh County, South Carolina Minutes of the
County Court 1785-1799.* Easley, South Carolina: Southern
Historical Press, 1980.

Hook, J.N. *Family Names: How Our Surnames Came to
America.* New York: MacMillan Publishing Company, 1982.

Johnson, James Dolphus, Jr. *Early Settlers of Pickens County,
Alabama.* Cullman, Alabama: Gregath Publishing Co., 1992.

Julich, Louise Milam. *Roster of Revolutionary Soldiers and
Patriots in Alabama.* Montgomery, Alabama: Daughters of the
American Revolution, 1979.

Kaye, Samuel H., et al. *By the Flow of the Inland Rivers: The
Settlement of Columbus, Mississippi to 1825.* N.p., n.d.

Langdon, Barbara R. *Fairfield County Marriages 1775-1879
Implied in Fairfield County, South Carolina Probate Record.*
Columbia, South Carolina: Langdon & Langdon, 1986.

Latham, Flora G. *Charles Holland Family and Descendents.*
Unpublished Notes.

Lawson, James. *Handbook of Indian Place Names in America.*
Wisconsin Dells: Lawson, 1970.

Lewis, William T. *The Centennial History: Winston County,
Mississippi.* Pasadena, Texas: Globe Publishers International,
1970.

Lincecum, Jerry Bryan, and Edward Hake Phillips, eds. *Adventures of a Frontier Naturalist: The Life and Times of Dr. Gideon Lincecum*. College Station, Texas: Texas A&M, 1994.

Lincecum, Jerry Bryan, Edward Hake Phillips, and Peggy A. Redshaw, eds. *Science on the Texas Frontier: Observations of Dr. Gideon Lincecum*. College Station, Texas: Texas A&M, 1997.

Linn, Jo White, comp. *Rowan County, North Carolina Will Abstracts*. Salisbury, North Carolina: Linn, 1971.

McGuire, Mrs. C.P., Sr. *Records of Pickens County, Alabama*. 3 Vols. Tuscaloosa: Willo Publishing Company, n.d.

Marshall, Mary Grantham. *Cemetery Records of Greene County, Alabama and Related Areas*. N.p., n.d.

Meek, Melton P., comp. *Adam Meek*. Lawton, Oklahoma: N.p., 1996.

Monroe County History Book Committee. *History of Monroe County, Mississippi*. Curtis Media. n.d.

Owen, Thomas M., comp. *Revolutionary Soldiers in Alabama*. Baltimore: Genealogical Publishing Company, 1975.

_____. *History of Alabama and Dictionary of Alabama Biography*. Chicago: S.J. Clarke Publishing Co., 1921.

Palmer, John R. *The Mangums of Virginia, North Carolina, South Carolina, Georgia, Alabama, Mississippi Tennessee, Arkansas, Texas, Utah and Adjoining States*. Santa Rosa, California: Palmer, 1992.

Parham, James Lynn, comp. *Pleasant Mangum and All His Kin*. Baltimore: Gateway Press,1997.

Peterson, David A., and Bama Sellars Kosirnik. *The History of Our Family in the Southern United States*. N.p., n.d.

Phillips, Charles, and Alan Axelrod, eds. *Encyclopedia of the American West*, Vol.3. New York: Simon & Schuster Macmillan, 1996.

Pickens, Albert James. *History of Alabama and Incidentally of Georgia and Mississippi: From the Earliest Period*. Spartanburg, South Carolina: Reprint Company, 1975.

Pioneers of Tuscaloosa Co., Alabama Prior to 1830. Tuscaloosa: Tuscaloosa Genealogical Society, 1981.

Pitchlynn, Peter. "A Man Between Nations: the Diary of Peter Pitchlynn." *Missouri Review*. Online <http://www.missouri.edu/~moreview/features/pitchlynn.html>. Printout dated 21 September 1998.

Power, Anabel. "Some Early Settlers of Lowndes County." *Jackson Daily News-Clarion Ledger*. Jackson, Mississippi. (November 16 and 23, 1958).

Priest, Ruby Maude Weeks, and Hazel Willis Weeks, comps. *Weeks: Background and Beginnings*. N.p., 1983.

Prout, W.E. *A Historical Documentation of Colbert, Waverly, and Pala Alto, Mississippi*. Columbus, Mississippi: Tombigbee River Valley Water Management District, 1975.

Ramenofsky, Ann F. "Death by Disease." *Archaeology*. 45, no. 2 (March/April 1992).

Ray, Worth S. *Austin Colony Pioneers: Including History of Bastrop, Fayette, Grimes, Montgomery and Washington Counties, Texas*. 1949. Reprint. Baltimore: Genealogical Publishing Company, 1995.

Records of Land Patents: Lowndes County, Mississippi 1820-1842. Columbus, Mississippi: The Columbus-Lowndes Genealogical Society, 1988.

Rowland, Dunbar, ed. *Mississippi: Compressing Sketches of Counties, Towns, Events, Institutions, and Persons Arranged in Cyclopedic Form.* 3 Vols. Atlanta: Southern Historical Publications, 1907.

Simonton, Ashbel Green. *Journal.* Unpublished. 1852-1854.

Slaughter, William W., and Michael Landon. *Trail of Hope: The Story of the Mormon Trail.* Salt Lake City: Shadow Mountain, 1997.

Smith, Elsdon C. *American Surnames.* New York: Chilton Book Company, 1969.

Smith, Nelson F. *History of Pickens County, Alabama, From Its First Settlement in 1817, to 1856.* Carrollton, Alabama: Pickens Republican, 1856.

Starnes, C.W. *The Starnes Family.* Decorah, Iowa: Anundsen Publishers, 1985.

Starnes, H. Gerald. *Of Them That Left a Name Behind.* Baltimore: Gateway Press, 1983.

Story, W.M., et al. *The Family Story: George Story and His Descendants 1725-1955.* N.p., n.d.

Taunton, Louis, and Nancy R. Parkes. *Winston County and Its People: A Collection of Family Histories.* Louisville, Mississippi: Winston County Genealogical and Historical Society, 1980.

Van Wagenen, Avis Stearns. *Genealogy and Memoirs of Charles and Nathaniel Stearns and Their Descendants.* N.p., 1982.

Virginia Land Records: From the Virginia Magazine of History and Biography, the William and Mary College Quarterly and Tylers Quarterly. Baltimore: Genealogical Publishing Company, 1982.

Virginia Military Records. Baltimore: Genealogical Publishing Company, 1983.

Walser, Richard. *Five Walsers: An Informal Account.* Raleigh: Wolf's Head Press,1976.

Watson, Larry S., ed. *Creek - Choctaw - Chickasaw Land Fraud in Public Land: Public Land Series #1 Reprint Senate Document #151, 23d Congress, 2d Session.* Washington, D.C.: Histree, 1990.

Wiese, O'Levia Neil Wilson, ed. *Cemetery Records of Greene County, Alabama and Related Areas: The Journal of Mrs. Mary Marshall.* N.p., 1982.

Williams, T.P. *Oktibbeha County, Mississippi in the Civil War 1861-1865.* Starkville, Mississippi: Golden Triangle Civil War Round Table, 1990.

Wiltshire, Betty C., comp. *Abstracts of Choctaw County, Mississippi Records.* Carrollton, Mississippi: Pioneer Publishing, 1993.

_____. *Fayette County, Alabama Marriage and Probate Records.* Carrollton, Mississippi: Pioneer Publishing, 1994.

Wood, C.L. *Dedication of U.S. Government Marker at the Grave of John Pitchlynn Sr.* Unpublished, 1929.

Wood, W.J. *Major Battles and Campaigns: Battles of the Revolutionary War, 1775-1781.* New York: DeCapo Press, 1995.

Index